Contents

Paper Introduction

How to Use the Materials

These Kaplan Publishing learning materials have been carefully designed to make your learning experience as easy as possible and to give you the best chances of success in your examinations.

The product range contains a number of features to help you in the study process. They include:

(1) Detailed study guide and syllabus objectives

(2) Description of the examination

(3) Study skills and revision guidance

(4) Complete text or essential text

(5) Question practice

The sections on the study guide, the syllabus objectives, the examination and study skills should all be read before you commence your studies. They are designed to familiarise you with the nature and content of the examination and give you tips on how to best to approach your learning.

The **complete text or essential text** comprises the main learning materials and gives guidance as to the importance of topics and where other related resources can be found. Each chapter includes:

- The **learning objectives** contained in each chapter, which have been carefully mapped to the examining body's own syllabus learning objectives or outcomes. You should use these to check you have a clear understanding of all the topics on which you might be assessed in the examination.

- The **chapter diagram** provides a visual reference for the content in the chapter, giving an overview of the topics and how they link together.

- The **content** for each topic area commences with a brief explanation or definition to put the topic into context before covering the topic in detail. You should follow your studying of the content with a review of the illustration/s. These are worked examples which will help you to understand better how to apply the content for the topic.

- **Test your understanding** sections provide an opportunity to assess your understanding of the key topics by applying what you have learned to short questions. Answers can be found at the back of each chapter.

- **Summary diagrams** complete each chapter to show the important links between topics and the overall content of the paper. These diagrams should be used to check that you have covered and understood the core topics before moving on.

- **Question practice** is provided at the back of each text.

Icon Explanations

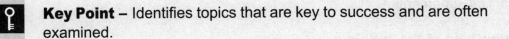

Definition – Key definitions that you will need to learn from the core content.

Key Point – Identifies topics that are key to success and are often examined.

Expandable Text – Expandable text provides you with additional information about a topic area and may help you gain a better understanding of the core content. Essential text users can access this additional content on-line (read it where you need further guidance or skip over when you are happy with the topic)

Illustration – Worked examples help you understand the core content better.

Test Your Understanding – Exercises for you to complete to ensure that you have understood the topics just learned.

Tricky topic – When reviewing these areas care should be taken and all illustrations and test your understanding exercises should be completed to ensure that the topic is understood.

On-line subscribers

Our on-line resources are designed to increase the flexibility of your learning materials and provide you with immediate feedback on how your studies are progressing. Ask your local customer services staff if you are not already a subscriber and wish to join.

If you are subscribed to our on-line resources you will find:

(1) On-line referenceware: reproduces your Complete or Essential Text on-line, giving you anytime, anywhere access.

(2) On-line testing: provides you with additional on-line objective testing so you can practice what you have learned further.

(3) On-line performance management: immediate access to youron-line testing results. Review your performance by key topics and chart your achievement through the course relative to your peer group.

Ask your local customer services staff if you are not already a subscriber and wish to join.

Paper introduction

Paper background

The aim of ACCA Paper F3 (UK), Financial Accounting, is to develop knowledge and understanding of the underlying principles and concepts relating to financial accounting and technical proficiency in the use of double-entry accounting techniques including the preparation of basic financial statements.

Objectives of the syllabus

- Explain the context and purpose of financial reporting.
- Define the qualitative characteristics of financial information and the fundamental bases of accounting.
- Demonstrate the use of double entry and accounting systems.
- Record transactions and events.
- Prepare a trial balance (including identifying and correcting errors).
- Prepare basic financial statements for incorporated and unincorporated entities.

Core areas of the syllabus

- The context and purpose of financial reporting
- The qualitative characteristics of financial information and the fundamental bases of accounting
- The use of double entry and accounting systems
- Recording transactions and events
- Preparing a trial balance
- Preparing basic financial statements

Syllabus objectives

We have reproduced the ACCA's syllabus below, showing where the objectives are explored within this book. Within the chapters, we have broken down the extensive information found in the syllabus into easily digestible and relevant sections, called Content Objectives. These correspond to the objectives at the beginning of each chapter.

B THE QUALITATIVE CHARACTERISTICS OF FINANCIAL INFORMATION AND THE FUNDAMENTAL BASES OF ACCOUNTING

1 The qualitative characteristics of financial reporting

(a) Define, understand and apply accounting concepts and qualitative characteristics:[1]   2 & 20

   (i) true and fair view

   (ii) going concern

   (iii) accruals

   (iv) consistency

   (v) materiality

   (vi) relevance

   (vii) reliability

   (viii) faithful representation

   (ix) substance over form

   (x) neutrality

   (xi) prudence

   (xii) completeness

   (xiii) comparability

   (xiv) understandability.

   xv. Business entity concept

(b) Understand the balance between qualitative characteristics.[1]   20

2 Alternative bases used in the preparation of financial information

(a) Identify and explain the main characteristics of alternative valuation bases e.g. historical cost, replacement cost, net realisable value, economic value.[1]   20

(b) Understand the advantages and disadvantages of historical cost accounting.[1]   20

(c) Understand the provision of Financial Reporting Standards governing financial statements regarding changes in accounting policies.[1]   18

(d) Identify the appropriate accounting treatment if a company changes a material accounting policy.[1]   18

KAPLAN PUBLISHING

C THE USE OF DOUBLE ENTRY AND ACCOUNTING SYSTEMS

1 Double entry bookkeeping principles including the maintenance of accounting records and sources of information

(a) Identify and explain the function of the main data sources in an accounting system.[1]   10

(b) Outline the contents and purpose of different types of business documentation, including: quotation, sales order, purchase order, goods received note, goods despatched note, invoice, statement, credit note, debit note, remittance advice, receipt.[1]   10

(c) Understand and apply the concept of double entry accounting and the duality concept.[1]   3

(d) Understand and apply the accounting equation.[1]   3

(e) Understand how the accounting system contributes to providing useful accounting information and complies with organisational policies and deadlines.[1]   1

(f) Identify the main types of business transactions, e.g. sales, purchases, payments, receipts.[1]   2, 3 & 10

2 Ledger accounts, books of prime entry and journals

(a) Identify the main types of ledger accounts and books of prime entry, and understand their nature and function.[1]   3

(b) Understand and illustrate the uses of journals and the posting of journal entries into ledger accounts.[1]   3

(c) Identify correct journals from given narrative.[1]   3

(d) Illustrate how to balance and close a ledger account.[1]   3

3 Accounting systems and the impact of information technology on financial reporting

(a) Understand the basic function and form of accounting records in a typical manual system.[1]   14

(b) Understand the basic function and form of accounting records in a typical computerised system.[1]   14

(c) Compare manual and computerised accounting systems.[1]   14

(d) Identify advantages and disadvantages of computerised accounting systems.[1]   14

(e) Understand the uses of integrated accounting software packages.[1]   14

D RECORDING TRANSACTIONS AND EVENTS

1 Sales and purchases

(a)	Record sale and purchase transactions in ledger accounts and in day books.[1]	3 & 10
(b)	Understand and record sales and purchase returns.[1]	3
(c)	Understand the general principles of the operation of a Value Added Tax (VAT).[1]	4
(d)	Calculate VAT on transactions and record the consequent accounting entries. (various rates of tax may be used) [1]	4
(e)	Account for discounts allowed and discounts received.[1]	3

2 Cash

(a)	Record cash transactions in ledger accounts.[1]	2, 10
(b)	Understand the need for a record of petty cash transactions.[1]	10
(c)	Describe the features and operation of a petty cash imprest system.[1]	10
(d)	Account for petty cash using imprest and non-imprest methods. [1]	10
(e)	Understand the importance of and identify controls and security over the petty cash system.[1]	10

3 Stock

(a)	Recognise the need for adjustments for stock in preparing financial statements.[1]	5
(b)	Record opening and closing stock.[1]	5
(c)	Identify the alternative methods of valuing stock.[1]	5
(d)	Understand and apply the ASB requirements for valuing stock.[1]	5
(e)	Recognise which costs should be included in valuing stock.[1]	5
(f)	Understand the use of continuous and period end stock records. [1]	5
(g)	Calculate the value of closing stock using FIFO (first in, first out) and AVCO (average cost).[1]	5
(h)	Understand the impact of accounting concepts on the valuation of stock.[1]	5
(i)	Identify the impact of stock valuation methods on profit and on assets.[1]	5

KAPLAN PUBLISHING

E PREPARING A TRIAL BALANCE

1 Trial balance

(a)	Identify the purpose of a trial balance.[1]	3 & 9
(b)	Extract ledger balances into a trial balance.[1]	3 & 9
(c)	Prepare extracts of an opening trial balance.[1]	3
(d)	Identify and understand the limitations of a trial balance.[1]	9

2 Correction of errors

(a)	Identify the types of error which may occur in bookkeeping systems.[1]	13
(b)	Identify errors which would be highlighted by the extraction of a trial balance.[1]	13
(c)	Understand the provision of Financial Reporting Standards governing financial statements regarding material errors which result in prior period adjustment.[1]	18
(d)	Prepare journal entries to correct errors.[1]	13
(e)	Calculate and understand the impact of errors on the profit and loss account and balance sheet.[1]	13

3 Control accounts and reconciliations

(a)	Understand the purpose of control accounts for debtors and creditors.[1]	10,11
(b)	Understand how control accounts relate to the double entry system.[1]	10
(c)	Prepare ledger control accounts from given information.[1]	10, 11
(d)	Perform control account reconciliations for debtors and creditors.[1]	11
(e)	Identify errors which would be highlighted by performing a control account reconciliation.[1]	11
(f)	Identify and correct errors in control accounts and ledger accounts.[1]	11

4 Bank reconciliations

(a)	Understand the purpose of bank reconciliations.[1]	12
(b)	Identify the main reasons for differences between the cash book and the bank statement.[1]	12
(c)	Correct cash book errors and/or omissions.[1]	12
(d)	Prepare bank reconciliation statements.[1]	12

3 Events after the balance sheet date

(a) Define an event after the balance sheet date in accordance with Financial Reporting Standards.[1] 18

(b) Classify events as adjusting or non-adjusting.[1] 18

(c) Distinguish between how adjusting and non-adjusting events are reported in the financial statements.[1] 18

4 Accounting for partnerships

(a) Understand and identify the typical content of a partnership agreement, including profit-sharing terms.[1] 16

(b) Understand the nature of: [1] 16

    (i) capital accounts

    (ii) current accounts

    (iii) division of profits.

(c) Calculate and record the partners' shares of profit/losses.[1] 16

(d) Account for guaranteed minimum profit shares.[1] 16

(e) Calculate and record partners' drawings.[1] 16

(f) Calculate and record interest on drawings.[1] 16

(g) Calculate and record interest on capital.[1] 16

(h) Calculate and record partner salaries.[1] 16

(i) Prepare an extract of a current account.[1] 16

(j) Prepare an extract of a capital account.[1] 16

(k) Prepare extracts of the profit and loss account, including division of profit, and balance sheet of a partnership.[1] 16

(l) Define goodwill, in relation to partnership accounts.[1] 16

(m) Identify the factors leading to the creation of goodwill in relation to partnership accounts.[1] 16

(n) Calculate the value of goodwill from given information.[1] 16

Note: Questions on partnerships may include the effect of admission of new partners.

5 Cash flow statements (excluding partnerships)

(a) Differentiate between profit and cash flow.[1] 19

(b) Understand the need for management to control cash flow.[1] 19

(c) Recognise the benefits and drawbacks to users of the financial statements of a cash flow statement.[1] 19

(d) Classify the effect of transactions on cash flows.[1] 19

(e) Calculate the figures needed for the cash flow statement including:[1]

    (i)   net cash flow from operating activites

    (ii) return on investments or servicing of finance

    (iii) taxation

    (iv) capital expenditure

    (v) equity dividends paid

    (vi) management of liquid resources

    (vii) financing

(f) Calculate the cash flow from operating activities using the indirect and direct method[1]

(g) Prepare extracts from cash flow statements from given information.[1]

(h) Identify the treatment of given transactions in a company's cash flow statement.[1]

6 Incomplete records

(a) Understand and apply techniques used in incomplete record situations:[1]

    (i)   use of accounting equation

    (ii) use of ledger accounts to calculate missing figures

    (iii) use of cash and/or bank summaries

    (iv) use of profit percentages to calculate missing figures.

The superscript numbers in square brackets indicate the intellectual depth at which the subject area could be assessed within the examination. Level 1 (knowledge and comprehension) broadly equates with the Knowledge module, Level 2 (application and analysis) with the Skills module and Level 3 (synthesis and evaluation) to the Professional level. However, lower level skills can continue to be assessed as you progress through each module and level.

The examination

Examination format

The syllabus is assessed by a two-hour paper or computer-based examination. Questions will assess all parts of the syllabus and will contain both computational and noncomputational elements:

	Number of marks
Forty 2-mark questions	80
Ten 1-mark questions	10
	90

Total time allowed: 2 hours

Paper-based examination tips

Spend the first few minutes of the examination reading the paper.

Divide the time you spend on questions in proportion to the marks on offer. One suggestion **for this exam** is to allocate 1 and 1/3 minutes to each mark available, so a 2 mark question should be completed in approximately 2 minutes 40 seconds.

Multiple-choice questions: Read the questions carefully and work through any calculations required. If you don't know the answer, eliminate those options you know are incorrect and see if the answer becomes more obvious. Guess your final answer rather than leave it blank if necessary.

Computer-based examination (CBE) – tips

Be sure you understand how to use the software before you start the exam. If in doubt, ask the assessment centre staff to explain it to you.

Questions are **displayed on the screen** and answers are entered using keyboard and mouse. At the end of the exam, you are given a certificate showing the result you have achieved.

Do not attempt a CBE until you have **completed all study material** relating to it. **Do not skip any of the material** in the syllabus.

Read each question very carefully.

Double-check your answer before committing yourself to it.

Answer every question – if you do not know an answer, you don't lose anything by guessing. Think carefully before you **guess.**

With a multiple-choice question, eliminate first those answers that you know are wrong. Then choose the most appropriate answer from those that are left.

Remember that only **one answer to a multiple-choice question can be right.** After you have eliminated the ones that you know to be wrong, if you are still unsure, guess. But only do so after you have double-checked that you have only eliminated answers that are definitely wrong.

Don't panic if you realise you've answered a question incorrectly.Getting one question wrong will not mean the difference between passing and failing.

Study skills and revision guidance

This section aims to give guidance on how to study for your ACCA exams and to give ideas on how to improve your existing study techniques.

Preparing to study

Set your objectives

Before starting to study decide what you want to achieve - the type of pass you wish to obtain. This will decide the level of commitment and time you need to dedicate to your studies.

Devise a study plan

Determine which times of the week you will study.

Split these times into sessions of at least one hour for study of new material. Any shorter periods could be used for revision or practice.

Put the times you plan to study onto a study plan for the weeks from now until the exam and set yourself targets for each period of study – in your sessions make sure you cover the course, course assignments and revision.

If you are studying for more than one paper at a time, try to vary your subjects as this can help you to keep interested and see subjects as part of wider knowledge.

When working through your course, compare your progress with your plan and, if necessary, re-plan your work (perhaps including extra sessions) or, if you are ahead, do some extra revision/practice questions.

Effective studying

Active reading

You are not expected to learn the text by rote, rather, you must understand what you are reading and be able to use it to pass the exam and develop good practice. A good technique to use is SQ3Rs – Survey, Question, Read, Recall, Review:

(1) **Survey** the chapter – look at the headings and read the introduction, summary and objectives, so as to get an overview of what the chapter deals with.

(2) **Question** – whilst undertaking the survey, ask yourself the questions that you hope the chapter will answer for you.

(3) **Read** through the chapter thoroughly, answering the questions and making sure you can meet the objectives. Attempt the exercises and activities in the text, and work through all the examples.

(4) **Recall** – at the end of each section and at the end of the chapter, try to recall the main ideas of the section/chapter without referring to the text. This is best done after a short break of a couple of minutes after the reading stage.

(5) **Review** – check that your recall notes are correct.

You may also find it helpful to re-read the chapter to try to see the topic(s) it deals with as a whole.

Note-taking

Taking notes is a useful way of learning, but do not simply copy out the text. The notes must:

- be in your own words
- be concise
- cover the key points
- be well-organised
- be modified as you study further chapters in this text or in related ones.

Trying to summarise a chapter without referring to the text can be a useful way of determining which areas you know and which you don't.

KAPLAN PUBLISHING

Three ways of taking notes:

Summarise the key points of a chapter.

Make linear notes – a list of headings, divided up with subheadings listing the key points. If you use linear notes, you can use different colours to highlight key points and keep topic areas together. Use plenty of space to make your notes easy to use.

Try a diagrammatic form – the most common of which is a mind-map. To make a mind-map, put the main heading in the centre of the paper and put a circle around it. Then draw short lines radiating from this to the main sub-headings, which again have circles around them. Then continue the process from the sub-headings to sub-sub-headings, advantages, disadvantages, etc.

Highlighting and underlining

You may find it useful to underline or highlight key points in your study text – but do be selective. You may also wish to make notes in the margins.

Revision

The best approach to revision is to revise the course as you work through it. Also try to leave four to six weeks before the exam for final revision. Make sure you cover the whole syllabus and pay special attention to those areas where your knowledge is weak. Here are some recommendations:

Read through the text and your notes again and condense your notes into key phrases. It may help to put key revision points onto index cards to look at when you have a few minutes to spare.

Review any assignments you have completed and look at where you lost marks – put more work into those areas where you were weak.

Practise exam standard questions under timed conditions. If you are short of time, list the points that you would cover in your answer and then read the model answer, but do try to complete at least a few questions under exam conditions.

Also practise producing answer plans and comparing them to the model answer.

If you are stuck on a topic find somebody (a tutor) to explain it to you.

Read good newspapers and professional journals, especially ACCA's Student Accountant – this can give you an advantage in the exam.

Ensure you **know the structure of the exam** – how many questions and of what type you will be expected to answer. During your revision attempt all the different styles of questions you may be asked.

Further reading

You can find further reading and technical articles under the student section of ACCA's website.

1

Introduction to accounting

Chapter learning objectives

Upon completion of this chapter you will be able to:

- define accounting
- explain the different types of business entity:
  - sole trader
  - partnership
  - limited liability company
- explain who users of the financial statements are and their information needs
- explain the nature, principles and scope of accounting.
- explain how the accounting system contributes to providing useful information and complies with organisational policies and deadlines.

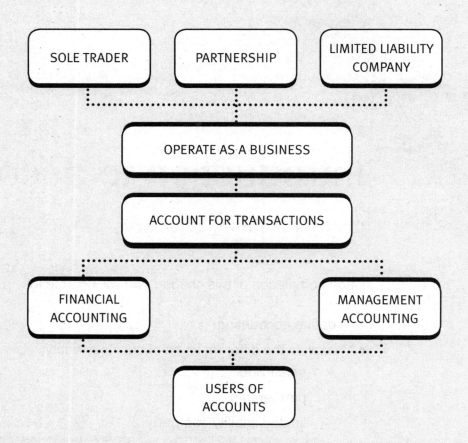

Analysing data is also an important feature of accounting. Financial statements are prepared so that we can examine and evaluate all information, in order to make key decisions.

KAPLAN PUBLISHING

1 Definition of accounting

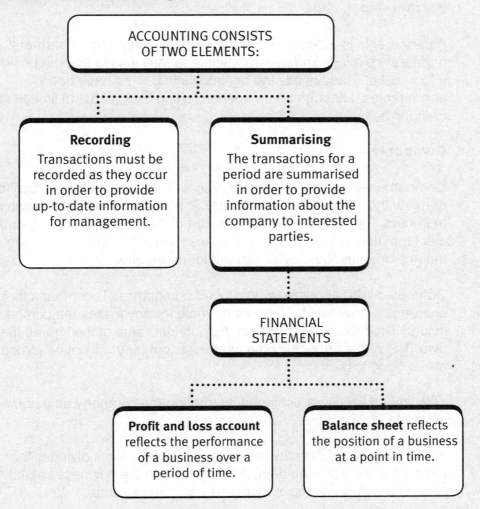

2 Types of business entity

A business can be organised in one of several ways:

- Sole trader – a business owned and operated by one person.
- Partnership – a business owned and operated by two or more people.
- Company – a business owned by many people and operated by many (though not necessarily the same) people.

Expandable text

Sole trader

The simplest form of business is the sole trader. This is owned and managed by one person, although there might be any number of employees. A sole trader is fully and personally liable for any losses that the businesses might make.

Partnership

A partnership is a business owned jointly by a numebr of partners. The partners are jointly and severally liable for any losses that the business might make. Traditionally the big accounting firms have been partnerships, although some are converting their status to limited liability companies.

Companies

Companies are owned by shareholders. There can be one shareholder or many thousands of shareholders. Shareholders are also known as members. Each shareholder owns part of the company. As a group, they elect the directors who run the business. Directors often own shares in their companies, but not all shareholders are directors.

Companies are almost always limited companies. This means that the shareholders will not be personally liable for any losses the company incurs. Their liability is limited to the nominal value of the shares that they own. The shares may become worthless, but they will not be forced to make good losses.

This limited liability is achieved by treating the company as a completely separate legal entity.

For all three types of entity, the money put up by the individual, the partners or the shareholders, is referred to as the business capital. In the case of a company, this capital is divided into shares.

3 Users of the financial statements

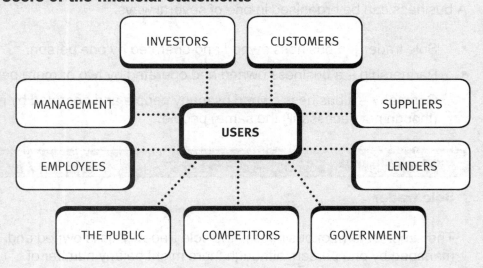

Different user groups are interested in a company's financial statements for different reasons:

Management need detailed information in order to control their business and plan for the future. Budgets will be based upon past performance and future plans. These budgets will then be compared with actual results. Information will also be needed about the profitability of individual departments and products. Management information must be very up to date and is normally produced on a monthly basis.

Investors and potential investors are interested in their potential profits and the security of their investment. Future profits may be estimated from the target company's past performance as shown in the income statement. The security of their investment will be revealed by the financial strength and solvency of the company as shown in the statement of financial position. The largest and most sophisticated groups of investors are the institutional investors, such as pension funds and unit trusts.

Employees and trade union representatives need to know if an employer can offer secure employment and possible pay rises. They will also have a keen interest in the salaries and benefits enjoyed by senior management. Information about divisional profitability will also be useful if a part of the business is threatened with closure.

Lenders need to know if they will be repaid. This will depend on the solvency of the company, which should be revealed by the statement of financial position. Long-term loans may also be backed by 'security' given by the business over specific assets. The value of these assets will be indicated in the statement of financial position.

Government agencies need to know how the economy is performing in order to plan financial and industrial policies. The tax authorities also use financial statements as a basis for assessing the amount of tax payable by a business.

Suppliers need to know if they will be paid. New suppliers may also require reassurance about the financial health of a business before agreeing to supply goods.

Customers need to know that a company can continue to supply them into the future. This is especially true if the customer is dependent on a company for specialised supplies.

Competitors wish to compare their own performance against that of other companies and learn as much as possible about their rivals in order to help develop strategic plans.

The public may wish to assess the effect of the company on the economy, local environment and local community. Companies may contribute to their local economy and community through providing employment and patronising local suppliers. Some companies also run corporate responsibility programmes through which they support the environment, economy and community by, for example supporting recycling schemes.

Test Your Understanding 1

Which of the following users do you think require the most detailed financial information to be made available to them?

(a) Competitors

(b) Management of the business

(c) Trade unions

(d) Investors

4 Types of accounting

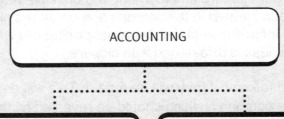

ACCOUNTING

Financial accounting	Management accounting
• Production of summary financial statements for external users.	• Production of detailed accounts, used by management to control the business and plan for the future.
• Prepared annually (six-monthly or quarterly in some countries).	• Normally prepared monthly, often on a rolling basis.
• Generally required by law.	• Not mandatory.
• Reflects past performance and current position.	• Includes budgets and forecasts of future activities, as well as reflecting past performance.
• Information calculated and presented in accordance with strict legal and accounting requirements.	• Information computed and presented in order to be relevant to managers.

Expandable text

Financial accounting

Financial accounting is concerned with the production of financial statements for external users. These are a report on the directors' stewardship of the funds entrusted to them by the shareholders.

Investors need to be able to choose which companies to invest in and compare their investments. In order to facilitate comparison, financial accounts are prepared using accepted accounting conventions and standards. Statements of Standard Accounting Practice (SSAPs) and Financial Reporting Standards (FRSs) help to reduce the differences in the way that companies draw up their financial statements

The financial statements are public documents, and therefore they will not reveal details about product profitability.

Management accounting

Management need much more detailed and up-to-date information in order to control the business and plan for the future. They need to be able to cost out products and production methods, assess profitability and so on. In order to facilitate this, management accounts present information in any way which may be useful to management, for example by operating unit or product line.

Management accounting is an integral part of management activity concerned with identifying, presenting and interpreting information used for:

- formulation of strategy
- planning and controlling activities
- decision making
- optimising the use of resources.

5 How an accounting system contributes to providing useful information

The main features of an accounting system and how it helps in providing information to the business are as follows:

- In a computerised system all the information about the business transactions can be quickly accessed. This will help in decision making.

- It provides details of transactions of the business in the relevant accounts.

- When the accounts are closed off the balances for each outstanding account are determined. This will give the value of assets and liabilities in the business.

- It gives a summary of outstanding balances.

- This summary can then be used for the preparation of financial statements.

- Normally the financial statements are prepared at periodic intervals. The accounting system will allow the business to obtain the data and also prepare the financial statements to determine profitability, liquidity, risks, etc. applicable to the business for a particular period. For internal reporting purposes this could be monthly whilst for external reporting purposes this is usually yearly.

6 Chapter summary

SOLE TRADER	PARTNERSHIP	COMPANY
Business owned and operated by one person.	Business owned and operated by two or more people.	Business owned by, and operated by, many people.

OPERATE AS A BUSINESS

ACCOUNT FOR TRANSACTIONS

FINANCIAL ACCOUNTING
Production of summary financial statements for external users.

MANAGEMENT ACCOUNTING
Production of detailed accounts for internal use.

USERS OF ACCOUNTS

- investors
- employees
- lenders
- government
- suppliers
- customers
- competitors
- the public.

- Management

Test your understanding answers

Test Your Understanding 1

(b) Management

They need detailed information in order to control their business and make informed decisions about the future. Management information must be very up to date and is normally produced on a monthly basis.

Other parties will need far less detail:

Competitors will be monitoring what the competition are currently planning and working on, but they will not be making the key decisions themselves.

Trade unions will only require information which relates to their job role. They will only be particularly interested in disputes.

Investors are interested in profitability and the security of their investment.

KAPLAN PUBLISHING

Balance sheet and profit and loss account

Chapter learning objectives

Upon completion of this chapter you will be able to:

- explain the main elements of financial statements:
  - balance sheet
  - profit and loss account
- explain the purpose of each of the main statements
- list the main types of business transactions
- explain how the balance sheet equation and business entity convention underpin the balance sheet
- define assets and liabilities
- identify examples of debtors and creditors
- explain how and why assets and liabilities are disclosed in the balance sheet
- draft a simple balance sheet in vertical format
- explain the matching convention and how it applies to income and expenses
- explain how and why income and expenses are disclosed in the profit and loss account
- illustrate how the balance sheet and profit and loss account are interrelated
- draft a simple profit and loss account in vertical format
- identify the two sides of each transaction (duality concept)
- determine the accounting equation after each transaction.

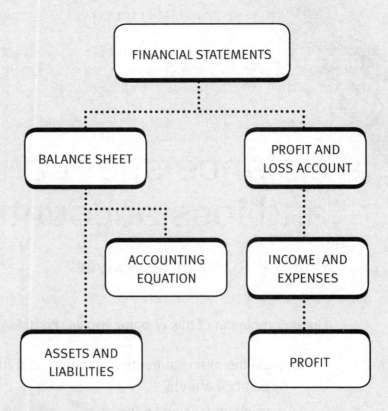

1 Financial statements

There are two elements to the financial statements:

- balance sheet, showing the financial position of a business at a point in time, and

- profit and loss account, showing the financial performance of a business over a period of time.

The financial statements show the effects of business transactions. The main types are:

- **sales of goods (either for cash or on credit)**

  If a sale is made for cash, then cash in the business will increase and a sales transaction will have also been created. The cash will be recorded in the balance sheet and the sale will be recorded in the profit and loss account.

  If a sale is made on credit, then the payment for the goods has not been made immediately. Therefore we are still owed for these items. The sale will still be recorded in the profit anf loss account, however a debtor will be recorded in the balance sheet.

- **purchase of stock for resale (either for cash or on credit)**

  If we buy stock for cash, then we are spendng money. This decrease in cash will be recorded in the balance sheet. The increase in stock that we now own will also be recorded as an asset in the balance sheet.

  If we buy stock on credit, then we will owe the supplier for these goods. This is called a creditor. Therefore stock will increase and also a creditor will be created. Both of these are entered onto the balance sheet.

- **purchase of fixed assets**

  If we buy a fixed asset (eg: a motor vehicle) then we are spending cash, so this will decrease. However, we have now gained a new asset, and both of these entires are recorded in the balance sheet.

- **payment of expenses such as utilities**

  Making this payment will reduce our cash balance and this will affect our balance sheet. We will have created an expense which we have made the payment for, untilities. This expense belongs on the profit and loss account.

- **introduction of new capital to the business**

  If the owner of the business introduces funds into the business, this is called capital. We have increased the capital within the business and also increased our cash or bank balances. Both of these entires are recorded on the balance sheet.

- **withdrawal of funds from the business by the owner.**

  If the owner then withdraws some of these funds back out of the business again, this is known as drawings. The capital will reduce and also the amount of funds within the bank account will too. Both of these are recorded on the balance sheet.

The business entity concept

- The business entity concept states that financial accounting information relates only to the activities of the business entity and not to the activities of its owner.

- The business entity is treated as separate from its owners.

Expandable text

The business entity concept

The business entity concept states that financial accounting information relates only to the activities of the business entity and not to the activities of its owner.

The business is seen as being separate from its owners, whatever its legal status. Thus, a company is both legally and for accounting purposes a separate entity distinct from its owners, the shareholders. On the other hand, the business of a sole trader is not a legal entity distinct from its proprietor; however, for accounting purposes, the business is regarded as being a separate entity and accounts are drawn up for the business separately from the trader's own personal financial dealings.

The entity concept is essential in order to be able to account for the business as a separate economic unit. Flows of money between the business and the proprietors are also separately identified from other money flows.

The correct terms for these cash movements are:

Cash movement from/to proprietors	Sole trader, partnership	Company
In	Either 'loans from proprietors' or increase in capital'	Share issue proceeds
Out	Either 'drawings' or 'reduction in capital'	Dividends

The key link between the owner and the business is the amount stated as capital which is the amount the business owes to the proprietor.

2 Balance sheet

The balance sheet can be shown in two formats:

- the vertical format and

- the horizontal format.

The vertical format is today the more popular form of presentation in the UK. The vertical format of the balance sheet for a soletrader is shown below: (see later in chapter 17 for companies)

W Wang

Balance sheet as at 31 December 20X6

	£	£
Fixed assets:		
Motor van		2,400
Current assets:		
Stock	2,390	
Debtors	1,840	
Cash at bank	1,704	
Cash in hand	56	
	_____	
	5,990	
Current liabilities:		
Creditors	(1,700)	
	_____	
Net current assets		4,290
Long term liabilities		(1,000)
		_____
Net assets		5,690
		_____
Capital account:		
Balance at 1 January 20X6		4,200
Net profit	3,450	
Increase in capital	1,000	
Less drawings	(2,960)	
	_____	
		1,490
		_____
Balance at 31 December 20X6		5,690
		_____

- The top half of the balance sheet shows the assets and liabilities of the business.
- The bottom half of the balance sheet shows the capital of the business.

The balance sheet equation

The balance sheet above shows the position of W Xang's business at one point in time – in this case at close of business on 31 December 20X6. A balance sheet will always satisfy the balance sheet or accounting equation as follows:

> ASSETS – LIABILITIES = PROPRIETOR'S CAPITAL

It follows that the accounting equation can be rewritten as:

> ASSETS = PROPRIETOR'S CAPITAL + LIABILITIES

The horizontal format balance sheet is an expansion of this form of the accounting equation.

Assets and liabilities

Assets are resources an entity controls as a result of past events and from which future economic benefits are expected to flow to the entity. Some examples are:

- stock, e.g. goods manufactured or purchased for resale
- debtors, e.g. money owed by credit customers, prepaid expenses
- cash
- fixed assets
- and is available for use in the business.

A liability is an entity's present obligation arising from a past event, the settlement of which will result in an outflow of economic benefits from the entity. This is something owed by the business to someone else, such as:

- creditors, e.g. amounts owed to credit suppliers, accrued expenses
- loans.

Equity is defined as the residual interest in the entity's assets after deducting its liabilities. You will become more familiar with this term when you come to look at Company accounts in chapter 17.

KAPLAN PUBLISHING

Capital is a type of liability. This is the amount that is due to the owner(s) of the business. It will increase each year by any new capital injected into the business and by the profit made by the business. It will decrease by any amounts withdrawn from the business by the owner(s).

Disclosure of assets and liabilities in the balance sheet

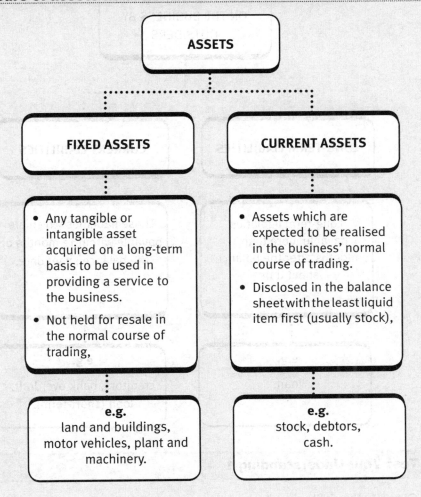

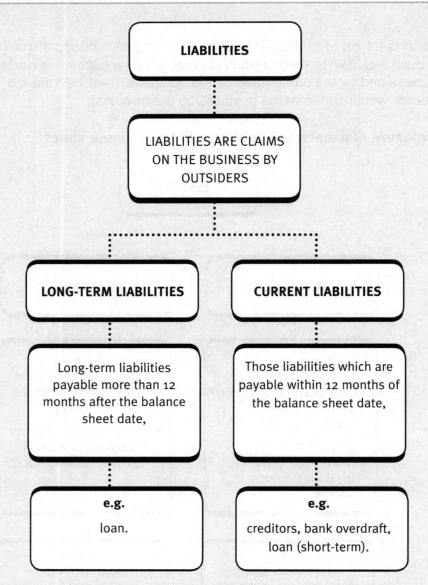

Test Your Understanding 1

Classify the following items into current and fixed assets and liabilities:

- land and buildings
- debtors
- cash
- loan repayable in two years' time
- creditors
- delivery van.

Test Your Understanding 2

List the following items showing the least liquid items first:

- cash in hand
- stock of finished goods
- cash at bank
- debtors
- stock of raw materials.

3 Profit and loss account

The format of the profit and loss account is shown below:

Mr W Xang

Profit and loss account for the year ended 31 December 20X6

	£	£
Sales		33,700
Opening stock	3,200	
Purchases	24,490	
	———	
	27,690	
Less: Closing stock	(2,390)	
	———	
Cost of sales		(25,300)
		———
Gross profit		8,400
Wages	3,385	
Rent	1,200	
Sundry expenses	365	
	———	
		(4,950)
		———
Net profit		3,450
		———

- **Income** is increases in economic benefits during the period in the form of inflows or enhancements of assets or decreases of liabilities that result in increases in equity, other than those relating to contributions from equity participants.

- **Expenses** are decreases in economic benefits during the period in the form of outflows or depletions of assets or increases of liabilities that result in decreases in equity, other than those relating to distributions to equity participants.

- The profit and loss account shows the performance of the business over a period of time, in this case for a full year.

- The profit and loss account is prepared following the accruals concept. This means that income and expenses are recorded as they are earned/incurred regardless of whether cash has been received/paid.

- Sales includes the income from goods sold in the year, regardless of whether those goods have been paid for.

- The cost of buying the goods sold must be deducted from the sales income. It is important that the cost of any goods remaining unsold is not included here.

- The current year's sales will include goods bought in the previous year, so this opening stock must be added to the current year's purchases.

- Some of this year's purchases will be unsold at 31 December 20X6 and this closing stock must be deducted from purchases to be set off against next year's sales.

- The profit and loss account is split into two parts, the first part (or trading account) gives gross profit and the second part, net profit.

- Gross profit divided by sales gives the gross profit margin ratio which illustrates the profitability of the business at a trading level.

Expandable text

The profit and loss account – wages and drawings

We must distinguish between wages and drawings. Wages relate to payments to third parties (employees) and represent a deduction or charge in arriving at net profit. Amounts paid to the proprietor (even if he calls them 'salary'!) must be treated as drawings. It would be wrong to treat drawings as a business expense as the amounts drawn are not used to further a sale. The whole of the profit belongs to the proprietor, and the drawings are that part of the profit the proprietor chooses to withdraw.

4 Relationship between the balance sheet and profit and loss account

The link between the balance sheet and profit and loss account is shown below:

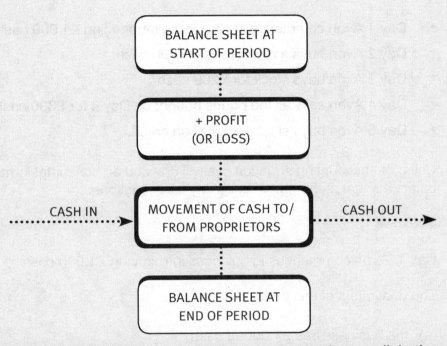

- The balance sheets are not isolated statements; they are linked over time with the profit and loss account.

- As the business records a profit in the profit and loss account, that profit is added to the capital section of the balance sheet, along with any capital introduced. Cash taken out of the business by the proprietor, called drawings, is deducted.

5 The accounting equation

ASSETS = PROPRIETOR'S CAPITAL + LIABILITIES

ASSETS – LIABILITIES = PROPRIETOR'S CAPITAL

- The accounting equation is a simple expression of the fact that at any point in time the assets of the business will be equal to its liabilities plus the capital of the business.

- It follows that assets less liabilities equals the capital of the business. Assets less liabilities is known as net assets.

- Each and every transaction that the business makes or enters into has two aspects to it and has a double effect on the business and the accounting equation. This is known as the duality concept.

Illustration 1 : The accounting equation

This illustration involves a series of transactions using the dual effect of transactions and then the accounting equation to build up a set of financial statements. The transactions are as follows:

- Day 1 Avon commences in business introducing £1,000 cash.
- Day 2 Avon buys a motor car for £400 cash.
- Day 3 Avon buys stock for £200 cash.
- Day 4 Avon sells all the goods bought on Day 3 for £300 cash.
- Day 5 Avon buys stock for £400 on credit.

Using the accounting equation, we will draw up an horizontal format balance sheet at the end of each day's transactions.

Solution

Day 1: Avon commences in business introducing £1,000 cash

The dual effect of this transaction is:

(a) the business has £1,000 of cash

(b) the business owes the owner £1,000 – this is capital.

Balance sheet Day 1

Assets	£	Capital and liabilities	£
Cash	1,000	Capital	1,000
	1,000		1,000

Day 2: Avon buys a motor car for £400 cash

The dual effect of this transaction is:

(a) the business has an asset of £400

(b) the business has spent £400 in cash

This transaction changes the form in which the assets are held.

Balance sheet Day 2

Assets	£	Capital and liabilities	£
Motor car	400	Capital	1,000
Cash			
(£1,000 – £400)	600		
	1,000		1,000

Note that the acquiring of an asset must lead to one of the following:

*   reducing another asset by a corresponding amount (as above)
*   incurring a corresponding liability (Day 5)
*   increasing the capital contributed by the proprietor (Day 1).

Day 3: Avon buys stock for £200 cash

The dual effect of this transaction is:

(a) the business has £200 of stock
(b) the business has spent £200 in cash.

Again this is merely a change in the form in which the assets are held. £200 is withdrawn from cash and invested in stock.

Balance sheet for Day 3

Assets	£	Capital and liabilities	£
Motor car	400	Capital	1,000
Stock	200		
Cash:			
(£600 – £200)	400		
	1,000		1,000

Day 4: Avon sells all the goods bought on Day 3 for £300 cash

This is an important new development. It is true that one asset (stock) is being replaced by another (cash), but the amounts do not correspond.

	£
Cash acquired (sale proceeds)	300
Asset relinquished (stock)	200
Difference (= profit)	100

Thus total assets have increased by £100. Since there are no liabilities involved, if the fundamental equation is to remain valid the capital must increase by £100.

Profit is the difference between purchase price and sale proceeds and it belongs to the proprietor(s) of the business. It is an increase in the capital of the business.

The dual effect of this transaction is:

(a) The business has received £300 of cash.

(b) The business has reduced stock by £200 and made a profit of £100.

Balance sheet for Day 4

Assets	£	Capital and liabilities	£
Motor car	400	Capital	1,000
Cash:			
(£400 + £300)	700	Add: Profit	100
	1,100		1,100

Day 5: buys stock for £400 on credit

The dual effect of this transaction is:

(a) The business has £400 of stock.

(b) The business has a liability to the supplier of £400.

Assets can be increased by a corresponding increase in liabilities as follows:

Balance sheet for Day 5

	£	Capital and Liabilities	£
Assets		**Capital and Liabilities**	
Motor car	400	Capital	1,000
Stock	400	Add: Profit	100
Cash	700	Creditors	400
	1,500		1,500

Note that the creditors are acting in effect as a source of finance for the business.

Test Your Understanding 3

Continuing from the illustration above, prepare the balance sheet at the end of each day after accounting for the transactions below:

Day 6 Avon sells half of the goods bought on Day 5 on credit for £250.

Day 7 Avon Pays £200 to his supplier.

Day 8 Avon receives £100 from a customer.

Day 9 Proprietor draws £75 in cash.

Day 10 Avon pays rent of £40 in cash.

Day 11 Avon receives a loan of £600 repayable in two years.

Day 12 Avon pays cash of £30 for insurance.

Your starting point is the balance sheet at the end of Day 5, from the illustration above.

Once you have dealt with each of the transactions, prepare a balance sheet at the end of Day 12 and a profit and loss account for the first 12 days of trading.

6 Chapter summary

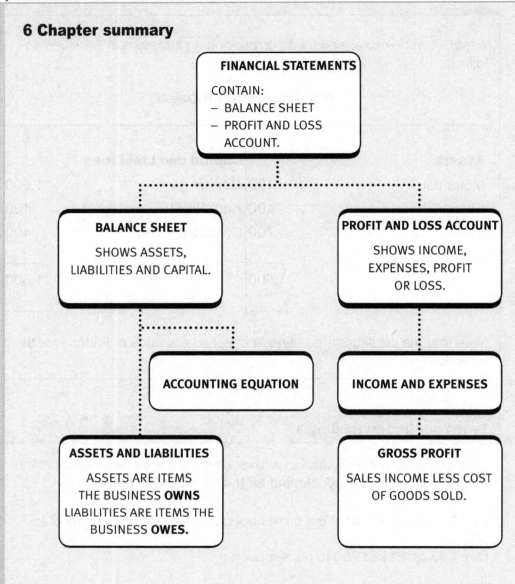

Test your understanding answers

Test Your Understanding 1

- Land and buildings – fixed asset.
- Debtors – current asset.
- Cash – current asset.
- Loan repayable in two years time – long-term liability.
- Creditors – current liability.
- Delivery van – fixed asset.

Test Your Understanding 2

- The correct order is:
- stock of raw materials
- stock of finished goods
- debtors
- cash at bank
- cash in hand.

Test Your Understanding 3

Day 6: sells half of the goods bought on Day 5 on credit for £250

This transaction introduces two new concepts:

- Sale on credit. Essentially this is the same as a sale for cash, except that the asset increased is not cash, but debtors.
- Sale of part of the stock. In practice this is the normal situation. The important accounting requirement is to separate:
- stock still held as an asset, from
- cost of stock sold.

Balance sheet for Day 6

Assets	£	Capital and liabilities	£
Motor car	400	Capital introduced	1,000
Stock	200	Add: Profit to date	
Debtors	250	(£100 + £50)	150
Cash	700		
			1,150
			400
	1,550		1,500

Day 7: Avon pays £200 to his supplier

The dual effect of this transaction is:

(a) The business has paid out £200 in cash.

(b) The business has reduced creditors (liability) by £200.

This is simply the reduction of one liability (creditors) and one asset (cash) by a corresponding amount (£200).

Balance sheet for Day 7

Assets	£	Capital and liabilities	£
Motor car	400	Capital	1,000
Stock	200	Add: Profit to date	150
Debtors	250		
Cash (£700 – £200)	500		
			1,150
		Creditors	
		(£400 – £200)	200
	1,350		1,350

Day 8: Avon receives £100 from a customer

The dual effect of this transaction is:

(a) The business has received £100 in cash.

(b) The debtors of the business have reduced by £100.

Balance sheet for Day 8

Assets	£	Capital and liabilities	£
Motor car	400	Capital	1,000
Stock	200	Add: Profit to date	150
Debtors			
(£250 – £100)	150		1,150
Cash (£500 + £100)	600	Creditors	200
	1,350		1,350

Day 9: Proprietor draws £75 in cash

This shows on the balance sheet as a reduction of capital, and as a reduction of cash.

Cash or other assets taken out of the business by the owner are called 'amounts withdrawn', or 'drawings'.

The dual effect of this transaction is:

(a) The business has reduced cash by £75.

(b) The business has a drawings balance of £75 which reduces capital.

Balance sheet for Day 9

Assets	£	Capital and liabilities	£
Motor car	400	Capital	1,000
Stock	200	Add: Profit to date	150
Debtors	150		
Cash (£600 – £75)	525		1,150
		Less: Drawings	(75)
			1,075
		Creditors	200
	1,275		1,275

Day 10: Avon pays rent of £40

This is an example of a business expense.

The dual effect of this transaction is:

(a) The business pays out £40 in cash.

(b) The business has a rent expense of £40 which reduces profit.

Balance sheet for Day 10

Assets	£	Capital and liabilities	£
Motor car	400	Capital	1,000
Stock	200	Add: Profit to date	
Debtors	150	(£150 – £40)	110
Cash (£525 – £40)	485		
			1,110
		Less: Drawings	(75)
			1,035
		Creditors	200
	1,235		1,235

Day 11: Avon receives a loan of £600 repayable in two years time'

The dual effect of this transaction is:

(a) The business receives £600 in cash.

(b) The business has a liability of £600.

Balance sheet for Day 11

Assets	£	Capital and liabilities	£
Motor car	400	Capital introduced	1,000
Stock	200	Add: Profit to date	110
Debtors	150		
Cash (£485 + £600)	1,085		
			1,110
		Less: Drawings	
			1,035
		Loan	600
		Creditors	200
	1,835		1,835

Day 12: Avon pays cash of £30 for insurance

The dual effect of this transaction is:

(a) The business pays out £30 in cash.

(b) The business has an insurance expense of £30 which reduces profit.

Balance sheet for day 12

Assets	£	Capital and liabilities	£
Motor car	400	Capital introduced	1,000
Stock	200	Add: Profit to date	
Debtors	150	(£110 – £30)	80
Cash (£1,085 – £30)	1,055		
	———		———
	1,805		
		Less: Drawings	(75)
			———
			1,005
		Loan	600
		Creditors	200
	———		———
	1,805		1,805

This marks the end of the transactions. The financial statements for the 12-day period can now be considered.

Avon, profit and loss account for the 12-day period

			£	£
Sales:	Cash			300
	Credit			250
				———
				550
Cost of sales:	Purchases:	Cash	200	
		Credit	400	
			———	
			600	
Less: Closing stock			(200)	
Cost of goods sold				(400)
				———
Gross profit				150
Rent			40	
Insurance			30	
			———	
				(70)
				———
Net profit				80

Avon, balance sheet as at end of Day 12

	£	£
Fixed asset:		
Motor car (at cost)		400
Current assets:		
Stock	200	
Debtors	150	
Cash	1,055	
	─────	
	1,405	
Less: Current liabilities: creditors	(200)	
		1,205
		─────
		1,605
Long-term liability: loan		(600)
		─────
		1,005
		─────
Capital account of Avon:		
Capital introduced		1,000
Net profit	80	
Less: drawings	(75)	
	─────	
Retained profit		5
		─────
		1,005
		─────

KAPLAN PUBLISHING

Double entry bookkeeping

Chapter learning objectives

Upon completion of this chapter you will be able to:

- explain the concept of double entry and the duality concept

- explain the debit and credit principle

- explain the meaning of the balance on each type of account

- record cash transactions in ledger accounts

- record credit sale and purchase transactions in ledger accounts

- illustrate how to account for discounts

- explain sales and purchase returns and demonstrate their recording

- illustrate how to balance a ledger account

- extract the ledger balances into a trial balance

- identify the purpose of a trial balance

- prepare a simple profit and loss account and balance sheet from a trial balance

- explain and illustrate the process of closing the ledger accounts in the accounting records when the financial statements have been completed.

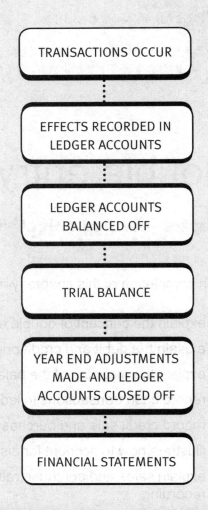

1 The duality concept and double entry bookkeeping

- Each transaction that a business enters into affects the financial statements in two ways, e.g.

A business buys a fixed asset for cash.

The two effects on the financial statements are:

(1) There is an increase in fixed assets.

(2) There is a decrease in cash.

- To follow the rules of double entry bookkeeping, each time a transaction is recorded, both effects must be taken into account.

- These two effects are equal and opposite such that the accounting equation will always prove correct:

$$\text{Assets } - \text{ Liabilities } = \text{Capital}$$

- Traditionally, one effect is referred to as the debit side (abbreviated to Dr) and the other as the credit side of the entry (abbreviated to Cr).

2 Ledger accounts, debits and credits

- Transactions are recorded in the relevant ledger accounts. There is a ledger account for each asset, liability, income and expense item.

- Each account has two sides – the debit and credit sides:

Debit	Name of account	Credit
(Dr)	e.g. cash, sales	(Cr)

Date	Narrative	£	Date	Narrative	£

- The duality concept means that each transaction will affect two ledger accounts.

- One account will be debited and the other credited.

- Whether an entry is to the debit or credit side of an account depends on the type of account and the transaction:

Debit	Credit
Increase in:	Increase in:
Expense	Income
Asset	Liability
Drawings	Capital

Summary of steps to record a transaction

(1) Identify the two items that are affected.

(2) Consider whether they are being increased or decreased.

(3) Decide whether each account should be debited or credited.

(4) Check that a debit entry and a credit entry have been made and they are both for the same amount.

Recording cash transactions

Cash transactions are those where payment is made or received immediately.

Cheque payments of receipts are classed as cash transactions.

Double entry involves the bank ledger:

- a debit entry is where funds are received

- a credit entry is where funds are paid out.

Test Your Understanding 1

Show the following transactions in ledger accounts. (Tip: the ledger accounts you need are bank, rent, drawings and sales.)

(1) Kamran pays £80 for rent by cheque.

(2) Kamran sells goods for £230 cash which he banks.

(3) He then takes £70 out of the business for his personal living expenses.

(4) Kamran sells more goods for cash, receiving £3,400.

Test Your Understanding 2

Yusuf enters into the following transactions in his first month of trading:

(1) Buys goods for cash for £380.

(2) Pays £20 in sundry expenses.

(3) Makes £1,000 in sales.

(4) Receives a bank loan of £5,000.

(5) Pays £2,600 for fixtures and fittings.

What is the total entry to the credit side of the cash T account?

A   £6,000

B   £6,380

C   £3,000

D   £2,620

Recording credit sales and purchases

Credit sales and purchases are transactions where goods or services change hands immediately, but payment is not made or received until some time in the future.

Money that a business is owed is accounted for in the debtors ledger.

Money that a business owes is accounted for in the creditors ledger.

Test Your Understanding 3

Norris notes down the following transactions that happened in June.

(1) Sell goods for cash for £60.

(2) Pay insurance premium by cheque – £400.

(3) Sell goods for £250 – the customer will pay in a month.

(4) Pay £50 for petrol for the delivery van.

(5) Buy £170 goods for resale on credit.

(6) Take £57 out of the business for living expenses.

(7) Buy another £40 goods for resale, paying cash.

(8) Buy a new computer for the business for £800.

Record these transactions using ledger accounts.

Test Your Understanding 4

For each of the following individual transactions state the two ledger accounts affected, and whether the ledger account should be debited or credited:

(1) Ole purchases goods for £5,000, and pays by cheque.

(2) Ole makes a sale to a customer for £500. The customer pays in 30 days' time.

(3) Ole pays a telephone bill amounting to £40, and pays by cheque.

(4) Ole receives bank interest income of £150.

(5) Ole purchases stationery for £12 and pays cash.

(6) Ole makes a sale to a customer for £400. The customer pays cash.

3 Recording sales and purchases returns

- It is normal for customers to return unwanted goods to a business; equally the business will occasionally have cause to return unwanted goods to their supplier.

- The double entries arising will depend upon whether the returned goods were initially purchased on credit:

	Originally a credit transaction	Originally a cash transaction
Sales returns(returns outwards)	Dr Sales returns Cr Debtors	Dr Sales returns Cr Cash
Purchases returns (returns outwards) returns	Dr Creditors Cr Purchases returns	Dr Cash Cr Purchases

Test Your Understanding 5

For each of the following, state the double entry required to record the transaction in the accounts:

(1) Alfie invests £10,000 of his life savings into a business bank account.

(2) He then buys goods from Isabel, a supplier for £1,000 and pays by cheque.

(3) A sale is made for £400 – the customer pays by cheque.

(4) Alfie makes a sale for £600 and the customer promises to pay in the future.

(5) Alfie then buys goods from his supplier, Kamen, for £500 on credit.

(6) Alife pays a telephone bill of £150 by cheque.

(7) The credit customer pays the balance on her account.

(8) Alfie pays Isabel £340.

(9) Bank interest of £30 is received.

(10) A cash customer returned £20 goods to Alfie for a refund.

(11) Alfie sent goods of £100 back to Kamen.

4 Accounting for discounts

Discounts may be given in the case of credit transactions for prompt payment:

- A business may give its customer a discount – known as **discount allowed**.

- A business may receive a discount from a supplier – known as **discount received**.

KAPLAN PUBLISHING

The correct double entries are:

Discount allowed

Dr Discount allowed (expense)	X
Cr Debtors	X

The expense is shown beneath gross profit in the profit and loss account, alongside other expenses of the business.

Discount received

Dr Creditors	X
Cr Discount received (income)	X

The income is shown beneath gross profit in the profit and loss account.

Trade discounts

Trade discounts are given to try and increase the volume of sales being made by the supplier. By reducing the selling price, buying items in bulk then becomes more attractive. If you are able to source your products cheaper, you can then also sell them on to the consumer cheaper too. For example, if we were to buy over 1000 items, the supplier might be able to drop the price of those items by 5%.

Early settlement discounts

This type of discount encourages people to pay for items much quicker. If you pay for the goods within a set time limit, then you will receive a % discount. For example, a cash discount of 3% is offered to any customers who pay within 14 days.

Whilst offering this discount makes the cash flow in quicker, it is still a 'lost cost' to the business who offers such a discount.

Test Your Understanding 6

George owes a supplier, Herbie, £2,000 and is owed £3,400 by a customer, Iris. George offers a cash discount to his customers of 2.5% if they pay within 14 days and Herbie has offered George a cash discount of 3% for payment within ten days.

George pays Herbie within ten days and Iris takes advantage of the cash discount offered to her.

What ledger entries are required to record these discounts?

		£		£
A	Dr Creditors	60	Dr Discount allowed	85
	Cr Discount received	60	Cr Debtors	85
B	Dr Discount allowed	60	Dr Creditors	85
	Cr Debtors	60	Cr Discount received	85
C	Dr Creditors	50	Dr Discount allowed	102
	Cr Discount received	50	Cr Debtors	102
D	Dr Discount allowed	50	Dr Creditors	102
	Cr Debtors	50	Cr Discount received	102

5 Balancing off a balance sheet ledger account

Once the transactions for a period have been recorded, it will be necessary to find the balance on the ledger account:

(1) Total both sides of the T account and find the larger total.

(2) Put the larger total in the total box on the debit and credit side.

(3) Insert a balancing figure to the side of the T account which does not currently add up to the amount in the total box. Call this balancing figure 'balance c/f' (carried forward) or 'balance c/d' (carried down).

(4) Carry the balance down diagonally and call it 'balance b/f' (brought forward) or 'balance b/d' (brought down).

Test Your Understanding 7

Balance off the following account:

Cash				
	£			£
Capital	10,000	Purchases		200
Sales	250	Rent		150
		Electricity		75

KAPLAN PUBLISHING

Test Your Understanding 8

Balance off the following account:

	Bank		
	£		£
Capital	10,000	Purchases	1,000
Sales	300	Rent	2,500
		Electricity	750
		New van	15,000

6 The trial balance

- Once all ledger accounts have been balanced off a trial balance is prepared.

- A trial balance is a list of the 'balance b/f' on the ledger accounts according to whether they are on the debit or credit side.

Trial balance as at 31 December 20X5

Name of account	Dr £	Cr £
Sales		X
Purchases	X	
Debtors	X	
Creditors		X
Capital		X
	X	X

What does the trial balance prove?

The trial balance will balance if for every debit entry made, an equal credit entry was made and the balances were correctly extracted and cast (added up!).

- The purpose of a trial balance is:

- to check that for every debit entry made, an equal credit entry has been made

- as a first step in preparing the financial statements.

Note that a number of adjustments will be made after the trial balance is extracted. These adjustments do not therefore appear in the trial balance.

7 Closing off the ledger accounts

Balance sheet ledger accounts

- Assets/liabilities at the end of a period = assets/liabilities at start of the next period, e.g. the cash at bank at the end of one day will be the cash at bank at the start of the following day.

- Balancing the account will result in:

- – a balance c/f (being the asset/liability at the end of the accounting period).

- – a balance b/f (being the asset/liability at the start of the next accounting period).

Profit and loss account ledger account

- At the end of a period any amounts that relate to that period are transferred out of the income and expenditure accounts into another ledger account called the profit and loss account.

- This is done by closing the account.

- Do not show a balance c/f or balance b/f but instead put the balancing figure on the smallest side and label it 'profit and loss account.'

Capital account

- At the start of the next accounting period the capital account will have an opening balance, i.e. a balance b/f equal to the amount that is owed to the owner at the start of that period.

- This amount is equal to what was owed to the owner at the start of the previous period, plus any capital that the owner introduced in the period, plus any profits earned in the period less any drawings taken out in the period.

- Therefore we transfer the balance on the profit and loss account and the balance on the drawings account to the capital account at the end of the period so that it will have the correct opening balance at the start of the next period.

Capital

	£		£
		Balance b/f	X
Loss for year	X	Profit for year	X
Drawings	X	Cash injections	X
Balance c/f	X		
	—		—
	X		X
	—		
		Balance b/f	X

Test Your Understanding 9

Oddjob had £7,800 capital invested in his business at the start of the year. During the course of the year he took £3,100 cash out of the business and also paid his wife, who did some secretarial work for him, £500. The business' profit for the year was £8,900. Oddjob also paid £350 for a new suit using the business cheque book during the year.

What is the balance on the capital account at the end of the year?

A   £12,750

B   £13,250

C   £13,600

D   £13,100

8 Opening balances in the ledger accounts

- If a business has been in operation in the previous year, then at the beginning of any accounting period it will have assets and liabilities such as cash and fixed assets.

- Any opening amounts are shown in balance sheet ledger accounts as opening balances.

- The opening balance on an asset account is a debit entry.

- The opening balance on a liability account is a credit entry.

- Transactions during the year are then entered as normal in the ledger account, and at the year end it is balanced off taking into account the opening balance.

Note: profit and loss account ledger accounts do not have an opening balance.

Test Your Understanding 10

Johnny had debtors of £4,500 at the start of 20X5. During the year to 31 December 20X5 he makes credit sales of £45,000 and receives cash of £46,500 from credit customers.

What is the balance on the debtors account at 31 December 20X5?

A   £6,000Dr

B   £6,000Cr

C   £3,000Dr

D   £3,000Cr

9 Preparation of financial statements

The process seen thus far is as follows:

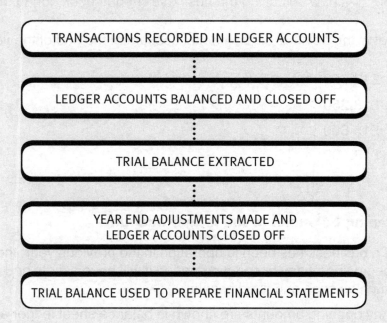

TRANSACTIONS RECORDED IN LEDGER ACCOUNTS

LEDGER ACCOUNTS BALANCED AND CLOSED OFF

TRIAL BALANCE EXTRACTED

YEAR END ADJUSTMENTS MADE AND LEDGER ACCOUNTS CLOSED OFF

TRIAL BALANCE USED TO PREPARE FINANCIAL STATEMENTS

Examination questions may draw on any particular stage of this process.

Test Your Understanding 11

Closing off the accounts

Matthew set up a business and in the first nine days of trading the following transactions occurred:

1 January	Matthew introduces £10,000 capital by cheque.
2 January	Matthew buys supplies worth £4,000 and pays by cheque.
3 January	Matthew buys a delivery van for £2,000 and pays by cheque.
4 January	Matthew buys £1,000 of purchases on credit.
5 January	Matthew sells goods for £1,500 and receives a cheque of that amount.
6 January	Matthew sells all his remaining goods for £5,000 on credit.
7 January	Matthew pays £800 to his supplier by cheque.
8 January	Matthew pays rent of £200 by cheque.
9 January	Matthew draws £100 for living expenses from the business bank account.

A   Complete the relevant ledger accounts.

B   Extract a trial balance.

C   Prepare the profit and loss account for the first nine days.

D   Prepare the balance sheet as at 9 January.

10 Chapter summary

TRANSACTIONS OCCUR

**TWO EFFECTS RECORDED
IN LEDGER ACCOUNTS**

Debit = credit

Dr = increase in	Cr = increase in
Expense	Liability
Asset	Income
Drawings.	Capital.

LEDGER ACCOUNTS BALANCED OFF

1. Total both sides and find the larger total.
2. Put the larger total in both total boxes.
3. Insert a balancing figure as required in balance sheet accounts, call this balancing figure 'Balance c/f'. For income and expense accounts, take this balancing figure to the profit and loss account T account.
4. For balance sheet accounts, carry the balance down diagonally and call it 'balance b/f'.

TRIAL BALANCE

Is extracted. Double entry has been correctly upheld as long as total debits = total credits.

**YEAR-END ADJUSTMENTS AND LEDGER
ACCOUNTS CLOSED OFF**

- Balance sheet accounts result in a balance c/f.
- Profit and loss accounts are closed off to the profit and loss account ledger account.
- The balance on the profit and loss account and drawings ledger accounts are transferred to the capital account.

FINANCIAL STATEMENTS

Test your understanding answers

Test Your Understanding 1

Bank

	£		£
Sales (2)	230	Rent (1)	80
Sales (4)	3,400	Drawings (3)	70

Sales

	£		£
		Bank (2)	230
		Bank (4)	3,400

Rent

	£		£
Bank (1)	80		

Drawings

	£		£
Bank (3)	70		

Test Your Understanding 2

The correct answer is C

Cash

	£		£
Sales	1,000	Purchases	380
Loan	5,000	Sundry expenses	20
		Fixtures and fittings	2,600
		Bal c/fwd	3,000
	6,000		6,000

Test Your Understanding 3

Bank

	£		£
Sales (1)	60	Insurance (2)	400
		Motor expenses (4)	50
		Drawings (6)	57
		Purchases (7)	40
		Fixed assets (8)	800

Sales

	£		£
		Bank (1)	60
		Debtors (3)	250

Insurance (expense)

	£		£
Bank (2)	400		

Debtors

	£		£
Sales (3)	250		

Motor expenses

	£		£
Bank (4)	50		

Purchases

	£		£
Creditors (7)	170		
Cash (7)	40		

Creditors

	£		£
		Purchases (5)	170

Drawings

	£		£
Bank (6)	57		

Fixed asset (computer)

	£		£
Bank (8)	800		

Test Your Understanding 4

			£	£
1	Dr	Purchases	5,000	
	Cr	Bank		5,000
2	Dr	Debtors	500	
	Cr	Sales		500
3	Dr	Telephone expense	40	
	Cr	Bank		40
4	Dr	Bank	150	
	Cr	Interest income		150
5	Dr	Stationery expense	12	
	Cr	Cash		12
6	Dr	Cash	400	
	Cr	Sales		400

Test Your Understanding 5

			£	£
1	Dr	Bank	10,000	
	Cr	Capital		10,000
2	Dr	Purchases	1,000	
	Cr	Bank		1,000
3	Dr	Bank	400	
	Cr	Sales		400
4	Dr	Debtors	600	
	Cr	Sales		600
5	Dr	Purchases	500	
	Cr	Creditors		500
6	Dr	Telephone expense	150	
	Cr	Bank		150
7	Dr	Bank	600	
	Cr	Debtors		600
8	Dr	Creditors	340	
	Cr	Bank		340
9	Dr	Bank	30	
	Cr	Interest income		30
10	Dr	Sales returns	20	
	Cr	Bank		20
11	Dr	Creditors	100	
	Cr	Purchases returns		100

Test Your Understanding 6

The correct answer is A

Creditors

	£		£
Cash (97% x 2,000)	1,940	Balance b/f	2,000
Discount received	60		
	2,000		2,000

Debtors

	£		£
Balance b/f	3,400	Cash (97.5% x 3,400)	3,315
		Discount allowed	85
	3,400		3,400

Discount received

	£		£
		Creditors	60

Discount allowed

	£		£
Debtors	85		

Test Your Understanding 7

Cash

	£		£
Capital	10,000	Purchases	200
Sales	250	Rent	150
		Electricity	75
		Balance c/f	9,825
	10,250		10,250
Balance b/f	9,825		

Test Your Understanding 8

Bank

	£		£
Capital	10,000	Purchases	1,000
Sales	300	Rent	2,500
		Electricity	750
		New van	15,000
Balance c/f	8,950		
	19,250		19,250
		Balance b/f	8,950

Note that a balance on the credit side of a bank account denotes an overdraft.

KAPLAN PUBLISHING

Test Your Understanding 9

The correct answer is B

Capital

	£		£
Drawings	3,100	Balance b/f	7,800
Drawings (suit)	350	Profit for the year	8,900
Balance c/f	13,250		
	16,700		16,700
		Balance b/f	13,250

Test Your Understanding 10

The correct answer is C

Debtors

	£		£
Balance b/f	4,500		
Sales	45,000	Cash received	46,500
		Balance c/f	3,000
	49,500		49,500
Balance b/f	3,000		

Test Your Understanding 11

Bank

			£			£
(a) 1 Jan	Capital		10,000	2 Jan	Purchases	4,000
5 Jan	Sales		1,500	3 Jan	Delivery van	2,000
				7 Jan	Creditors	800
				8 Jan	Rent	200
				9 Jan	Drawings	100
					Balance c/f	4,400
			11,500			11,500
Balance b/f			4,400			

Capital

		£			£
Balance c/f		10,000	1 Jan	Bank	10,000
		10,000			10,000
			Balance b/f		10,000

Purchases

		£		£
2 Jan	Bank	4,000	P&L	5,000
4 Jan	Creditors	1,000		
		5,000		5,000

Delivery van

		£		£
3 Jan	Bank	2,000	Balance c/f	2,000
		2,000		2,000
Balance b/f		2,000		

Creditors

		£			£
7 Jan	Bank	800	4 Jan	Purchases	1,000
	Balance c/f	200			
		1,000			1,000
				Balance b/f	1,000

Sales

		£			£
	P&L	6,500	5 Jan	Bank	1,500
			6 Jan	Debtors	5,000
		6,500			6,500

Debtors

		£		£
7 Jan	Sales	5,000	Balance c/f	5,000
		5,000		5,000
Balance b/f		5,000		

Rent

		£		£
8 Jan	Bank	200	P&L	200
		200		200

Drawings

		£		£
9 Jan	Bank	100	Balance c/f	100
		100		100
Balance b/f		100		

(b) Trial balance as at 9 January

	Dr	Cr
	£	£
Bank	4,400	
Capital		10,000
Purchases	5,000	
Delivery van	2,000	
Creditors		200
Sales		6,500
Debtors	5,000	
Rent	200	
Drawings	100	
	16,700	16,700

KAPLAN PUBLISHING

(c) Profit and loss account for the period ended 9 January

	£	£
Sales		6,500
Cost of sales		
Opening inventory		–
Purchases	5,000	
Closing inventory		–
		(5,000)
Gross profit		1,500
Expenses		
Rent		(200)
Net profit		1,300

(d) Balance sheet as at 9 January

	£	£
Fixed assets		
Delivery van		2,000
Current assets		
Inventory	–	
Debtors	5,000	
Bank		
	4,400	
	————	
		9,400
Current liabilities		
Creditors		(200)
		————
		11,200
		————
Capital		10,000
Profit		1,300
Drawings		(100)
		————
		11,200
		————

KAPLAN PUBLISHING

Value added tax

Chapter learning objectives

Upon completion of this chapter you will be able to:

- explain the general principles of the operation of value added tax (VAT)
- calculate correctly VAT on transactions
- enter VAT on sales and purchases into the ledger accounts.

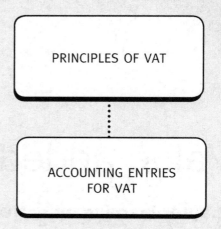

1 Principles of VAT

VAT is a form of indirect taxation.

- A business that is registered for VAT is essentially a collection agent for the government.
- VAT is charged on purchases (input tax) and sales (output tax).
- VAT is excluded from the reported sales and purchases of the business.
- Periodically the business pays the VAT to the tax authorities.
- If output tax exceeds input tax, the business pays the excess to the tax authorities.
- If input tax exceeds output tax, the business is repaid the excess by the tax authorities.
- VAT is sometimes called goods and services tax.
- VAT is charged on most goods and services.

2 Calculation of VAT

- The standard rate of VAT is 17.5%, charged on the selling price.
- The following is therefore true:

Net selling price (tax exclusive price)	100.0%
VAT	17.5%
Gross selling price (tax inclusive price)	117.5%

- The net selling price is the amount that the business wishes to achieve.
- The gross selling price is the price charged to customers.
- The difference is paid to the tax authorities.

Please note: in the exam any rate of VAT could be used in a question, it will not always be 17.5%.

Illustration 1 : Calculation of VAT

Calculation of VAT

Orlando sells the following goods:

(1) to Bruno at a tax inclusive price of £470
(2) to Cosmo at a tax exclusive price of £700.

How much VAT is Orlando collecting on behalf of the government?

The rate of VAT to be used is 17.5%.

Solution

VAT can be calculated using the relevant percentage depending on whether the price is tax inclusive or exclusive.

Sales to Bruno (sales price tax inclusive) 17.5% / 117.5% * £470 = £70

Sales to Cosmo (sales price tax exclusive) 17.5% / 100% * £700 = £122.50

Total VAT collected: £70 + £122.50 = £192.50

Test Your Understanding 1

Lorenzo purchases goods for £170,625 (including VAT) and sells goods for £230,500 (including VAT).

What amount of VAT is ultimately payable to the tax authorities?

A   £8,918

B   £14,926

C   £4,471

D   £10,479

The VAT rate is 17.5%.

3 Accounting entries for VAT

The usual bookkeeping entries for purchases and sales are only slightly amended by VAT, the main addition being the introduction of a VAT account, which is a debtor or creditor account with the tax authorities.

VAT paid on purchases (input tax)

Dr Purchases	Cost excluding VAT (net cost)
Dr VAT	VAT
Cr Creditors/cash	Cost including VAT (gross cost)

- The purchases account does not include VAT because it is not an expense – it will be recovered.

- The creditors account does include VAT, as the supplier must be paid the full amount due.

VAT charged on sales (output tax)

Dr Debtors/cash	Sales price including VAT (gross selling price)
Cr Sales	Sales price excluding VAT (net selling price)
Cr VAT	VAT

- The sales account does not include VAT because it is not income – it will have to be paid to the tax authorities.

- The debtors account does include VAT, as the customer must pay the full amount due.

Payment of VAT

Dr VAT	Amount owing
Cr Cash	Amount owing

- If output tax exceeds input tax, a payment must be made to the tax authorities.

Receipt of VAT

Dr Cash	Amount Recieved
Cr VAT	Amount Recieved

- If input tax exceeds output tax, there will be a receipt from the tax authorities.

VAT on discounts

The VAT is calculated on the sales price less the early settlement discount, whether this discount is taken or not.

Dr Debtors/cash – gross selling price (sales price including VAT)

Cr Sales – net selling price

Cr VAT – VAT amount is calculated on the sales price less the discount being offered, whether it is taken or not.

Test Your Understanding 2

A Cleo's purchases and sales analysis shows the following information for the last quarter of his financial year:

		Net	VAT	Total
		£	£	£
Purchases	(all on credit)	180,000	31,500	211,500
Sales	(all on credit)	260,000	45,500	305,500

Record these transactions in the ledger accounts.

Test Your Understanding 3

Valerie's business is registered for VAT purposes. During the quarter ending 31 March 20X6, she made the following sales, all of which were subject to VAT at 17.5%:

£10,000 excluding VAT

£7,402 including VAT

£9,870 including VAT

£11,632 including VAT

She also made the following purchases all of which were subject to VAT at 17.5%:

£15,000 excluding VAT

£12,455 including VAT

£11,338 including VAT

£6,745 excluding VAT

What is the balance on the VAT account on 31 March 20X6?

A   £7,639 Dr

B   £1,742 Dr

C   £7,639 Cr

D   £1,875 Cr

4 Chapter summary

PRINCIPLES OF VAT

- It is charged on purchases and sales.

- It is excluded from the reported sales and purchases of the business.

- The business is a collection agent for the government.

- It is paid periodically to the tax authorities (or it is repaid to the business if taxable purchases exceed sales).

ACCOUNTING ENTRIES FOR VAT

- Sales and purchases ledger accounts are net of VAT.

- Debtors and creditors ledger accounts are inclusive of VAT as the business collects the VAT from customers and pays it to suppliers.

- The VAT account is a payable (or receivable) account in the balance sheet.

Test your understanding answers

The correct answer is A

	£
Output tax:	
Sales (including VAT)	230,500
VAT (17.5/117.5)	34,330
	————
Input tax:	
Purchases (including VAT)	170,625
VAT (17.5/117.5)	25,412
	————
Payable to tax authorities:	
Output tax – Input tax	
(34,330 – 25,412)	8,918
	————

Test Your Understanding 2

Sales

	£		£
		Debtors	260,000
			———
			260,000
			———

Note that sales are recorded excluding VAT, as this is not income for the business.

Purchases

	£		£
Creditors	180,000		
	———		
	180,000		
	———		

Note that purchases are recorded net of VAT, as this is not a cost to the business.

Debtors

	£		£
Sales/VAT	305,500		
	———		
	305,500		
	———		

Debtors are recorded including VAT (the gross amount) as the customer must pay the business the cost of the goods plus the VAT.

Creditors

	£		£
		Purchases/VAT	211,500
			———
			211,500
			———

As with debtors, the creditors must be recorded inclusive of VAT, as the business needs to pay its suppliers the gross amount.

VAT account (a personal account with tax authorities)

	£		£
Creditors	31,500	Debtors	45,500
Balance c/f	14,000		
	45,500		45,500
		Balance b/f	14,000

Note: As the balance on the VAT account represents a normal trade liability it is included in accounts payable on the balance sheet.

Test Your Understanding 3

The correct answer is B

VAT

Purchases:	£	Sales:	£
15,000 x 17.5%	2,625	10,000 x 17.5%	1,750
12,455 x 17.5/117.5	1,855	7,402 x 17.5/117.5	1,102
11,338 x 17.5/117.5	1,689	9,870 x 17.5/117.5	1,023
6,745 x 17.5%	1,180	11,632.50 x 17.5/117.5	1,732
		Balance c/f	1,742
	7,349		7,349
Balance b/f	1,742		

Stock

Chapter learning objectives

Upon completion of this chapter you will be able to:

- explain the need for adjustments for stock in preparing financial statements

- illustrate profit and loss accounts with opening and closing stock

- explain and demonstrate how opening and closing stock are recorded in the stock account

- explain the Statement of Standard Accounting Practice (SSAP 9) requirement regarding the valuation of closing stock

- define the cost and net realisable value (NVR) of closing stock

- discuss alternative methods of valuing stock

- explain and demonstrate how to calculate the value of closing stock from given movements in stock levels, using FIFO (first in first out) and AVCO (average cost)

- assess the effect of using either FIFO or AVCO on both profit and asset value

- explain the Accounting Standards Board (ASB) requirements for inventories

- explain the use of continuous and period-end stock records.

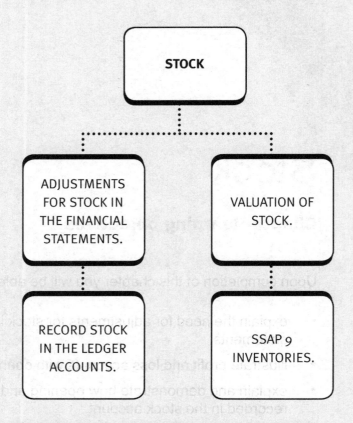

1 Adjustments for stock in the financial statements

- To be able to prepare a set of financial statements, stock must be accounted for at the end of the period.

- Opening stock must be included in cost of sales as these goods are available for sale along with purchases during the year.

- Closing stock must be deducted from cost of sales as these goods are left on hand at the period end and have not been sold.

Expandable text

In order to be able to prepare a set of financial statements, it is first necessary to learn how to account for any items of goods held at the end of the year, i.e. closing stock. (In some countries stock is referred to as 'inventory'.)

Example

A trader starts in business and by the end of his first year he has purchased goods costing £21,000 and he has made sales totalling £25,000. Goods which cost him £3,000 have not been sold by the end of the year.

What profit has he made in the year?

Solution

The unsold goods are referred to as closing stock. This stock is deducted from purchases in the profit and loss account.

Gross profit is thus:

	£	£
Sales		25,000
Purchases	21,000	
Less: Closing stock	(3,000)	
Cost of sales		(18,000)
Gross profit		7,000

Closing stock of £3,000 will appear on the balance sheet as an asset.

Illustration 1 : Adjustments for stock

Peter buys and sells washing machines. He has been trading for many years. On 1 January 20X7, his opening stock is 30 washing machines which cost £9,500. He purchased 65 machines in the year amounting to £150,000 and on 31 December 20X7 he has 25 washing machines left in stock with a cost of £7,500. Peter has sold 70 machines with a sales value of £215,000 in the year.

Calculate the gross profit for the year ended 31 December 20X7.

Solution

- Gross profit is sales revenue less cost of sales.

- We must match the 70 machines sold with the cost of those machines and exclude from cost of sales the machines that are left in stock.

- Opening stock must be included in cost of sales as some of the goods sold during the year come from the goods the trader started off with at the beginning of the year.

- We can calculate the gross profit as follows:

	£	£
Sales		215,000
Opening stock (at cost)	9,500	
Purchases (at cost)	150,000	
	159,500	
Less: Closing stock (at cost)	(7,500)	
Cost of sales		(152,000)
Gross profit		63,000

2 Recording stock in the ledger accounts

- Stock is only recorded in the ledger accounts at the end of the accounting period.

- In the stock ledger account the **opening stock** will be the brought down balance from the previous period. This must be transferred to the profit and loss account ledger account with the following entry:

  Dr Profit and loss account (ledger account)

  Cr Stock (ledger account).

- The **closing stock** is entered into the ledger accounts with the following entry:

  Dr Stock (ledger account)

  Cr Profit and loss account (ledger account).

- Once these entries have been completed, the profit and loss account ledger account contains both opening and closing stock and the stock ledger account shows the closing stock for the period to be shown in the balance sheet.

Illustration 2 : Recording stock in the ledger accounts

Continuing from the previous illustration, we will now see how the ledger accounts for stock are prepared.

We will look at the ledger accounts at the following times:

(a) Immediately before extracting a trial balance at 31 December 20X7.

(b) Immediately after the year-end adjustments and closing off of the ledger accounts.

(a) **Ledger accounts before extracting a trial balance**

Stock account

20X7	£		£
1 Jan Balance b/f	9,500		

The stock is an asset and therefore is a debit entry in the stock account.

Purchases account

20X7	£		£
Various suppliers	150,000		

Sales account

	£	20X7	£
		Various customers	215,000

- The balance of £9,500 in stock account originated from last year's balance sheet when it appeared as closing stock. This figure remains unchanged in the stock account until the very end of the year when closing stock at 31 December 20X7 is considered.

- The closing stock figure is not usually provided to us until after we have extracted the trial balance at 31 December 20X7.

- The purchases and sales figures have been built up over the year and represent the year's accumulated transactions.

- The trial balance will include opening stock, purchases and sales in respect of the stock transactions.

(b) Ledger accounts reflecting the closing stock

Closing stock for accounting purposes has been valued at £7,500.

Step 1

The profit and loss account forms part of the double entry. At the year end the accumulated totals from the sales and purchases accounts must be transferred to it using the following journal entries:

Dr Sales	£215,000
Cr Profit and loss account	£215,000
Dr Profit and loss account	£215,000
Cr Purchases	£150,000

These transfers are shown in the ledger accounts below.

Step 2

The opening stock figure (£9,500) must also be transferred to the profit and loss account account in order to arrive at cost of sales.

Dr Profit and loss account	£9,500
Cr Stock	£9,500

Step 3

The profit and loss account cannot be completed (and hence gross profit calculated) until the closing stock is included.

Dr Stock	£7,500
Cr Profit and loss account	£7,500

After summarising and balancing off, the ledger then becomes:

Stock

20X7	£	20X7	£
1 Jan Balance b/f	9,500	31 Dec Profit and loss account	9,500
31 Dec Profit and loss account	7,500	31 Dec Balance c/f	7,500
	17,000		17,000
20X8			
1 Jan Balance b/f	7,500		

Purchases

20X7	£	20X7	£
Various dates		31 Dec Profit and loss account	
Creditors	150,000		150,000

Sales revenue account

20X7	£	20X7	£
31 Dec Profit and loss account	215,000	Various dates Debtors	215,000

Profit and loss account (T account form)

20X7	£	20X7	£
31 Dec		31 Dec Sales	215,000
Purchases	150,000	Stock	7,500
Stock	9,500		
Gross profit c/f	63,000		
	222,500		222,500
		Gross profit b/f	63,000

Key points:

- The sales and the purchases accounts are cleared out to and summarised in the profit and loss account.

- Opening stock is cleared out to the profit and loss account and closing stock is entered into the stock account and the profit and loss account.

- The balance on the stock account remains at the end of the period and is listed in the balance sheet under current assets as stock.

- The first part of the profit and loss account can be balanced at this stage to show the gross profit figure carried down and brought down.

- The above layout of the profit and loss account is not particularly useful, but it assists the appreciation of the actual double entry processes and the realisation that the profit and loss account is part of the double entry.

The more common layout of the first part of the profit and loss account is:

	£	£
Sales		215,000
Opening stock	9,500	
Add: Purchases	150,000	
	159,500	
Less: Closing stock	(7,500)	
Cost of sales		(152,000)
Gross profit		63,000

Expandable text

Recording stock in ledger accounts

After the financial statements have been completed, it is usual to balance the various ledger accounts.

Note particularly the treatment of the stock account. The balance carried forward (c/f) is a balance at the end of the year which will be entered on the balance sheet representing closing stock.

This is brought forward (b/f) at the beginning of the following year, representing the opening stock for the next accounting period. This illustrates two key features in bookkeeping:

- any balance carried forward at the end of an accounting period should be included on the balance sheet

- any balance carried forward at the end of an accounting period will become the opening balance at the beginning of the next accounting period.

Test Your Understanding 1

The trading position of a simple cash-based business for its first week of trading was as follows:

	£
Capital introduced by the owner	1,000
Purchases for cash	800
Sales for cash	900

At the end of the week there were goods which had cost £300 left in stock.

Write up the ledger accounts for the first week, including the profit and loss account, and then prepare a vertical profit and loss account together with a balance sheet at the end of the first week.

Test Your Understanding 2

The business described in the previous activity now continues into its second week. Its transactions are as follows:

	£
Sales for cash	1,000
Purchases for cash	1,100

The goods left in stock at the end of this second week originally cost £500.

Write up the ledger accounts for the second week, including the profit and loss account, and then prepare a vertical profit and loss account together with a balance sheet at the end of the second week.

3 Stock drawings

It is not unusual for a sole trader to take stock from their business for their own use. This type of transaction is a form of drawings.

The correct double entry to account for such drawings is:

Dr Drawings	cost of stock taken
Cr Cost of sales	cost of stock taken

The credit entry ensures that the cost of stock taken is not included as part of the cost of stock sold in the profit and loss account.

4 Valuation of stock

Stock consists of:

- goods purchased for resale
- consumable stores (such as oil)
- raw materials and components (used in the production process)
- partly-finished goods (usually called work-in-progress – WIP)
- finished goods (which have been manufactured by the business).

Stock is included in the balance sheet at:

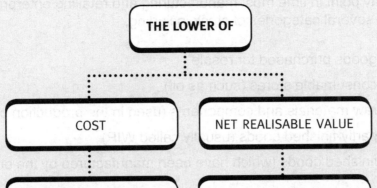

THE LOWER OF

COST

- All the expenditure incurred in bringing the product or service to its present location and condition.
- This includes cost of purchase – material costs, import duties, freight and cost of **conversion** – this includes **direct costs** and **production overheads**.

NET REALISABLE VALUE

- Revenue expected to be earned in the future when the goods are sold, less any selling costs.

Expandable text

Stock valuation

Introduction

It can be a complicated procedure to arrive at the valuation placed on closing stock, because:

- initially the existence of the stock, and the quantities thereof, have to be ascertained by means of a stock count
- following on from this, a valuation has to be placed on the stock which, as will be seen, may differ according to whatever accounting policy a company adopts.

The valuation of stock is governed by SSAP 9 Stock and long-term contracts.

Definition of stock and WIP

At any point in time most manufacturing and retailing enterprises will hold several categories of stock including:

- goods purchased for resale
- consumable stores (such as oil)
- raw materials and components (used in the production process)
- partly-finished goods (usually called WIP)
- finished goods (which have been manufactured by the enterprise).

The matching and prudence concept

The concept of matching justifies the carrying forward of purchases not sold by the end of the accounting period, to leave the remaining purchases to be 'matched' with sales.

When it comes to placing a value on the stock carried forward, we have a further concept to consider: the prudence concept.

If it weren't for this concept, we would carry forward stock at its cost to the business. The prudence concept, however, requires the application of a degree of caution in making estimates under conditions of uncertainty.

In the context of the value of stock, this means that if goods are expected to be sold below cost after the balance sheet date (for example, because they are damaged or obsolete), account must be taken of the loss in order to prepare the balance sheet.

The amount at which stock should be stated in the balance sheet is the lower of cost and NRV.

Cost

Cost includes all the expenditure incurred in bringing the product or service to its present location and condition.

This includes:

- cost of **purchase** – material costs, import duties, freight
- cost of **conversion** – this includes **direct costs** and **production overheads**. These terms are explained in the following example.

Example

Gordano is a small furniture manufacturing company. All of its timber is imported from Scandinavia and there are only three basic products – a dining table, a cupboard and a bookcase. At the end of the year the company has 200 completed bookcases in stock. For final accounts purposes, these will be stated at the lower of cost and NRV. How is 'cost' arrived at?

Solution

'Cost' will include several elements:

- **Cost of purchase.** First of all we must identify the timber used in the manufacture of bookcases (as opposed to dining tables and cupboards). The relevant costs will include the cost of the timber, the import duty and all the insurance and freight expenses associated with transporting the timber from Scandinavia to the factory.

- **Cost of conversion.** This will include costs which can be directly linked to the bookcases produced during the year. This includes labour costs 'booked' and sundry material costs (e.g. hinges and screws). Production overheads present particular problems. Costs such as factory heating and light, salaries of supervisors and depreciation of equipment are likely to relate to the three product ranges. These costs must be allocated to these product ranges on a reasonable basis. In particular, any percentage additions to cover overheads must be based on the normal level of production. If this proviso was not made, the stock could be overvalued at the end of a period of low production, because there would be a smaller number of items over which to spread the overhead cost.

These groups of cost must relate to either:

- bookcases sold during the year, or
- bookcases in stock at the year end (i.e. 200 bookcases).

Test Your Understanding 3

Cole's business sells three products X, Y and Z. The following information was available at the year end:

	X	Y	Z
	£	£	£
Cost	7	10	19
NRV	10	8	15
Units	100	200	300

What is the value of the closing stock?

A	£8,400
B	£6,800
C	£7,100
D	£7,200

Test Your Understanding 4

In what circumstances might the NRV of stocks be lower than their cost?

5 Methods of calculating cost of stock

Method	Key points:	
Unit cost	This is the actual cost of purchasing identifiable units of stock.	Only used when items of stock are individually distinguishable and of high value.
FIFO: first in **first out**	For costing purposes, the first items of stock received are the first ones sold.	When a sale is made, the cost of sales is the cost of the oldest goods purchased.
AVCO: average **cost**	The cost of an item of stock is calculated by taking the average of all stock held.	The average cost can be calculated periodically or continuously.

Expandable text

Methods of arriving at cost

With the exception of the unit cost method, the techniques mentioned below are not designed to ascertain the identity of individual items of stock, but make assumptions as to which items are deemed to be in closing stock.

Unit cost is the actual cost of purchasing identifiable units of stock.

This method is only likely to be used in situations where stock items are of high value and individually distinguishable. Examples would include jewellery retailers and art dealers, where in each case the proprietors would need to value each item individually.

FIFO

In **FIFO**, the assumption is made for costing purposes that the first items of stock received are the first items to be sold.

Thus every time a sale is made, the cost of goods sold is identified as representing the cost of the oldest goods remaining in stock.

AVCO

Under the weighted average cost formula, the cost of each item is determined from the weighted average of the cost of similar items at the beginning of the period and the cost of similar items purchased or produced during the period.

This calculation can be carried out periodically, or continuously after every purchase.

Note that the use of LIFO (last in first out) is no longer permissible internationally.

Test Your Understanding 5

Sam started her business on 1 January and provides details of the following transactions:

Purchases

1 January	5 units at £4/unit
3 January	5 units at £5/unit
4 January	5 units at £5.50/unit

She then sold 7 units for £10/unit on 5 January.

(a) Calculate the value of the closing stock at the end of the first week of trading using the FIFO and the AVCO method.

(b) Prepare the profit and loss account for the first week of trading under both the FIFO and AVCO bases.

Test Your Understanding 6

A business is commenced on 1 January and purchases are made as follows:

Month	No. of units	Unit price	Value
		£	£
Jan	380	2.00	760
Feb	400	2.50	1,000
Mar	350	2.50	875
Apr	420	2.75	1,155
May	430	3.00	1,290
Jun	440	3.25	1,430
	2,420		6,510

In June, 1,420 articles were sold for £7,000.

What is the cost of closing stock and gross profit for the period using the FIFO method:

	Closing stock	Gross profit
	£	£
A	2,690	3,180
B	2,310	2,800
C	3,077	3,567

The impact of valuation methods on profit and the balance sheet.

Different valuation methods will result in different closing stock values.

This will in turn impact both profit and balance sheet asset value.

Similarly any incorrect valuation of stock will impact the financial statements.

If stock is overvalued then:

- assets are overstated in the balance sheet
- profit is overstated in the profit and loss account (as cost of sales is too low)

If stock is undervalued then:

- assets are understated in the balance sheet
- profit is understated in the profit and loss account (as cost of sales is too high).

6 SSAP 9 Stock and long-term contracts

The key requirements of SSAP 9 are:

- stock is valued at the lower of cost and net realisable value
- cost includes costs of purchase, costs of conversion and other costs incurred in bringing the stock to its present location and condition
- costs which must be excluded from the cost of stock are:
  - selling costs
  - storage costs
  - abnormal waste of materials, labour or other costs
  - administrative overheads.

- cost should be unit cost (if identifiable), FIFO or weighted average
- disclosures must be made about the accounting policy for stock and classification of stock included in the financial statements.

Keeping stock records

A business may choose to keep stock records on a continuous basis throughout the year or only count stock at the period end.

Expandable text

SSAP 9 Stock and long-term contracts

SSAP 9 lays down the rules to be applied when valuing stock and specifies disclosure requirements for the financial statements.

The basic principle of SSAP 9 is that stock should be valued at the lower of cost and NRV.

The requirements of SSAP 9 for arriving at cost

The cost of inventories should include all costs of purchase, costs of conversion and other costs incurred in bringing the stock to its present location and condition.

For goods purchased for resale and for raw materials, arriving at cost is reasonably easy. Cost of purchase includes import duties, other taxes (unless recoverable) and transport costs. Trade discounts are obviously to be deducted.

For manufactured goods or WIP, the problem becomes more complex. Cost must include direct labour and an allocation of fixed and variable overheads. (Fixed overheads are those that remain fairly constant regardless of the volume of production, like factory rent, while variable overheads are those which vary according to the level of production, such as indirect labour or lubricating oils for plant.)

The allocation of fixed overheads needs to be based on the normal level of production.

Overhead expenses which must be excluded are:

- selling costs (excluded because they relate to goods sold, not those held in stock)
- storage costs
- abnormal wastage of materials, labour or other production costs
- administrative overheads.

Measurement of cost

As we saw above, there are several ways of deciding which items are deemed to be held in stock:

- unit cost
- FIFO
- AVCO.

Other possibilities are:

- standard cost
- selling price less gross margin.

Standard cost means the cost taking the normal levels of materials, labour, efficiency and capacity utilisation as determined by the costing system of the business.

Selling price less gross margin may be convenient for retailers for whom the selling price is more accessible than the cost price. The stock is taken at selling price and then reduced to cost by deducting the appropriate percentage gross margin.

Since the objective is to value stock at cost or a close approximation of cost, unit cost is required for goods whose costs can be specifically identified. For other goods, SSAP 9 nominates FIFO or weighted average as appropriate treatments. Standard cost, or selling price less gross margin, could only be used if it was clear that the resulting stock figures approximated to the actual cost.

NRV

The comparison between cost and NRV must be made item by item, not on the total stock value. It may be acceptable to consider groups of items together if all are worth less than cost.

Continuous and period-end stock records

In preparing the financial statements, the calculation of what is in closing stock can be a major exercise for a business. The business may need to count its stock at the balance sheet date. A formal title for the sheets recording the stock count is 'period-end stock records'.

An alternative would be to have records which show the amount of stock at any date, i.e. continuous stock records. These records may take a variety of forms but, in essence, a record of each item of stock would be maintained showing all the receipts and issues for that item.

The merits of **continuous stock** records are as follows:

- There is better information for stock control.

- Excessive build-up of certain lines of stock, and having insufficient stock of other lines are avoided.

- Less work is needed to calculate stock at the end of the accounting period.

The merits of **period-end stock** records are as follows:

- They are cheaper in most situations than the costs of maintaining continuous stock records.

- Even if there is a continuous stock record, there will still be a need to check the accuracy of the information on record by having a physical check of some of the stock lines.

Test Your Understanding 7

SSAP 9 defines the items that may be included in computing the value of a stock of finished goods manufactured by a business.

Which one of the following lists consists only of items which may be included in the balance sheet value of such stock according to SSAP 9?

A   Foreman's wages, carriage inwards, carriage outwards, raw materials.

B   Raw materials, carriage inwards, costs of storage of finished goods, plant depreciation.

C   Plant depreciation, carriage inwards, raw materials, foreman's wages.

D   Carriage outwards, raw materials, foreman's wages, plant depreciation.

7 Chapter summary

STOCK

VALUED AT THE LOWER OF COST
AND NRV

ADJUSTMENTS FOR STOCK

OPENING STOCK
MUST BE TRANSFERRED TO
THE PROFIT AND LOSS ACCOUNT.
CLOSING STOCK MUST BE
ENTERED INTO THE ACCOUNTS AT
THE YEAR END.

VALUATION OF STOCK

METHODS USED:
- UNIT COST
- FIFO
- AVCO.

**SSAP 9 STOCK AND
LONG-TERM CONTRACTS**

PROVIDES RULES ON VALUATION
OF STOCK AS WELL AS
DISCLOSURE REQUIREMENTS

**RECORD STOCK IN THE LEDGER
ACCOUNTS**

CLOSING STOCK:
DR STOCK A/C
CR PROFIT AND LOSS ACCOUNT
LEDGER
DRAWINGS OF STOCK:
DR DRAWINGS
CR COST OF SALES.

Test your understanding answers

Test Your Understanding 1

First, the transactions are entered into the ledger accounts, and the accounts are balanced. Sales and purchases are then transferred to the profit and loss account ledger account.

Capital

	£		£
		Cash	1,000

Cash

	£		£
Capital	1,000	Purchases	800
Sales	900	Balance c/f	1,100
	——		——
	1,900		1,900
	——		——
Balance b/f	1,100		

Sales

	£		£
Profit and loss account	900	Cash	900
	——		——

Purchases

	£		£
Cash	800	Profit and loss account	800
	——		——

Next, the closing stock must be accounted for in the stock account and the profit and loss account account. There is no opening stock as this is the first week of trading for the business.

Stock

	£		£
Profit and loss account	300		

Profit and loss account

	£		£
Purchases	800	Sales	900
Gross profit c/f	400	Closing stock	300
	1,200		1,200
		Gross profit b/f	400

The profit and loss account is prepared in the vertical format by rearranging the profit and loss account ledger account.

Profit and loss account for Week One

	£	£
Sales revenue		900
Cost of goods sold:		
Purchases	800	
Less: Closing stock	(300)	
		(500)
Gross profit		400

The balance sheet is prepared by listing the balances brought down from the ledger accounts

Balance sheet as at Week One

	£
Stock	300
Cash	1,100
	1,400
Capital	1,000
Profit for the week	400
	1,400

Test Your Understanding 2

First, the ledger accounts must be written up. You must remember that there are opening balances on the balance sheet accounts (cash and capital) but the profit and loss account accounts have no opening balances as they were transferred to the profit and loss account in week one.

Cash

	£		£
Balance b/f	1,100	Purchases	1,100
Sales revenue	1,000	Balance c/f	1,100
	2,100		2,100
Balance b/f	1,000		

Sales

	£		£
Profit and loss account	1,000	Cash	1,000

Purchases

	£		£
Cash	1,100	Profit and loss account	1,100

Profit and loss account

	£		£
Purchases	1,100	Sales revenue	1,000

The opening stock must be transferred to the profit and loss account, and the closing stock entered into the ledger accounts (stock and profit and loss account) leaving the balance brought down which will be included in the balance sheet.

Stock

	£		£
Balance b/f	300	Profit and loss account	300
Profit and loss account	500	Balance c/f	500

Profit and loss account

	£		£
Purchases	1,100	Sales revenue	1,000
Opening stock	300	Closing stock	500
Gross profit c/f	100		
	1,500		1,500
		Gross profit b/f	100

Profit and loss account for Week Two

	£	£
Sales revenue		1,000
Cost of goods sold:		
Opening stock	300	
Purchases	1,100	
	1,400	
Less: Closing stock	(500)	
		(900)
Gross profit		100

Balance sheet as at Week Two

	£
Stock	500
Cash	1,000
	1,500
Capital at start of week two	1,400
Profit for week two	100
	1,500

Test Your Understanding 3

The correct answer is B

X	£7	(cost)	x	100	=	£700
Y	£8	(NRV)	x	200	=	£1,600
Z	£15	(NRV)	x	300	=	£4,500
Total						£6,800

Test Your Understanding 4

NRV may be relevant in special cases, such as where goods are slow-moving, damaged or obsolete. However, most items of stock will be stated at cost.

Test Your Understanding 5

Units purchased (5 x 3)	=	15
Units sold	=	7
Closing stock	=	8

(a) FIFO

		£
3 units @ £5	=	15
5 units @ £5.50	=	27.50
		42.50

AVCO

Average cost per unit:

$$\frac{(5 \times £4) + (5 \times £5) + (5 \times £5.50)}{15} = £4.83 \quad 15$$

Closing stock	=	8 x £4.83
	=	£38.64

(b) FIFO

	£	£
Sales (7 x £10)		70
Cost of sales		
Purchases (5 x £4) + (5 x £5) + (5 x £5.50)	72.50	
Less: Closing stock	(42.50)	
		(30)
Profit		40

AVCO

	£	£
Sales (7 x £10)		70
Cost of Sales		
Purchases (5 x £4) + (5 x £5) + (5 x £5.50)	72.50	
Less: Closing stock	(38.64)	
		(33.86)
Profit		36.14

Test Your Understanding 6

The correct answer is C

Stock valuation (stock in hand 2,420 – 1,420 = 1,000 units)

FIFO – stock valued at latest purchase prices

		£
440	articles at £3.25	1,430
430	articles at £3.00	1,290
130	articles at £2.75	357
1,000		3,077

B   Effect of different stock methods on trading results

	No. of units	£	FIFO £
Sales	1,420		7,000
	2,420	6,510	
Purchases			
Less:			
Closing stock	(1,000)	(3,077)	
Cost of goods sold	1,420		(3,433)
Gross profit			3,567

Test Your Understanding 7

The correct answer is C

The other three answers contain items which cannot be included in stock according to SSAP 9.

6

Accruals and prepayments

Chapter learning objectives

Upon completion of this chapter you will be able to:

- explain the need for adjustments for accruals and prepayments in preparing financial statements

- illustrate the process of adjusting for accruals and prepayments in preparing financial statements.

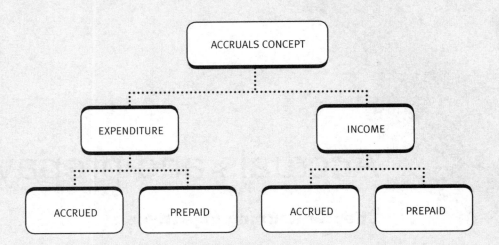

1 Accruals basis of accounting

The accruals basis of accounting means that to calculate the profit for the period, we must include all the income and expenditure relating to the period, whether or not the cash has been received or paid or an invoice received/not received.

Profit is therefore:

Income earned	X
Expenditure incurred	(X)
	___
Profit	X

Expandable text

The accruals concept is that income and expenses should be matched together and dealt with in the profit and loss account for the period to which they relate, regardless of the period in which the cash was actually received or paid. Therefore, all of the expenses involved in making the sales for a period should be matched with the sales income and dealt with in the period in which the sales themselves are accounted for.

Sales

The sales revenue for an accounting period is included in the profit and loss account when the sales are made. This means that when a sale is made on credit, it is recognised in the profit and loss account when the agreement is made and the invoice is sent to the customer rather than waiting until the cash for the sale is received. This is done by setting up debtor in the balance sheet for the amount of cash that is due from the sale (debit debtors and credit sales).

Purchases

Similarly purchases are matched to the period in which they were made by accounting for all credit purchases when they took place and setting up a creditor in the balance sheet for the amount due (debit purchases and credit creditors).

Cost of sales

The major cost involved in making sales in a period is the actual cost of the goods that are being sold. As we saw in the previous chapter, we need to adjust for opening and closing stock to ensure that the sales made in the period are matched with the actual costs of those goods. Any goods unsold are carried forward to the next period so that they are accounted for when they are actually sold.

Expenses

The expenses of the period that the business has incurred in making its sales, such as rent, electricity, telephone, must also be matched with the sales for the period. This means that the actual expense incurred in the period should be included in the profit and loss account rather than simply the amount of the expense that has been paid for in cash.

2 Accrued expenditure

An accrual arises where expenses of the business, relating to the year, have not been paid by the year end.

In this case, it is necessary to record the extra expense relevant to the year and create a corresponding balance sheet liability (called an accrual):

Dr Expense account   X
Cr Accrual   X

Accrued expenditure will reduce profit in the profit and loss account and will also create a current liability on the balance sheet.

For example, if we were to put through an accrual of £500 for telephone expenses. The double entry would be:

Dr Telephone expenses   £500
Cr Accruals   £500

The additional telephone expense would reduce profits by £500. The additional accrual would increase our current liabilities by £500.

Illustration 1 : Accrued expenditure

Accrued expenditure

A business' electricity charges amount to £12,000 pa. In the year to 31 December 20X5, £9,000 has been paid. The electricity for the final quarter is paid in January 20X6.

What year-end accrual is required and what is the electricity expense for the year?

Show the relevant entries in the ledger accounts.

Solution

- The total expense charged to the profit and loss account in respect of electricity should be £12,000.

- The year-end accrual is the £3,000 expense that has not been paid in cash.

The double entry required is:

Dr Electricity expense	£3,000
Cr Accrual	£3,000

Ledger accounts and accrued expenses

Method 1: know the accrual

Electricity expense

	£		£
Cash	9,000		
Accrual c/f	3,000	Profit and loss account (ß)	12,000
	―――		―――
	12,000		12,000
	―――		―――
		Accrual b/f	3,000

Method 2: know the profit and loss account charge

Electricity expense

	£		£
Cash	9,000		
Accrual (ß)	3,000	Profit and loss account	12,000
	12,000		12,000

Test Your Understanding 1

John Simnel's business has an accounting year end of 31 December 20X1. He rents factory space at a rental cost of £5,000 per quarter, payable in arrears.

During the year to 31 December 20X1 his cash payments of rent have been as follows:

31 March (for the quarter to 31 March 20X1)	£5,000
29 June (for the quarter to 30 June 20X1)	£5,000
2 October (for the quarter to 30 September 20X1)	£5,000

The final payment due on 31 December 20X1 for the quarter to that date was not paid until 4 January 20X2.

Show the ledger accounts required to record the above transactions.

3 Prepaid expenditure

A **prepayment** arises where some of the following year's expenses have been paid in the current year.

In this case, it is necessary to remove that part of the expense which is not relevant to this year and create a corresponding balance sheet asset (called a prepayment):

Dr Prepayment	X
Cr Expense account	X

Prepaid expenditure increases profit on the profit and loss account and also creates a current asset to be included on the balance sheet.

For example, if we were to put a prepayment of £1000 in our financial statments for insurance, the double entry would be:

Dr Prepayments £1000

Cr Insurance expense £1000

The prepayments side would increase our current assets by the £1000. The insurance expense would decrease by the £1000, and hence increase our overall profits.

Illustration 2 : Prepaid expenditure

Prepaid expenditure

The annual insurance charge for a business is £24,000 pa. £30,000 was paid on 1 January 20X5 in respect of future insurance charges.

What is the year-end prepayment and what is the insurance expense for the year?

Show the relevant entries in the ledger accounts.

Solution

- The total expense charged to the profit and loss account in respect of insurance should be £24,000.

- The year-end prepayment is the £6,000 that has been paid in respect of 20X6.

The double entry required is:

Dr prepayment	£6,000
Cr Insurance expense	£6,000

Insurance – expense

	£		£
Cash	30,000	Profit and loss account	24,000
		Prepayments c/f	6,000
	30,000		30,000
Prepayments b/f	6,000		

Test Your Understanding 2

Tubby Wadlow pays the rental expense on his market stall in advance. He starts business on 1 January 20X5 and on that date pays £1,200 in respect of the first quarter's rent. During his first year of trade he also pays the following amounts:

3 March (in respect of the quarter ended 30 June)	£1,200
14 June (in respect of the quarter ended 30 September)	£1,200
25 September (in respect of the quarter ended 31 December)	£1,400
13 December (in respect of the first quarter of 20X6)	£1,400

Show these transactions in the rental expense account.

4 Proforma expense T account

Expense

	£		£
Balance b/f (opening prepaid expense)	X	Balance b/f (opening accrued expense)	X
Bank (total paid during the year)	X	Profit and loss account (total expense for the year)	X
Balance c/f (closing accrued expense)	X	Balance c/f (closing prepaid expense)	X
	X		X
Balance b/f (opening prepaid expense)	X	Balance b/f (opening accrued expense)	X

Test Your Understanding 3

On 1 January 20X5, Willy Mossop owed £2,000 in respect of the previous year's electricity. Willy made the following payments during the year ended 31 December 20X5:

6 February	£2,800
8 May	£3,000
5 August	£2,750
10 November	£3,100

At 31 December 20X5, Willy calculated that he owed £1,800 in respect of electricity for the last part of the year.

What is the electricity charge to the profit and loss account?

A   £1,800

B   £11,450

C   £11,650

D   £13,450

5 Accrued income

Accrued income arises where income has been earned in the accounting period but has not yet been received.

In this case, it is necessary to record the extra income in the profit and loss account and create a corresponding asset in the balance sheet (called accrued income):

Dr Accrued income (B/S)	X
Cr Income (P&L)	X

Accrued income creates an additional current asset on our balance sheet. It also creates additional income on our profit and loss account, and hence this will increase overall profits.

Illustration 3 : Accrued income

Accrued income

A business earns bank interest income of £300 per month. £3,000 bank interest income has been received in the year to 31 December 20X5.

What is the year-end asset and what is the bank interest income for the year?

Show the relevant entries in the ledger accounts.

Solution

- The total amount credited to the profit and loss account in respect of interest should be £3,600.

- The year-end accrued income asset is the £600 that has not yet been received.

The double entry required is:

Dr Accrued income (B/S)	£600
Cr Bank interest income	£600

Bank interest income

	£		£
Profit and loss account	3,600	Bank	3,000
		Accrued income c/f	600
	———		———
	3,600		3,600
	———		———
Accrued income b/f	600		

6 Prepaid income

Prepaid income arises where income has been received in the accounting period but which relates to the next accounting period.

In this case, it is necessary to remove the income not relating to the year from the profit and loss account and create a corresponding liability in the balance sheet (called prepaid income):

Dr Income (P&L)	X
Cr Prepaid income (B/S)	X

Prepaid income reduces income on the profit and loss account and hence reduces overall profits too. It also creates a current liability on our balance sheet.

Illustration 4 : Prepaid income

Prepaid income

A business rents out a property at an income of £4,000 per month. £64,000 has been received in the year ended 31 December 20X5.

What is the year-end liability and what is the rental income for the year?

Show the relevant entries in the ledger accounts.

Solution

- The total amount credited to the profit and loss account in respect of rent should be £48,000.

- The year-end prepaid income liability is the £16,000 that has been received in respect of next year.

The double entry required is:

Dr Rental income	£16,000
Cr Prepaid income (B/S)	£16,000

Rental income

	£		£
Profit and loss account	48,000	Cash	64,000
Prepaid income c/f	16,000		
	_____		_____
	64,000		64,000
	_____		_____
		Prepaid income b/f	16,000

7 Proforma income T account

Income

	£		£
Balance b/f (opening accrued income)	X	Balance b/f (opening prepaid income)	X
Profit and loss account (total revenue for the year)	X	Cash (total received during the year)	X
Balance c/f (closing prepaid income)	X	Balance c/f (closing accrued income)	X
	——		——
	X		X
	——		——
Balance b/f (opening accrued income)	X	Balance b/f (opening prepaid income)	X

Test Your Understanding 4

Libby Farquar receives income from two rental units as follows:

		Unit 1		Unit 2
Period	£	Received	£	Received
1.10.X4 – 31.12.X4	2,100	30.9.X4	1,300	2.1.X5
1.1.X5 – 31.3.X5		27.12.X4	1,300	4.4.X5
	2,150			
1.4.X5 – 30.6.X5	2,150	25.3.X5	1,300	1.7.X5
1.7.X5 – 30.9.X5	2,200	21.6.X5	1,400	6.10.X5
1.10.X5 – 31.12.X5	2,200	21.9.X5	1,400	2.1.X6
1.1.X6 – 31.3.X6	2,200	29.12.X5	1,400	4.4.X6

What is Libby's rental income in the profit and loss account for the year ended 31 December 20X5?

A £5,400

B £8,700

C £14,000

D £14,100

8 Chapter summary

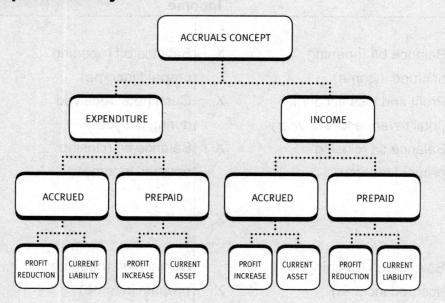

Test your understanding answers

Test Your Understanding 1

Rental expense

	£		£
31 March cash	5,000		
29 June cash	5,000		
2 October cash	5,000		
Accrual c/f	5,000	Profit and loss account	20,000
	20,000		20,000
		Accrual b/f	5,000

Test Your Understanding 2

Rental expense

	£		£
1 January cash	1,200		
3 March cash	1,200		
14 June cash	1,200		
25 September cash	1,400	Profit and loss account	5,000
13 December cash	1,400	Prepayment c/f	1,400
	6,400		6,400
Prepayment b/f	1,400		

Test Your Understanding 3

The correct answer is B

Electricity expense

	£		£
6 February cash	2,800	Accrual b/f	2,000
8 May cash	3,000		
5 August cash	2,750		
10 November	3,100	Profit and loss account	11,450
Accrual c/f	1,800		
	_____		_____
	13,450		13,450
	_____		_____
		Accrual b/f	1,800

Test Your Understanding 4

The correct answer is D

Rental income (unit 1)

	£		£
		Prepaid income b/f	2,150
		25.3.X5 cash	2,150
		21.6.X5 cash	2,200
Profit and loss account	8,700	21.9.X5 cash	2,200
Prepaid income c/f	2,200	29.12.X5 cash	2,200
	_____		_____
	10,900		10,900
	_____		_____
		Prepaid income b/f	2,200

Rental income (unit 2)			
	£		£
Accrued income b/f	1,300	2.1.X5 cash	1,300
		4.4.X5 cash	1,300
		1.7.X5 cash	1,300
Profit and loss account	5,400	6.10.X5 cash	1,400
		Accrued income c/f	1,400
	6,700		6,700
Accrued income b/f	1,400		

Total income: £8,700 + £5,400 = £14,100

7

Irrecoverable debts and allowances for debtors

Chapter learning objectives

Upon completion of this chapter you will be able to:

- identify the benefits and costs of offering credit facilities to customers
- explain the purpose of an aged debtors analysis
- explain the purpose of credit limits
- prepare the bookkeeping entries to write off a bad debt
- record an irrecoverable debt recovered
- identify the impact of irrecoverable debts on the profit and loss account and balance sheet
- prepare the bookkeeping entries to create and adjust an allowance for debtors
- illustrate how to include movements in the allowance for debtors in the profit and loss account and how the closing balance of the allowance should appear in the balance sheet.

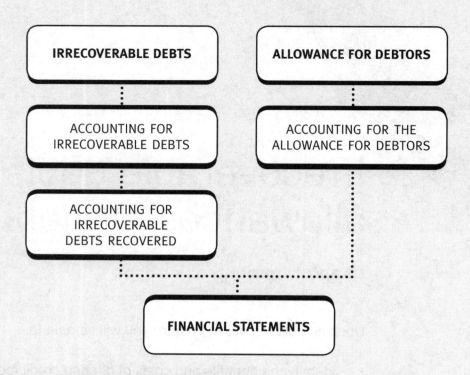

1 The provision of credit facilities

The majority of businesses will sell to their customers on credit and state a defined time within which they must pay (a credit period). The main benefits and costs of doing so are as follows:

Benefits

- The business may be able to enter new markets.
- There is a possibility of increased sales.
- Customer loyalty may be encouraged.

Costs

- It can be costly since the business is accepting payment later.
- Cash flow of the business may deteriorate.
- There is a potential risk of irrecoverable debts.

Aged debtors analysis

Where credit facilities are offered, it is normal for a business to maintain an aged debtors analysis.

- Analysis is usually a list, ordered by name, showing how much each customer owes and how old their debts are.

- The credit control function of a business uses the analysis to keep track of outstanding debts and follow up any that are overdue.

- Timely collection of debts improves cash flow and reduces the risk of them becoming irrecoverable.

Credit limits

It is also normal for a business to set a credit limit for each customer. This is the maximum amount of credit that the business is willing to provide.

The use of credit limits may:

- reduce risk to business of irrecoverable debts by limiting the amount sold on credit

- help build up the trust of a new customer

- be part of the credit control strategy of a business.

2 Irrecoverable debts

- The accruals concept dictates that when a sale is made, it is recognised in the accounts, regardless of whether or not the cash has been received.

- If sales are made on credit, there may be problems collecting the amounts owing from customers.

- Some customers may refuse to pay their debt or be declared bankrupt and be unable to pay the amounts owing.

- Some customers may be in financial difficulties or may dispute the amount owed and there may be some doubt as to whether their debt will be paid.

- If it is highly unlikely that the amount owed by a customer will be received, then this debt is known as a **bad or irrecoverable debt.** As it will probably never be received, it is written off by writing it out of the ledger accounts completely.

- If there is some doubt whether a customer can or will pay his debt, an **allowance for debtors** will be created. These debts are not yet irrecoverable, but in line with the prudence concept, the possible loss is accounted for immediately, whilst the amount of the original debt will still remain in the ledger account just in case the customer does eventually pay.

Please note: the terms 'bad' and 'irrecoverable' debts may both be used in the real exam, but they have the same meaning.

Expandable text

Debtors and irrecoverable debts

If a sale is for cash, the customer pays for the goods immediately when the sale is made. If the sale is on credit terms the customer will probably take the goods with him or arrange to have them delivered but he will not pay for the goods at that time. Instead, the customer will be given or sent an invoice detailing the goods and their price and the normal payment terms. This will tell the customer when he is expected to pay for those goods.

Under the accruals concept, a sale is included in the ledger accounts at the time that it is made.

For a cash sale, this will be when the cash or cheque is paid by the customer and the double entry will be:

> Dr Cash account

> Cr Sales account

For a sale on credit, the sale is made at the time that the invoice is sent to the customer and therefore the accounting entries are made at that time as follows:

> Dr Debtors

> Cr Sales account

When the customer eventually settles the invoice the double entry will be:

> Dr Cash account

> Cr Debtors

This then clears out the balance on the customer's account.

The problem that businesses face with credit sales is that of the collectability of the amounts owing on sales invoices. If a customer is fraudulent and disappears without trace before payment of the amount due, then it is unlikely that such amounts will ever be recovered. If a customer is declared bankrupt, then again it is unlikely that he will be able to pay the amounts due. If a customer is having financial difficulties or is in liquidation, then there is likely to be some doubt as to his eventual ability to pay.

If a business is faced with a situation where it is highly unlikely that the amount owing by a customer will be received, then this debt is known as a bad or irrecoverable debt. As it will probably never be received, it is written off by writing it out of the ledger accounts completely.

In other cases, we may have some doubt about whether a customer can or will pay his debt, but without being quite certain that the debt is bad. It is still hoped that such a debt will be received and therefore it will remain in the ledger accounts. However, in order to be prudent, such a debt will be allowed for by creating an allowance for debtors. This means that the possible loss from not receiving the cash will be accounted for immediately, whilst the amount of the original debt will still remain in the ledger account just in case the customer does eventually pay.

3 Accounting for irrecoverable debts

An **irrecoverable debt** is a debt which is, or is considered to be, uncollectable.

With such debts it is prudent to remove them from the accounts and to charge the amount as an expense for irrecoverable debts to the profit and loss account. The original sale remains in the accounts as this did actually take place.

The double entry required to achieve this is:

Dr Irrecoverable debts expense account

Cr Debtors

Test Your Understanding 1

Araf & Co have total debtors at the end of their accounting period of £45,000. Of these it is discovered that one, Mr Xiun who owes £790, has been declared bankrupt, and another who gave his name as Mr Jones has totally disappeared owing Araf & Co £1,240.

Calculate the effect in the financial statements of writing off these debts as bad.

4 Accounting for irrecoverable debts recovered

There is a possible situation where a debt is written off as irrecoverable in one accounting period, perhaps because the customer has been declared bankrupt, and the money, or part of the money, due is then unexpectedly received in a subsequent accounting period.

When a debt is written off the double entry is:

Dr Irrecoverable debts expense account

Cr Debtors (removing the debt from the accounts)

When cash is received from a customer the double entry is:

Dr Cash

Cr Debtors

When an irrecoverable debt is recovered, the credit entry (above) cannot be taken to debtors as the debt has already been taken out of the debtors balance.

Instead the accounting entry is:

Dr Cash account

Cr Irrecoverable debts expense account

Some businesses may wish to keep a separate 'bad debts recovered' account to separate the actual cost of bad debts in the period.

Expandable text

Irrecoverable debts recovered

There is a possible situation where a debt is written off as irrecoverable in one accounting period, perhaps because the debtor has been declared bankrupt, and the money, or part of the money, due is then unexpectedly received in a subsequent accounting period.

When a debt is written off the double entry is:

Dr Irrecoverable debts expense account (an expense in the profit and loss account)

Cr Debtors account (removing the debt from the accounts)

The full double entry for the cash being received from that customer in a subsequent accounting period is:

Dr Debtors account (to reinstate the debt that had been cancelled when it was written off)

Cr Irrecoverable debts expense account

and

Dr Cash account

Cr Debtors account

Note that this second entry is the usual double entry for cash received from a customer.

This double entry can be simplified to:

Dr Cash account

Cr Irrecoverable debts expense account

This is because the debit and the credit to the debtors account cancel each other out. However, it may be useful to pass the transaction through the customer's account so that the fact that the debt was eventually paid, or partly paid, is recorded there.

Note that some businesses may keep an irrecoverable debts recovered account so that the expense for irrecoverable debts is kept separate from any irrecoverable debts recovered.

Test Your Understanding 2

Celia Jones had debtors of £3,655 at 31 December 20X7. At that date she wrote off a debt from Lenny Smith of £699. During the year to 31 December 20X8, Celia made credit sales of £17,832 and received cash from her customers totalling £16,936. She also received the £699 from Lenny Smith that had already been written off in 20X7.

What is the final balance on the debtors account at 31 December 20X7 and 20X8?

	20X7	20X8
	£	£
A	2,956	3,852
B	2,956	3,153
C	3,655	4,551
D	3,655	3,852

5 Allowance for debtors

There may be debts in the accounts where there is some cause for concern but they are not yet definitely irrecoverable.

It is prudent to recognise the possible expense of not collecting the debt in the profit and loss account, but the debtor must remain in the accounts in case the customer does in fact pay.

An allowance is set up which is a credit balance. This is netted off against trade debtors in the balance sheet to give a net figure for debtors that are probably recoverable.

There are two types of debts that may be potentially irrecoverable in the organisation's accounts:

- There will be some specific debts where the customer is known to be in financial difficulties, is disputing their invoice, or is refusing to pay for some other reason (poor service for example) and therefore the amount owing may not be recoverable. The allowance for such a debt is known as a **specific allowance**.

- The past experience and history of a business will indicate that not all of its trade debtors will be recoverable in full. It may not be possible to identify the amount that will not be paid but an estimate may be made that a certain percentage of customers are likely not to pay. An additional allowance will be made for these items, often known as a **general allowance**.

6 Accounting for the allowance for debtors

An allowance for debtors is set up with the following journal:

Dr Irrecoverable debts expense account

Cr Allowance for debtors account

If there is already an allowance for debtors in the accounts (opening allowance), only the**movement in** the profit is charged to the profit and loss account (closing allowance less opening allowance).

As the allowance can increase or decrease, there may be a debit or a credit in the irrecoverable debts account so the above journal may be reversed.

When calculating and accounting for a movement in the allowance for debtors, the following steps should be taken:

(1) Write off irrecoverable debts.

(2) Calculate the debtors balance as adjusted for the write-offs.

(3) Ascertain the specific allowance for debtors required.

(4) Deduct the debt specifically allowed for from the debtors balance (be sure to deduct the full amount of debt rather than the amount of specific allowance).

(5) Multiply the remaining debtors balance by the general allowance percentage to give the general allowance required: %(closing debtors – irrecoverable debts – debts specifically provided for).

(6) Add the specific and general allowances required together.

(7) Compare with the brought forward allowance.

(8) Account for the change in allowance.

Test Your Understanding 3

On 31 December 20X1, Jake Williams had debtors of £10,000. From past experience Jake estimated that the equivalent of 3% of these customers were likely never to pay their debts and he therefore wished to make an allowance for this amount.

During 20X2, Jake made sales on credit totalling £100,000 and received cash from his customers of £94,000. He still considered that the equivalent of 3% of the closing debtors may never pay and should be allowed for.

During 20X3, Jake made sales of £95,000 and collected £96,000 from his debtors. At 31 December 20X3, Jake still considered that the equivalent of 3% of his debtors should be allowed for.

Calculate the allowance for debtors and the irrecoverable debt expense as well as the closing balance of debtors for each of the years 20X1, 20X2 and 20X3.

Test Your Understanding 4

John Stamp has opening balances at 1 January 20X6 on his trade debtors account and allowance for debtors account of £68,000 and £3,400 respectively. During the year to 31 December 20X6, John Stamp makes credit sales of £354,000 and receives cash from his debtors of £340,000.

At 31 December 20X6, John Stamp reviews his debtors listing and acknowledges that he is unlikely ever to receive debts totalling £2,000. These are to be written off as irrecoverable. Past experience indicates that John should also make an allowance equivalent to 5% of his remaining debtors after writing off the irrecoverable debts.

What is the amount charged to John's profit and loss account for irrecoverable debt expense in the year ended 31 December 20X6?

A   £2,700

B   £6,100

C   £2,600

D   £6,000

What will the effect be of Irrecoverable debts on both the profit and loss account and the balance sheet?

Test Your Understanding 5

Gordon's debtors owe a total of £80,000 at the year end. These include £900 of long overdue debts that might still be recoverable, but for which Gordon has created an allowance for debtors'. Gordon has also provided an allowance of £1,582, which is the equivalent of 2% of the other debtors' balances.

What best describes Gordon's allowance for debtors as at his year end?

A   A specific allowance of £900 and an additional allowance of £1,582 based on past history.

B   A specific allowance of £1,582 and an additional allowance of £900 based on past history.

C   A specific allowance of £2,482.

D   A general allowance of £2,482.

7 Chapter summary

IRRECOVERABLE DEBTS

- Amounts that the business will not receive from its customers.
- May be bankruptcy, fraud or disputes.

ALLOWANCE FOR DEBTORS

- There may be some doubt as to the collectability of some of the business's debtors balances.
- An allowance is made to recognise the possible expense of not receiving the cash

ACCOUNTING FOR IRRECOVERABLE DEBTS

To recognise the expense in the profit and loss account:

Dr Irrecoverable debts expense

Cr Debtors

ACCOUNTING FOR THE ALLOWANCE FOR DEBTORS

To record an increase or setting up the allowance:

Dr   Irrecoverable debts expense

Cr   Allowance for debtors

The journal entry is reversed if the allowance is reduced.

ACCOUNTING FOR IRRECOVERABLE DEBTS RECOVERED

The debt has been taken out of debtors, the journal is:

Dr   Cash

Cr   Irrecoverable debts expense

FINANCIAL STATEMENTS

BALANCE SHEET

Debtors	X
Allowance for debtors	(X)
Net debtors	X

PROFIT AND LOSS ACCOUNT

Charge for irrecoverable debts

=

Irrecoverable debts written off

+/−

Change in allowance for debtors

Test your understanding answers

Test Your Understanding 1

Step 1

Enter the opening balance in the debtors account.

Step 2

As the two debts are considered to be irrecoverable, they must be removed from debtors by the following journal:

Dr Irrecoverable debts expense

Cr Debtors

Debtors

	£		£
Balance at period end	45,000	Irrecoverable debts	
		– Mr Xiun	790
		Irrecoverable debts	
		– Mr Jones	1,240
		Balance c/f	42,970
	45,000		45,000
Balance b/f	42,970		

Step 3

Balance the debtors account; the closing balance will appear in the balance sheet as the period end debtors figure.

Irrecoverable debts expense

	£		£
Debtors			
– Mr Xiun	790		
Debtors			
– Mr Jones	1,240	Profit and loss account	2,030
	2,030		2,030

Step 4

Balance the irrecoverable debts expense account and write off the balance to the profit and loss account as an expense for the period.

Note that the sales account has not been altered and the original sales to Mr Xiun and Mr Jones remain. This is because these sales actually took place and it is only after the sale that the expense of not being able to collect these debts has occurred.

Test Your Understanding 2

The correct answer is A

20X7

Debtors

	£		£
31 Dec	3,655	Irrecoverable debts	
		– Lenny Smith	699
		Balance c/f	2,956
	3,655		3,655
Balance b/f	2,956		

Irrecoverable debts expense

	£		£
Debtors		Profit and loss account	699
– Lenny Smith	699		
	___		___
	699		699
	___		___

20X8

Debtors

	£		£
Balance b/f	2,956		
Sales	17,832	Cash received	16,936
		Balance c/f	3,852
	_____		_____
	20,788		20,788
	_____		_____
Balance b/f	3,852		

Irrecoverable debts expense

	£		£
Profit and loss account	699	Cash	699
	___		___
	699		699
	___		___

Test Your Understanding 3

20X1

Debtors

	£		£
At 31 December	10,000	Balance c/f	10,000
	10,000		10,000
Balance b/f	10,000		

Provision required: £10,000 x 3% = £300

Allowance for debtors

	£		£
Balance c/f	300	31 Dec	
		Irrecoverable debts	300
	300		300
		Balance b/f	300

Irrecoverable debts expense

	£		£
31 Dec		31 Dec	
Allowance for debtors	300	Profit and loss account	300
	300		300

Balance sheet presentation

	£	£
Current assets		
Debtors		10,000
Less: Allowance for debtors		(300)
		─────
		9,700

20X2

Debtors

	£		£
Balance b/f	10,000		
Sales	100,000	Cash	94,000
		Balance c/f	16,000
	─────		─────
	110,000		110,000
	─────		─────
Balance b/f	16,000		

Allowance required: £16,000 x 3%
= £480

Allowance for debtors

	£		£
		Balance b/f	300
Balance c/f	480	31 Dec	
		Increase in allowance	180
	───		───
	480		480
	───		───
		Balance b/f	480

Irrecoverable debts expense

	£		£
31 Dec		31 Dec	
Allowance for debtors	180	Profit and loss account	180
	——		——
	180		180
	——		——

Balance sheet presentation

	£	£
Current assets		
Debtors	16,000	
Less: Allowance for debtors	(480)	
	——	
	15,520	

20X3

Debtors

	£		£
Balance b/f	16,000		
Sales	95,000	Cash	96,000
		Balance c/f	15,000
	———		———
	111,000		111,000
	———		———
Balance b/f	15,000		

Allowance required: £15,000 x 3% = £450

Allowance for debtors

	£		£
31 Dec		Balance b/f	480
Decrease in allowance	30		
Balance c/f	450		
	——		——
	480		480
	——		——
		Balance b/f	450

Irrecoverable debts expense

	£		£
31 Dec		31 Dec	
Profit and loss account	30	Allowance for debtors	30
	30		30

Balance sheet presentation

	£	£
Current assets		
Debtors	15,000	
Less: Allowance for debtors	(450)	
		14,550

Test Your Understanding 4

The correct answer is C

Debtors

20X6	£	20X6	£
1 Jan Balance b/f	68,000	31 Dec Cash	340,000
31 Dec			
Sales	354,000	31 Dec	
		Irrecoverable debts	2,000
		31 Dec	
		Balance c/f	80,000
	422,000		422,000
20X7			
1 Jan Balance b/f	80,000		

Irrecoverable debts expense

20X6	£	20X6	£
31 Dec Debtors	2,000		
31 Dec Allowance for debtors	600	31 Dec Profit and loss account	2,600
	2,600		2,600

Allowance for debtors

20X6	£	20X6	£
		1 Jan Balance b/f	3,400
31 Dec Balance c/f	4,000	31 Dec Irrecoverable debts	600
	4,000		4,000
		20X7	
		1 Jan Balance b/f	4,000

Note that only one irrecoverable debts expense account is used both to write off irrecoverable debts and to increase or decrease the allowance for debtors. There is no need to use separate accounts for each type of expense.

Working – Allowance for debtors

5% x £80,000 = £4,000

The **balance sheet** will show a debtors balance of 80,000. Underneath this separately the allowance for debtors c/f balance of 4,000 will be deducted to give a sub-total of £76,000.

The **profit and loss account** will show the £2,600 as an expense. This expense will cause a decrease in overall profits.

Test Your Understanding 5

The correct answer is A

There is a specific allowance for the debt of £900 which has still not been written off as irrecoverable, and an additional allowance equivalent to 2% of the remaining balance based on past history.

8

Fixed assets

Chapter learning objectives

Upon completion of this chapter you will be able to:

- define fixed assets
- distinguish between capital and revenue expenditure
- explain the function and purpose of an asset register
- explain and illustrate the ledger entries to record the acquisition of fixed assets
- define and explain the purpose of depreciation
- explain the straight-line and reducing balance methods of depreciation and make necessary calculations
- explain and illustrate how depreciation expense and accumulated depreciation are recorded in ledger accounts
- explain and illustrate how depreciation is presented in the profit and loss account and balance sheet
- explain the relevance of consistency and subjectivity in accounting for depreciation
- make the necessary adjustments if changes are made in the estimated useful life/residual value of a fixed asset
- explain and illustrate the ledger entries to record the disposal of fixed assets for cash
- explain and illustrate the ledger entries to record the disposal of fixed assets through part exchange
- explain and illustrate the inclusion of profits or losses on disposal in the profit and loss account

- explain and record the revaluation of a fixed asset in ledger accounts and in the balance sheet

- explain the impact of a revaluation on accounting for depreciation and disposal of a fixed asset

- explain and illustrate how fixed asset balances and movements are disclosed in company financial statements.

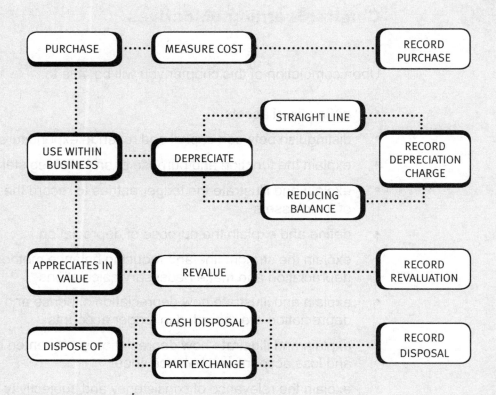

1 Fixed assets

Fixed assets are distinguished from current assets by the following characteristics:

- long-term in nature
- not normally acquired for resale
- could be tangible or intangible
- used to generate income directly or indirectly for a business
- not normally liquid assets (i.e. not easily and quickly converted into cash without a significant loss in value).

Current assets are those assets which will be settled within 12 months of the balance sheet date. They include cash, stock, debtors and prepayments.

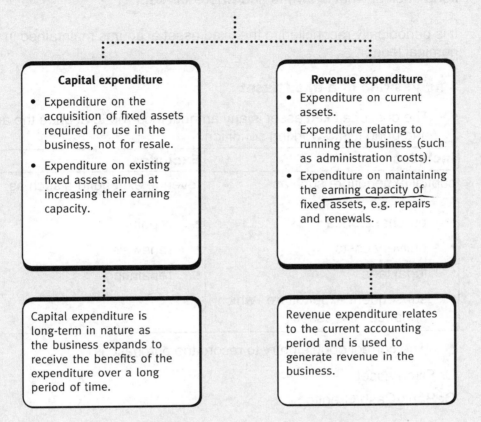

2 Capital and revenue expenditure

It follows that a business' expenditure may be classified as one of two types:

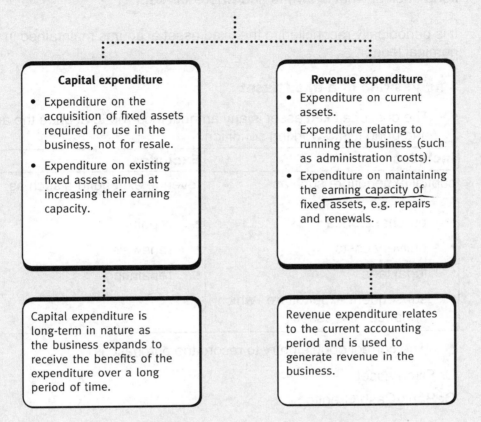

Capital expenditure

- Expenditure on the acquisition of fixed assets required for use in the business, not for resale.
- Expenditure on existing fixed assets aimed at increasing their earning capacity.

Revenue expenditure

- Expenditure on current assets.
- Expenditure relating to running the business (such as administration costs).
- Expenditure on maintaining the earning capacity of fixed assets, e.g. repairs and renewals.

Capital expenditure is long-term in nature as the business expands to receive the benefits of the expenditure over a long period of time.

Revenue expenditure relates to the current accounting period and is used to generate revenue in the business.

3 Fixed asset registers

Fixed asset registers are, as the name suggests, a record of the fixed assets held by a business. These form part of the internal control system of an organisation.

Details held on such a register may include:

- cost
- date of purchase
- description of asset
- serial/reference number
- location of asset
- depreciation method
- expected useful life
- net book value (NBV).

Function of fixed asset registers

A fixed asset register is maintained in order to control fixed assets and keep track of what is owned and where it is kept.

It is periodically reconciled to the fixed asset accounts maintained in the nominal ledger.

4 Acquisition of a fixed asset

- The cost of a fixed asset is any amount incurred to acquire the asset and bring it into working condition.

Includes	Excludes
capital expenditure such as	revenue expenditure such as
 • purchase price • delivery costs • legal fees • subsequent expenditure which enhances the asset	 • repairs • renewals • repainting

- The correct double entry to record the purchase is:

Dr Fixed asset   X
Cr Bank/Cash/Creditors   X

- A separate cost account should be kept for each category of fixed asset, e.g. motor vehicles, fixtures and fittings.

Expandable text

Subsequent expenditure on the fixed asset can only be recorded as part of the cost (or capitalised), if it enhances the benefits of the asset, i.e. increases the revenues capable of being generated by the asset.

An example of subsequent expenditure which meets this criterion and so can be capitalised is an extension to a shop building which provides extra selling space.

An example of subsequent expenditure which does not meet this criterion is repair work. Any repair costs must be debited to the profit and loss account (or expensed).

Test Your Understanding 1

Acquisition of a fixed asset

Bilbo Baggins started business providing limousine taxi services on 1 January 20X5. In the year to 31 December he incurred the following costs:

	£
Office premises	250,000
Legal fees associated with purchase of office	10,000
Cost of materials and labour to paint office in Bilbo's favourite colour, purple	300
Mercedes E series estate cars	116,000
Number plates for cars	210
Delivery charge for cars	180
Road licence fee for cars	480
Drivers' wages for first year of operation	60,000
Blank taxi receipts printed with Bilbo Baggins' business name and number	450

What amounts should be capitalised as 'Land and buildings' and 'Motor vehicles'?

	Land and buildings	Motor vehicles
	£	£
A	260,000	116,390
B	250,000	116,870
C	250,300	116,390
D	260,300	116,870

5 Depreciation

- **FRS 15** defines depreciation as 'the measure of the cost or revalued amount of the economic benefits of the tangible fixed asset that has been consumed during the period'.

- In simple terms, depreciation is a mechanism to reflect the cost of using a fixed asset.

- Depreciation matches the cost of using a fixed asset to the revenues generated by that asset over its useful life.

- This is achieved by recording a depreciation charge each year, the effect of which is twofold ('the dual effect'):

  - Reduce the balance sheet value of the fixed asset by cumulative depreciation to reflect the wearing out.

  - Record the depreciation charge as an expense in the profit and loss account to match the revenue generated by the fixed asset.

Expandable text

Depreciation may arise from:

- use

- physical wear and tear

- passing of time, e.g. a ten-year lease on a property

- obsolescence through technology and market changes, e.g. plant and machinery of a specialised nature

- depletion, e.g. the extraction of a mineral from a quarry.

The purpose of depreciation is not to show the asset at its current value in the balance sheet; nor is it intended to provide a fund for the replacement of the asset. It is simply a method of allocating the cost of the asset over the periods estimated to benefit from its use (the useful economic life).

Land normally has an unlimited life and so does not require depreciation, but buildings should be depreciated.

Depreciation of an asset begins when it is available for use.

6 Methods of calculating depreciation

The method of depreciation is always matched with the pattern of the use of the asset. This varies depending on the type of asset which is being depreciated.

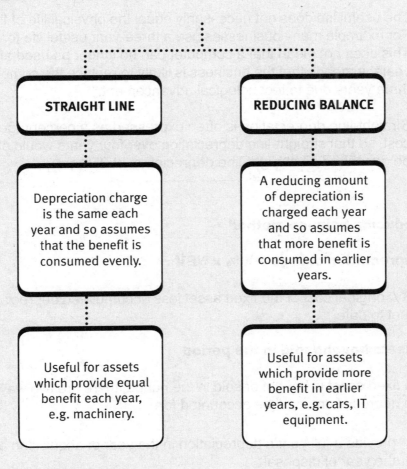

STRAIGHT LINE	REDUCING BALANCE
Depreciation charge is the same each year and so assumes that the benefit is consumed evenly.	A reducing amount of depreciation is charged each year and so assumes that more benefit is consumed in earlier years.
Useful for assets which provide equal benefit each year, e.g. machinery.	Useful for assets which provide more benefit in earlier years, e.g. cars, IT equipment.

Straight-line method

$$\text{Depreciation charge} = \frac{\text{Cost} - \text{Residual Value}}{\text{Useful economic life}}$$

Or

$$\text{X\% x cost}$$

Residual value: the estimated disposal value of the asset at the end of its useful economic life.

Useful economic life: the estimated number of years during which the business will use the asset.

Expandable text

The residual value may be a second-hand value or scrap value. It is unlikely to be a significant amount and is often zero.

The useful life does not necessarily equal the physical life of the asset. For example many businesses use a three-year useful life for computers. This does not mean that a computer can no longer be used after three years; it means that the business is likely to replace the computer after three years due to technological advancement.

Straight-line depreciation is often expressed as a percentage of original cost, so that straight-line depreciation over four years would alternatively be described as straight-line depreciation at 25% pa.

Reducing balance method

Depreciation charge = X % x NBV

NBV: original cost of the fixed asset less accumulated depreciation on the asset to date.

Assets bought/sold in the period

If a fixed asset is bought or sold in the period, there are two ways in which the depreciation could be accounted for:

- provide a full year's depreciation in the year of acquisition and none in the year of disposal

- monthly or pro rata depreciation, based on the exact number of months that the asset has been owned.

Illustration 1 : Reducing balance method

Dev, a trader, purchased an item of plant for £1,000 on 1 August 20X1 which he depreciates on the reducing balance at 20% pa. What is the depreciation charge for each of the first five years if the accounting year end is 31 July?

Solution

Year	Depreciation charge % x NBV	Depreciation charge £	Cumulative depreciation £
1	20% x £1,000	200	200
2	20% x £(1,000 – 200)	160	360
3	20% x £(1,000 – 360)	128	488
4	20% x £(1,000 – 488)	102	590
5	20% x £(1,000 – 590)	82	672

Test Your Understanding 2

Karen has been running a successful nursery school 'Little Monkeys' since 20X1. She bought the following assets as the nursery grew:

- a new oven for the nursery kitchen at a cost of £2,000 (purchased 1 December 20X4).

- a minibus to take the children on trips for £18,000 (purchased 1 June 20X4).

She depreciates the oven at 10% straight line and the minibus at 25% reducing balance. A full year's depreciation is charged in the year of purchase and none in the year of disposal.

What is the total depreciation charge for the year ended 31 October 20X6?

A £2,531

B £2,700

C £4,231

D £2,731

Test Your Understanding 3

The following information relates to Bangers & Smash, a car repair business:

	Machine 1	**Machine 2**
Cost	£12,000	£8,000
Purchase date	1 August 20X5	1 October 20X6
Depreciation method	20% straight line pro rata	10% reducing balance pro rata

What is the total depreciation charge for the years ended 31 December 20X5 and 20X6?

	20X5	**20X6**
	£	£
A	2,400	2,600
B	1,000	2,600
C	2,400	3,200
D	1,000	3,200

7 Accounting for depreciation

Whichever method is used to calculate depreciation, the accounting remains the same:

Dr Depreciation expense (P&L)	X
Cr Accumulated depreciation(B/S)	X

- The depreciation expense account is a profit and loss account account and therefore is not cumulative.

- The accumulated depreciation account is a balance sheet account and as the name suggests is cumulative, i.e. reflects all depreciation to date.

- On the balance sheet it is shown as a reduction against the cost of fixed assets:

	£
Cost	X
Accumulated depreciation	(X)
NBV	X

Illustration 2 : Accounting for depreciation

Santa runs a large toy shop in Windsor. In the year ended 31 August 20X5, she bought the following fixed assets:

- A new cash register for £5,000. This was purchased on 1 December 20X4, in time for the Christmas rush, and was to be depreciated at 10% straight line.
- A new delivery van, purchased on 31 March 20X5, at a cost of £22,000. The van is to be depreciated at 15% reducing balance.

Santa charges depreciation on a monthly basis.

- What is the depreciation charge for the year ended 31st August 20X5?
- Show the relevant ledger accounts and balance sheet presentation at that date.

Solution

Cash register Depreciation charge: 10% x £5,000 x 9/12 = £375

Delivery van Depreciation charge: 15% x £22,000 x 5/12 = £1,375

Cost (Cash register)

	£		£
Cost	5,000	Balance c/f	5,000
	5,000		5,000
Balance b/f	5,000		

Cost (delivery van)

	£		£
Cost	22,000	Balance c/f	22,000
	———		———
	22,000		22,000
	———		———
Balance b/f	22,000		

Accumulated depreciation (cash register)

	£		£
Balance c/f	375	Depreciation expense 20X5	375
	———		———
	375		375
	———		———
		Balance b/f	375

Accumulated depreciation (delivery van)

	£		£
Balance c/f	1,375	Depreciation expense 20X5	1,375
	———		———
	1,375		1,375
	———		———
		Balance b/f	1,375

Depreciation expense

	£		£
Accumulated depreciation (cash register)	375		
Accumulated depreciation (delivery van)	1,375	Profit and loss account	1,750
	———		———
	1,750		1,750
	———		———

Balance sheet extract at 31 August 20X5

	Cash register £	Delivery Van £
Cost	5,000	22,000
Accumulated depreciation	(375)	(1,375)
NBV	4,625	20,625

Test Your Understanding 4

Coco acquired two fixed assets for cash on 1 August 20X5 for use in her party organising business:

- a 25-year lease on a shop for £200,000
- a chocolate fountain for £4,000.

The fountain is to be depreciated at 25% pa using the reducing balance method.

A full year of depreciation is charged in the year of acquisition and none in the year of disposal.

Show the ledger account entries for these assets for the years ending 31 October 20X5, 20X6 and 20X7.

8 Consistency and subjectivity when accounting for depreciation

The following are all based on estimates made by the management of a business:

- depreciation method
- residual value
- useful economic life.

Different estimates would result in varying levels of depreciation and, consequently, profits.

It can be argued that these subjective areas could therefore result in manipulation of the accounts by management.

In order to reduce the scope for such manipulation and increase consistency of treatment, **FRS 15 Tangible fixed assets** requires the following:

- depreciation method may only be changed if the new method gives a fairer presentation of the results and financial position.

- residual value and useful economic life should be reviewed at each year end and changed if expectations differ from previous estimates.

Illustration 3 : Changes to estimates

Alfie purchased a fixed asset for £100,000 on 1 January 20X2 and started depreciating it over five years. Residual value was taken as £10,000.

At 1 January 20X3 a review of asset lives was undertaken and the remaining useful economic life was estimated at eight years. Residual value was nil.

Calculate the depreciation charge for the year ended 31 December 20X3 and subsequent years.

Solution

Initial depreciation charge pa	=	$\dfrac{£100,000 - £10,000}{5 \text{ years}}$
	=	£18,000
NBV at date of change	=	£100,000 − (£18,000 x 1yrs)
	=	£82,000
New depreciation charge	=	$\dfrac{£82,000 - \text{nil}}{8 \text{ years}}$
	=	£10,250

Test Your Understanding 5

Alberto bought a wood-burning oven for his pizza restaurant for £30,000 on 1 January 20X0. At that time he believed that the oven's useful economic life would be 20 years after which it would have no value.

On 1 January 20X3, Alberto revises his estimations: he now believes that he will use the oven in the business for another 12 years after which he will be able to sell it second-hand for £1,500.

What is the depreciation charge for the year ended 31 December 20X3?

A   £2,000

B   £2,125

C   £1,875

D   £2,375

9 Disposal of fixed assets

Profit/loss on disposal

An accounting profit or loss will arise on the disposal of a fixed asset.

Proceeds (cash or part exchange allowance)	>	NBV at disposal date	Profit
Proceeds (cash or part exchange allowance)	<	NBV at disposal date	Loss
Proceeds (cash or part exchange allowance)	=	NBV at disposal date	Neither profit nor loss

A disposals T account is required when recording the disposal of a fixed asset. This is a profit and loss account account which reflects any profit or loss on disposal.

Disposal for cash consideration

This is a three step process:

(1) Remove the original cost of the fixed asset from the 'fixed asset' account.

Dr	Disposals	original cost
Cr	Fixed assets	original cost

(2) Remove accumulated depreciation on the fixed asset from the 'accumulated depreciation' account.

Dr	Acc'd dep'n	acc'd dep'n
Cr	Disposals	acc'd dep'n

(3) Record the cash proceeds.

Dr	Cash	proceeds
Cr	Disposals	proceeds

The balance on the disposals T account is the profit or loss on disposal:

Disposals

Original cost	X	Accumulated depreciation	X
		Proceeds	X
Loss on disposal	ß	Profit on disposal	ß
	X		X

The profit or loss on disposal can also be calculated as proceeds less NBV of asset at disposal.

Test Your Understanding 6

Percy Throwerp runs a landscape gardening business. On 1 February 20X2, he purchased a sit-on lawnmower costing £3,000. He depreciates it at 10% straight line on a monthly basis. A few years later he decides to replace it with one with an enclosed cabin for when it rains. He sells the lawnmower to an old friend Alan Titchmuck for £2,000 on 31 July 20X5.

How much is charged to Percy's profit and loss account in respect of the asset for the year ended 31 December 20X5?

Disposal through a part-exchange agreement

A part-exchange agreement arises where an old asset is provided in part payment for a new one, the balance of the new asset being paid in cash.

The procedure to record the transaction is very similar to the three-step process seen for a cash disposal. There is however a fourth step:

(1) Remove the original cost of the fixed asset from the 'fixed asset' account.

Dr	**Disposals**	**original cost**
Cr	**Fixed assets**	**original cost**

(2) Remove accumulated depreciation on the fixed asset from the 'accumulated depreciation' account.

Dr	**Acc'd dep'n**	**acc'd dep'n**
Cr	**Disposals**	**acc'd dep'n**

(3) Record the part-exchange allowance (PEA) as proceeds.

Dr	**Fixed assets (= part of cost of new asset)**	**PEA**
Cr	**Disposals (= sale proceeds of old asset)**	**PEA**

(4) Record the cash paid for the new asset.

Dr	**Fixed assets**	**cash**
Cr	**Cash**	**Cash**

Again, the balance on the disposals T account is the profit or loss on disposal:

Disposals

Original cost	X	Accumulated depreciation	X
		PEA	X
Profit on disposal	ß	Loss on disposal	ß
	X		X

Expandable text

There are two debits to the fixed asset account in respect of the new asset:

- PEA
- cash balance.

Together these are the cost of the new asset. If preferred you can show the total as one debit (however do not forget to record both credits).

Test Your Understanding 7

Bindi Bobbin runs a business altering and repairing clothes. When she started business on 1 January 20X2, she bought a Soopastitch II sewing machine for £2,500. She depreciates sewing machines using the straight-line method at a rate of 20% pa, and she charges a full year of depreciation in the year of acquisition and none in the year of disposal.

The business has now grown such that she needs a faster machine, and she will upgrade to the Soopastitch V during December 20X5. The Soopastitch salesman has offered her a part-exchange deal as follows:

PEA for Soopastitch II   £750

Balance to be paid in cash for Soopastitch V   £4,850

Show the ledger entries for the year ended 31 December 20X5 to reflect this transaction.

10 Revaluation of fixed assets

- Some fixed assets such as land and buildings rise in value over time. Businesses may choose to reflect the current value of the asset in their balance sheet. This is known as revaluing the asset.

- The difference between the NBV of the asset and the revalued amount (normally a gain) is recorded in a revaluation reserve in the balance sheet.

- This gain is not recorded in the profit and loss account because it is unrealised, i.e. it is not realised in the form of cash.

- Revaluations are also included in the statement of total recognised gains and losses (STRGL), which is covered later in the text within chapter 17.

Expandable text

If the fair value of a fixed asset can be measured reliably, it can be carried at its fair value at the date of revaluation, less any subsequent depreciation and subsequent impairment losses. The revaluation should be repeated regularly to ensure that the fair value of the asset does not differ materially from the carrying amount.

An upward revaluation should be credited to revaluation surplus, unless it reverses a previous downward revaluation which was charged as an expense.

A downward revaluation should be charged as an expense, unless it reverses a previous upward revaluation, when it may be charged against the revaluation surplus for that same asset.

If one asset in a class is revalued, all assets of that class must be revalued. This is to prevent selective revaluation of only those assets that have increased in value.

Illustration 4 : Revaluation of fixed assets

Vittorio owns land which originally cost £250,000. No depreciation has been charged on the land in accordance with FRS 15 . Vittorio wishes to revalue the land to reflect its current market value, which he has been advised is £600,000.

What is the double entry to record this revaluation?

Solution

The land is currently held at cost of £250,000. This needs to be increased by £350,000 to reflect the new valuation of £600,000. Therefore the double entry required is:

Dr	Land cost	£350,000
Cr	Revaluation reserve	£350,000

Illustration 5 : Revaluation of fixed assets

Hamish runs a kilt-making business in Scotland. He has run the business for many years from a building which originally cost £300,000 and on which £100,000 total depreciation has been charged to date. Hamish wishes to revalue the building to £750,000.

What is the double entry required to record the revaluation?

Solution

The current balances in the accounts are:

Building cost	£300,000
Accumulated depreciation	£100,000

- The building cost account needs to be raised by £450,000 to £750,000.

- On revaluation, the accumulated depreciation account is cleared out.

Therefore the double entry required is:

Dr Building cost	£450,000
Dr Accumulated depreciation	£100,000
Cr Revaluation reserve	£550,000

The gain of £550,000 reflects the difference between the NBV pre-revaluation of £200,000 and the revalued amount of £750,000.

Cost (building)

	£		£
Balance b/f	300,000		
Revaluation reserve	450,000	Balance c/f	750,000
	750,000		750,000
Balance b/f	750,000		

Accumulated depreciation (building)

	£		£
Revaluation reserve	100,000	Balance b/f	100,000
	100,000		100,000

Revaluation reserve

	£		£
		Cost (building)	450,000
Balance c/f	550,000	Accumulated depreciation (building)	100,000
	550,000		550,000

In summary:

Revaluation surplus = Revalued amount – NBV

For a non-depreciated asset:

Dr Fixed asset	revaluation surplus
Cr Revaluation reserve	revaluation surplus

For a depreciated asset:

Dr Accumulated depreciation	depreciation to date
Dr Fixed asset	new value – original cost
Cr Revaluation reserve	revaluation surplus

Test Your Understanding 8

Max owns a fish-finger factory. The premises were purchased on 1 January 20X1 for £450,000 and depreciation charged at 2% pa straight line.

Max now wishes to revalue the factory premises to £800,000 on 1 January 20X7 to reflect the market value.

What is the balance on the revaluation reserve after this transaction?

A   £350,000

B   £395,000

C   £404,000

D   £413,000

11 Depreciation and disposal of a revalued asset

Depreciation of a revalued asset

- When a fixed asset has been revalued, the charge for depreciation should be based on the revalued amount and the remaining useful life of the asset.

- this charge will be higher than depreciation prior to the revaluation

- the excess of the new depreciation charge over the old depreciation charge should be transferred from the revaluation reserve to the profit and loss reserve (within the capital section of the balance sheet)

  Dr Revaluation reserve   X

  Cr Profit and loss reserve   X

Illustration 6 : Depreciation of a revalued asset

Eddie owns a retail unit in central Springfield. He bought it 25 years ago for £100,000, depreciating it over 50 years. At the start of 20X6 he decides to revalue the unit to £800,000. The unit has a remaining useful economic life of 25 years.

What accounting entries should be made in 20X6?

Solution

On revaluation at start of 20X6

Dr Retail unit cost	£700,000
Dr Accumulated depreciation	£50,000
Cr Revaluation reserve	£750,000

Depreciation for 20X6

Dr Depreciation expense(£800,000/25 yrs)	£32,000
Cr Accumulated depreciation	£32,000

Reserves transfer for 20X6

Dr Revaluation reserve (£32,000 – £2,000)	£30,000
Cr Profit and loss reserve	£30,000

Disposal of a revalued asset

- The disposal of a revalued asset is recorded as already seen.

Test Your Understanding 9

Depreciation of a revalued asset

Spartacus United football club's balance sheet at 31 December 20X7 includes the following information:

	£
Stadium cost	1,500,000
Depreciation	(450,000)
	—————
	1,050,000
	—————

Depreciation has been provided at 2% on the straight-line basis.

The stadium is revalued on 30 June 20X8 at £1,380,000. There is no change in its remaining estimated future useful life.

What is the depreciation charge for the year ended 31 December 20X8?

Test Your Understanding 10

Tiger Trees owns and runs a golf club. Some years ago Tiger purchased land next to the existing course with the intention of creating a smaller nine-hole course. The cost of the land was £260,000. Tiger hasn't yet built the additional course but has revalued this land to £600,000. He has now decided that building the new course is uneconomical and has found a buyer who is willing to pay £695,000 for the land.

What are the ledger entries on disposal?

12 Disclosure of fixed asset balances in company financial statements

Balance sheet	Profit and loss account	Notes to the accounts
Aggregate net book NBV of fixed assets disclosed on the face of the balance sheet.	Depreciation charge included within relevant expense categories.	• Disclosure of depreciation methods and rates used • Fixed assets disclosure • Details of revaluations.

Expandable text

FRS 15 Property, plant and equipment contains a number of disclosure requirements relating to fixed assets. Here are the main ones:

(1) The measurement bases used for arriving at the carrying amount of the asset (e.g. cost or valuation): if more than one basis has been used, the amounts for each basis must be disclosed.

(2) Depreciation methods used, with details of useful lives or the depreciation rates used.

(3) The gross amount of each asset heading and its related accumulated depreciation (aggregated with accumulated impairment losses) at the beginning and end of the period.

KAPLAN PUBLISHING

(4) A reconciliation of the carrying amount at the beginning and end of the period, showing:
- – additions
- – assets classified as held for sale
- – disposals
- – revaluations
- – depreciation.

(5) Any commitments for future acquisition of property, plant and equipment.

(6) If assets are stated at revalued amounts, the following should be disclosed:
- – the effective date of the revaluation
- – whether an independent valuer was involved
- – the methods and assumptions applied in estimating the items' fair value
- – the carrying amount that would have been recognised had the assets been carried at cost
- – the revaluation surplus, indicating the change for the period.

13 Chapter summary

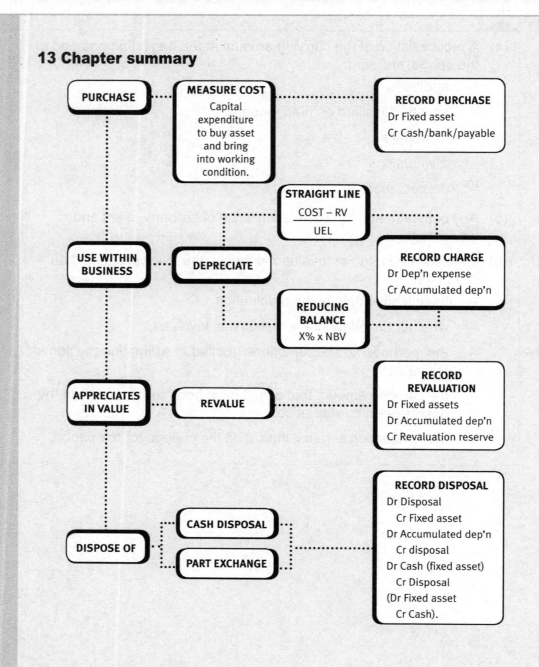

Test your understanding answers

Test Your Understanding 1

The correct answer is A

Land and buildings

	£
Office premises	250,000
Legal fees	10,000
	260,000

- the cost of the purple paint does not form part of the cost of the office and so should not be capitalised. Instead it should be taken to the profit and loss account as a revenue expense.

Motor vehicles

	£
3 Mercedes E series	116,000
Number plates	210
Delivery charges	180
	116,390

- The number plates are one-off charges which form part of the purchase price of any car.
- The road licence fee, drivers' wages and receipts are ongoing expenses, incurred every year. They cannot be capitalised, but should be taken to the profit and loss account as expenses.

Test Your Understanding 2

The correct answer is D

Oven		**20X6**
		£
£2,000 x 10%		200

Minibus

20X4: 25% x £18,000	= £4,500	
20X5: 25% x £(18,000 – 4,500)	= £3,375	
20X6: 25% x £(18,000 – 7,875)	= £2,531	2,531

Total depreciation charge		**2,731**

Test Your Understanding 3

The correct answer is B

Machine 1		£	£
20X5: 20% x £12,000 x 5/12	=	1,000	
20X6: 20% x £12,000	=	2,400	
Machine 2			
20X6: 10% x £8,000 x 3/12	=		
		200	

Total Depreciation charge		
20X5:		1,000
20X6: £2,400 + £200		2,600

Test Your Understanding 4

Leases (cost)

	£		£
1.8.X5 cash	200,000	Balance c/f	200,000
	200,000		200,000
Balance b/f	200,000		

Fixtures and fittings (cost)

	£		£
1.8.X5 cash	4,000	Balance c/f	4,000
	4,000		4,000
Balance b/f	4,000		

Depreciation charge

	£		£
X5 accumulated depreciation	9,000	Profit and loss account	9,000
X6 accumulated depreciation	8,750	Profit and loss account	8,750
X7 accumulated depreciation	8,563	Profit and loss account	8,563

Accumulated depreciation (leases)

	£		£
		X5 depreciation	
Balance c/f	8,000	charge	8,000
	8,000		8,000
		Balance b/f	8,000
Balance c/f	16,000	X6 depreciation charge	8,000
	16,000		16,000
		Balance b/f	16,000
Balance c/f	24,000	X7 depreciation charge	8,000
	24,000		24,000
		Balance b/f	24,000

Accumulated depreciation (fixtures and fittings)

	£		£
		X5 depreciation	
Balance c/f	1,000	charge	1,000
	1,000		1,000
		Balance b/f	1,000
Balance c/f	1,750	X6 depreciation charge	750
	1,750		1,750
		Balance b/f	1,750
Balance c/f	2,313	X7 depreciation charge	563
	2,313		2,313
		Balance b/f	2,313

Annual depreciation workings:

Note, details of the depreciation method and rate for the lease are not given in the question. We are however told that the lease term is 25 years. This suggests that it would be appropriate to use the straight-line method with a useful economic life of 25 years.

20X5	Lease: £200,000/25 years	=	8,000
	Fountain: £4,000 x 25%	=	1,000
			9,000
20X6	Lease: £200,000/25 years	=	8,000
	Fountain: £3,000 x 25%	=	750
			8,750
20X7	Lease: £200,000 / 25 years	=	8,000
	Fountain: £2,250 x 25%	=	563
			8,563

Test Your Understanding 5

The correct answer is A

Initial depreciation charge $= \dfrac{£30,000}{20 \text{ years}} = £1,500$

NBV at date of change $= £30,000 - (£1,500 \times 3\text{yrs})$
$= £25,500$

New depreciation charge $= \dfrac{£25,500 - £1,500}{12 \text{ years}}$
$= £2,000 \text{ pa}$

Test Your Understanding 6

1	Dr Disposals	£3,000
	Cr Fixtures and Fittings Cost	£3,000
2	Dr Accumulated depreciation	£1,050
	Cr Disposals	£1,050

Depreciation working:

X2	10 % x 3,000 x 11/12	=	275
X3	10% x 3,000	=	300
X4	10% x 3,000	=	300
X5	10% x 3,000 x 7/12	=	175
			1050

3	Dr Cash	£2,000
	Cr Disposals	£2,000

Disposals

	£		£
31.7.X5 Fixtures and fittings cost	3,000	Accumulated depreciation	1,050
Profit on disposal (ß)	50	Cash proceeds	2,000
	3,050		3,050

The charge to the profit and loss account for the year ended 31 December 20X5 is:

	£
Depreciation charge for the year	175
profit/loss on disposal	(50)

Note: As depreciation is charged monthly, it is necessary to charge an amount to the profit and loss account for the period 1 January 20X5 to the disposal date 31 July 20X5.

Test Your Understanding 7

Sewing machine cost

	£		£
Balance b/f	2,500	Disposal	2,500
New asset			
PEA	750		
Cash	4,850	Balance c/f	5,600
	–––––		–––––
	8,100		8,100
	–––––		–––––
Balance b/f	5,600		

Sewing machine accumulated depreciation

	£		£
Disposal	1,500	Balance b/f	1,500
		Depreciation	
Balance c/f	1,120	charge X5	1,120
	–––––		–––––
	2,620		2,620
	–––––		–––––
		Balance b/f	1,120

Depreciation b/f working:

£2,500 x 20% x 3 years = £1,500

Disposals

	£		£
		Sewing machine	
		accumulated	
Sewing machine cost	2,500	depreciation	1,500
		PEA	750
		Loss on disposal (ß)	250
	–––––		–––––
	2,500		2,500
	–––––		–––––

Depreciation charge

	£		£
Sewing machine accumulated depreciation	1,120	Profit and loss account	1,120

Depreciation charge working:

£5,600 x 20% = £1,120

Test Your Understanding 8

The correct answer is C

Factory cost

	£		£
Balance b/f	450,000		
Revaluation	350,000	Balance c/f	800,000
	800,000		800,000
	800,000		

Accumulated depreciation

	£		£
Revaluation (2% x £450,000 x 6yrs)	54,000	Balance b/f	54,000
	54,000		54,000

Revaluation reserve

	£		£
		Factory cost	350,000
Balance c/f	404,000	Accumulated depreciation	54,000
	404,000		404,000
		Balance b/f	404,000

Test Your Understanding 9

Depreciation must continue to be charged on the original cost until the date of revaluation. Thereafter it is charged on the revalued amount:

£

		£	
First half of 20X8	2% × £1,500,000 × 6/12	15,000	Note that this is part of the depreciation cleared out on revaluation and so is not part of the accumulated depreciation balance at the year end.
Second half of 20X8	$\dfrac{1,380,000}{6/12 \ \ 34.5\text{yrs}} \times$	20,000	This amount will form the accumulated depreciation at the year end.
Total depreciation charge for 20X8		35,000	

Test Your Understanding 10

Land cost

	£		£
Balance b/f	600,000	Disposal	600,000

Disposal

	£		£
Land cost	600,000	Proceeds	695,000
Profit on disposal	95,000		

9

From trial balance to financial statements

Chapter learning objectives

Upon completion of this chapter you will be able to:

- illustrate the process of adjusting the financial statements for accruals and prepayments, depreciation bad and doubtful debts.

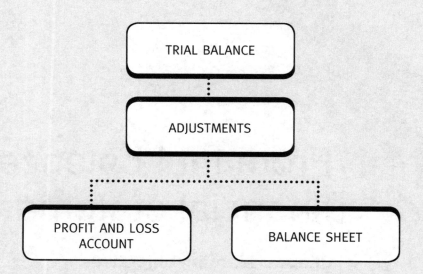

1 Trial balance

In this chapter we will bring together the material from the previous chapters and produce a set of financial statements from a trial balance.

This will involve adjusting for the following items:

- closing stock
- depreciation
- accruals and prepayments
- bad debts and the provision for doubtful debts.

Once these adjustments have been made, the profit and loss account and balance sheet can be prepared.

When making the adjustments we must make sure that each transaction contains the correct double entry.

Purpose of the trial balance

The purpose of the trial balance is

- to check that for every debit entry made, an equal credit entry has been made
- as a first step in preparing the financial statements.

Limitations of the trial balance

Although the trial balance is useful in ensuring that double entry has been maintained, it will not:

- identify errors such as mispostings to the wrong account or a double entry for the wrong amount
- identify where errors have been made, or what those errors are.

2 Adjustments

Here is a reminder of the accounting entries for the adjustments we need to make when preparing the financial statements:

Closing stock

Dr Stock (B/S)

Cr Stock included in cost of sales (P&L)

With the closing stock at the end of the period.

Depreciation

Dr Expenses (P&L)

Cr Accumulated depreciation (B/S)

With depreciation charge for the year for each class of asset.

Accruals

Dr Expenses (P&L)

Cr Accruals (B/S)

With each accrued expense.

Prepayments

Dr Prepayments (B/S)

Cr Expenses (P&L)

With each prepaid expense.

Irrecoverable debts

Dr Irrecoverable debt expense (P&L)

Cr Debtors (B/S)

With the total of debtors written off.

Allowance for debtors

Dr Irrecoverable debt (P&L)

Cr Allowance for debtors (B/S)

With the increasee in the allowance for the period.

Illustration 1 : Adjustments

In this example, we will account for the period-end adjustments and prepare a set of financial statements from trial balance.

The trial balance of Tyndall at 31 May 20X6 is as follows:

Trial balance of Tyndall at 31 May 20X6

	£	£
Capital account		15,258
Drawings by proprietor	5,970	
Purchases	73,010	
Returns inwards	1,076	
Returns outwards		3,720
Discounts	1,870	965
Credit sales		96,520
Cash sales		30,296
Customs duty	11,760	
Carriage inwards	2,930	
Carriage outwards	1,762	
Salesman's commission	711	
Salesman's salary	3,970	
Office salaries	7,207	
Bank charges	980	
Loan interest	450	
Light and heat	2,653	
Sundry expenses	2,100	
Rent	3,315	
Insurance	4,000	
Printing and postage	2,103	
Advertising	1,044	
Irrecoverable debts	1,791	
Allowance for debtors		437
Stock	7,650	
Debtors	10,760	
Creditors		7,411

	£	£
Cash at bank	2,634	
Cash in hand	75	
New delivery van (less trade-in)	2,200	
Motor expenses	986	
Furniture and equipment:		
Cost	8,000	
Depreciation at 1 June 20X5		2,400
Old delivery van:		
Cost	2,000	
Depreciation at 1 June 20X5		1,000
Loan account at 9%		
(repayable in five years)		5,000
	163,007	163,007

The following information is relevant:

(1) Closing stock has been valued for accounts purposes at £8,490.

(2) The motor van was sold on 31 August 20X5 and traded in against the cost of a new van. The trade-in price was £1,400 and the cost of the new van was £3,600. No entries have yet been made for this transaction apart from debiting the £2,200 cash paid to the New delivery van account.

(3) Straight-line depreciation is to be provided on a monthly basis at the following annual rates:

Motor vans   25%

Furniture and equipment   10%

(4) Past experience indicates that an allowance for debtors should be made equivalent to 5% of the closing debtors.

(5) An accrual of £372 is required in respect of light and heat.

(6) A quarter's rent to 30 June 20X6 amounting to £900 was paid on 2 April 20X6. Insurance for the year to 31 March 20X7 amounting to £1,680 was paid on 16 April.

Required:

Prepare a profit and loss account and a balance sheet for the year ended 31 May 20X6.

Solution

Step 1 Stock

The closing stock figure of £8,490 must be included in the financial statements. The accounting journal is:

Dr Stock (B/S)	£8,490
Cr Stock (Cost of sales in IS)	£8,490

Step 2 Fixed assets and depreciation

As well as calculating the depreciation for the year, we must also deal with the part-exchange of the van during the year.

Depreciation of van from 1 June 20X5 to 31 August 20X5:

Cost £2,000 x 25% x 3/12 = £125

Disposal of van:

The van has been part-exchanged against the cost of a new van. The trade-in value of £1,400 is equivalent to the disposal proceeds of the van. The new van has a total cost of £3,600 consisting of £1,400 trade-in allowance and £2,200 cash.

The double entry to record the disposal is:

Dr Delivery van accumulated depreciation account (1,000 + 125)	£1,125
Dr New delivery van cost account	£1,400
Cr Delivery van cost account	£2,000
Cr Profit on sale of asset	£525

This can be shown in the disposal account as follows:

Old delivery van – disposal

	£		£
Old delivery van – cost	2,000	Old delivery van – accumulated depreciation	1,125
Profit on disposal	525		
		New delivery van	1,400
	2,525		2,525

Don't forget to add on the depreciation for the first three months of the year when you are calculating the profit on disposal.

Note that this question specifically requires monthly depreciation. Some questions may state that there is no depreciation in the year of acquisition or year of disposal of an asset. Make sure you read the question carefully.

Depreciation of van from 1 September 20X5 to 31 May 20X6

Cost £3,600 x 25% x 9/12 = £675.

The total depreciation for the year for delivery vans is £800 (675 + 125).

Depreciation on furniture and equipment:

Cost £8,000 x 10% = £800.

Step 3 Irrecoverable debts

The trial balance shows us that:

- £1,791 has been written off in the year for Irrecoverable debts, and
- the balance on the allowance for receivables is £437.

The closing allowance should be 5% of closing debtors.

£10,760 x 5% = £538.

The charge to the profit and loss account is the movement between the opening and closing allowance.

£538 – £437 = £101 increase in the allowance which is debited to the profit and loss account .

The double entry to record this transactions is:

Dr	Irrecoverable debts expense	£101
Cr	Allowance for debtors	£101

The charge in the profit and loss account for Irrecoverable debts will amount to £ 1,892 inlcuding the debt already written off (£1,791 + £101).

Step 4 Light and heat

£372 needs to be accrued for light and heat expenses. The double entry is:

Dr Light and heat expense	£372
Cr Accruals	£372

This journal entry ensures that the business has recorded all of its expenses in the period.

Step 5 Rent

The rent has been paid in advance and part of the payment relates to the next accounting period. This must be taken out of expenses for the current period and shown in the balance sheet as a prepayment.

Rent prepaid (1/3 x £900) = £300.

Step 6 Insurance

Insurance has also been paid in advance and must be adjusted.

Insurance prepaid 10/12 x £1,680 = £1,400.

Step 7 Prepare the profit and loss account and balance sheet

Sales:	£	£
Credit sales		96,520
Cash sales		30,296
		126,816
Less: Sales returns		(1,076)
		125,740
Opening stock	7,650	
Purchases	73,010	
Less: Purchase returns	(3,720)	
Carriage inwards	2,930	
Customs duty	11,760	
Closing stock	(8,490)	
Cost of sales		(83,140)
Gross profit		42,600
Discount received		965
Profit on sale of van		525
		44,090

Less: Expenses:

Depreciation:

Van **(Step 2)**	800
Equipment **(Step 2)**	800
Irrecoverable debts **(Step 3)**	1,892
Light and heat (2,653 + 372)**(Step 4)**	3,025
Rent (3,315 – 300) **(Step 5)**	3,015
Insurance (4,000 – 1,400) **(Step 6)**	2,600
Discount allowed	1,870
Carriage outwards	1,762
Salesman's commission	711
Salesman's salary	3,970
Office salary	7,207
Bank charges	980
Loan interest	450
Sundry expenses	2,100
Printing and postage	2,103
Advertising	1,044
Motor expenses	986
	————
	(35,315)
	————
Net profit	8,775
	————

Balance sheet at 31 May 20X6

	Cost	Acc dep'n	NBV
	£	£	£
Fixed assets:			
Motor van (Step 2)	3,600	675	2,925
Furniture and equipment	8,000	3,200	4,800
	11,600	3,875	7,725
Current assets:			
Stock		8,490	
Debtors	10,760		
Less: Allowance for debtors (Step 3)	(538)		
		10,222	
Prepayments		1,700	
Cash at bank		2,634	
Cash in hand		75	
		23,121	
Current liabilities:			
Creditors	7,411		
Accruals	372		
		(7,783)	
Net current assets			15,338
Long–term liabilities:			
Loan			5,000
			18,063
Capital account:			
Balance at 1 June 20X5			15,258
Net profit			8,775
Less drawings by proprietor			(5,970)
			18,063

Test Your Understanding 1

Kevin Suri carries on business as a retail trader. The trial balance of his business as at 31 December 20X5 was as follows:

	Dr £	Cr £
Capital		225,600
Sales and purchases	266,800	365,200
Stock at 1 January 20X5	23,340	
Returns	1,200	1,600
Wages	46,160	
Rent	13,000	
Motor expenses	3,720	
Insurance	760	
Irrecoverable debts	120	
Allowance for debtors at 1 January 20X5		588
Discounts	864	1,622
Light and heat	3,074	
Bank overdraft interest	74	
Motor vehicles at cost	24,000	
– aggregate depreciation 1 Jan 20X5		12,240
Fixtures and fittings at cost	28,000	
– aggregate depreciation 1 Jan 20X5		16,800
Land	100,000	
Debtors and creditors	17,330	23,004
Bank	3,412	
Buildings at cost	100,000	
– aggregate depreciation 1 Jan 20X5		6,000
Drawings	20,800	
	652,654	652,654

You are given the following additional information:

(1) Stock at 31 December 20X5 was £25,680.

(2) Rent was prepaid by £1,000 and light and heat owed was £460 at 31 December 20X5.

(3) Land is to be revalued to £250,000 at 31 December 20X5.

(4) Following a final review of the debtors at 31 December 20X5, Kevin decides to write off another debt of £130. He also wishes to maintain the allowance for debtors at 3% of the year-end debtor balance.

(5) Depreciation is to be provided as follows:

(a) buildings – 2% pa, straight-line

(b) fixtures and fittings – straight-line method, assuming a useful economic life of five years with no residual value

(c) motor vehicles – 30% pa on a reducing-balance basis.

A full year's depreciation is charged in the year of acquisition and none in the year of disposal.

Prepare a profit and loss account for the year ended 31 December 20X5 and a balance sheet as at that date for Kevin Suri.

3 Chapter summary

```
          ┌─────────────────────────────┐
          │       TRIAL BALANCE         │
          │  • Lists out all the        │
          │    balances on the          │
          │    ledger accounts          │
          └─────────────────────────────┘
                       ┊
          ┌─────────────────────────────┐
          │        ADJUSTMENT           │
          │  • Closing stock            │
          │  • Depreciation             │
          │  • Accruals and             │
          │    prepayments              │
          │  • Irrecoverable debts      │
          │    and allowance for        │
          │    debtors.                 │
          └─────────────────────────────┘
              ┊                   ┊
┌──────────────────────┐   ┌──────────────────────┐
│  PROFIT AND LOSS     │   │    BALANCE SHEET     │
│     ACCOUNT          │   │  • Shows the financial│
│  • Shows the financial│  │    position of the   │
│    performance of the │  │    business.         │
│    business.         │   │                      │
└──────────────────────┘   └──────────────────────┘
```

Test your understanding answers

Test Your Understanding 1

Kevin Suri

Profit and loss account for the year ended 31 December 20X5

	£	£
Sales		365,200
Returns in		(1,200)
		———
		364,000
Cost of sales		
Opening stock	23,340	
Purchases	266,800	
Returns out	(1,600)	
	———	
	288,540	
Closing stock	(25,680)	
	———	
		(262,860)
		———
Gross profit		101,140
Sundry income		
Discount received		1,622
Decrease in allowance for debtors (588 – 516)		72
		———
		102,834

Expenses	
Wages	46,160
Rent (13,000 – 1,000)	12,000
Motor expenses	3,720
Insurance	760
Irrecoverable debts (120 + 130)	250
Discounts allowed	864
Light and heat (3,074 + 460)	3,534
Bank interest	74
Depreciation	
Buildings **(W1)**	2,000
Fixtures and fittings **(W1)**	5,600
Motor vehicles **(W2)**	3,528
	(78,490)
Net profit	24,344

Balance sheet as at 31 December 20X5

	Cost £	Acc dep'n £	NBV £
Fixed assets			
Land	250,000	–	250,000
Buildings	100,000	8,000	
			92,000
Fixtures and fittings	28,000	22,400	5,600
Motor vehicles	24,000	15,768	8,232
	402,000	46,168	355,832
Current assets			
Stock		25,680	
Debtors (17,330 – 130)	17,200		
Allowance for debtors	(516)		
			16,684
Prepayments		1,000	
Bank		3,412	
			46,776
Current liabilities:			
Creditors	23,004		
Accruals	460		
		(23,464)	
Net current assets			23,312
			379,144
Capital			225,600
Net profit			24,344
Revaluation surplus			
(250,000 – 100,000)			150,000
Less drawings by proprietor			(20,800)
			379,144

KAPLAN PUBLISHING

(W1) Depreciation –Straight line

	Buildings	Fixtures and fittings
Cost	£100,000	£28,000
Depreciation rate	X 2 %	X 20 %
Annual dep'n charge	£2,000	£5,600

(W2) Depreciation –reducing balance

	Motor Vehicles
Cost	£24,000
Accumulated depreciation	(£12,240)
NBV	£11,760
Depreciation rate	x 30%
Annual depreciation charge	£3,528

Books of prime entry and control accounts

Chapter learning objectives

Upon completion of this chapter you will be able to:

- identify the main data sources and records in an accounting system

- describe the contents and purpose of different types of business documentation

- outline the form of accounting records in a typical manual system

- record credit sale and purchase transactions including value added tax (VAT) using day books

- post day book totals to the ledger accounts

- explain the division of the ledger into sections

- explain the nature and purpose of control accounts for the debtors and creditors ledgers

- account for contras between trade debtors and creditors

- record cash transactions using the cash book

- explain the need for a record of petty cash transactions

- illustrate the typical format of the petty cash book

- explain the importance of using the imprest system to control petty cash

- list the necessary controls and security over petty cash that would normally be found in a business

- explain the uses of the journal

- illustrate the use of the journal and the posting of journal entries into ledger accounts.

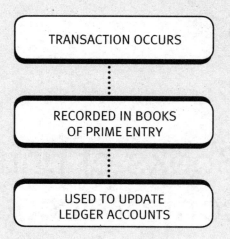

1 Business documentation

The table below summarises the main types of business documentation and sources of data for an accounting system, together with their content and purpose.

	Contents	Purpose
Quotation	Quantity/ description/ details of goods required.	To establish price from various suppliers and cross-refer to purchase requisition.
Purchase order	Details of supplier, e.g. name, address. Quantity/ description/ details of goods required and price. Terms and conditions of delivery, payment, etc.	To check to the quotation and delivery note. Sent to the supplier as request for supply
Sales order	Quantity/ description/ details of goods required.	Cross-checked with the order placed by customer. Sent to the stores/warehouse department for processing of th

Delivery note (Goods delivery note – GDN)	Details of supplier, e.g. name and address. Quantity and description of goods.	Provided by supplier. Checked with goods received and purchase order.
Goods received note (GRN)	Quantity and description of goods.	Produced by company receiving the goods as proof of receipt. Matched with delivery note and purchase order
Purchase invoice	Details of supplier, e.g. name and address. Contains details of goods, e.g. quantity, price, value, VAT, terms of credit, etc.	Issued by supplier as request for payment. Cross-checked with delivery note, and purchase ordr.
Supplier Stat	Details of supplier, e.g. name and address. Has details of date, invoice numbers and values, payments and refunds, amount owing.	Issued by supplier to show transaction in a period. Checked with other documents to ensure that the amount owing is corect.
Credte	Details of supplier, e.g name and address. Contains details of goods returned e.g. quantity, price, value, VAT, terms of credit, etc.	Issued by the supplier as evidence that credit is due. Checked with documents regarding goods

Debit not	Details of the supplier. Contains details of goods returned, e.g. quantity, price, value, VAT, terms of credit, etc.	Issued by the company receiving the goods. Cross-referred to the credit note issued by the supplier.
Remittance advice	Method of payment, invoice number, account number, date, etc.	Sent to supplier with, or as notification of, payment.
Receipt	Details of payment received.	Issued by the selling company indicating the payment received.

2 Accounting records

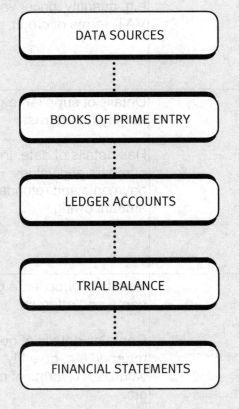

Books of prime entry

- If ledgers were updated each time a transaction occurred, the ledger accounts would quickly become cluttered and errors may be made.

- Therefore all transactions are initially recorded in a book of prime entry.

- Several books of prime entry exist, each recording a different type of transaction:

Book of prime entry	Transaction type
Sales day book	Credit sales
Purchases day book	Credit purchases
Sales returns day book on credit	Returns of goods sold
Purchases returns day book	Returns of goods bought
Cash book	All bank transactions
Petty cash book	All small cash transactions
The journal	All transactions not recorded elsewhere

- Entry of a transaction to a book of prime entry does not record the double entry required for that transaction.

- The book of prime entry is, however, the source for double entries to the ledger accounts.

- The double entry arising from the book of prime entry will be recorded periodically (daily, weekly, monthly) depending on the volume of transactions.

3 Ledger accounts and the division of the ledger

In a manual system, ledgers can be thought of as books containing the individual accounts:

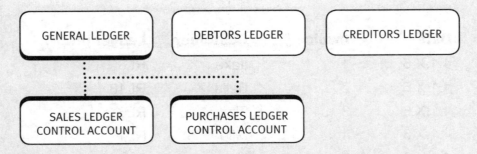

- The **general ledger** contains all accounts or a summary of all accounts necessary to produce the trial balance and financial statements.

- The **debtors ledger** contains an account for each credit customer to show how much each one owes.

- An account to summarise this information, the **sales ledger control account**, is normally contained within the general ledger.

- The **creditors ledger** contains an account for each credit supplier to show how much they are owed.

- An account to summarise this information, the **purchases ledger control account**, is normally contained within the general ledger.

Where there are individual accounts in a debtors or creditors ledger and a control account in the general ledger, only one can form part of the double entry system. The other exists for memorandum purposes. It is normally the case that the control accounts form part of the double entry system.

Expandable text

Not all businesses maintain a sales ledger control account and purchases ledger control account, however where they do it is usually these control accounts that form part of the double entry system.

Where control accounts are maintained, they are effective in reducing the time it takes to ascertain the total amount owed by debtors and owed to creditors. The scope for making errors when realising these numbers through totalling several individual accounts is also reduced.

Even where control accounts are maintained, a business must continue to keep a record of how much each customer owes them and how much they owe each supplier, therefore the debtors and creditors ledgers are always part of the accounting system.

4 Sales and purchases day books

Sales day book

The typical format of a sales day book is as follows:

Date	Invoice #	Customer	Ledger ref.	£
4.1.X6	1	Jake	RL3	4,500
4.1.X6	2	Bella	RL18	3,000
4.1.X6	3	Fizz	RL6	2,200
4.1.X6	4	Milo	RL1	10,000
4.1.X6	5	Max	RL12	500
Total for 4.1.X6				20,200

The format of the double entry resulting from the sales day book will depend upon whether the individual accounts in the debtors ledger or the sales ledger control account in the general ledger is part of the double entry system:

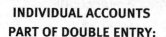

INDIVIDUAL ACCOUNTS PART OF DOUBLE ENTRY:	
Dr Jake (RL3)	£4,500
Dr Bella (RL18)	£3,000
Dr Fizz (RL6)	£2,200
Dr Milo (RL1)	£10,000
Dr Max (RL12)	£500
Cr Sales	£20,200

The total debtors of £20,200 should then be posted to the memorandum control account (assuming one is maintained).

SALES LEDGER CONTROL ACCOUNT PART OF DOUBLE ENTRY:	
Dr SLCA	£20,200
Cr Sales	£20,200

Care must then be taken to update the individual memorandum accounts with the new amounts that Jake, Bella, Fizz, Milo and Max owe.

Purchases day book, sales returns day book and purchases returns day book

The format of the remaining day books is similar to that of the sales day book. The double entries arising are:

	Individual accounts part of double entry	Control accounts part of double entry
Purchases day book	Dr Purchases Cr Individual accounts in creditors ledger. Total purchases also posted to the purchases ledger control account.	Dr Purchases Cr Purchases ledger control account. Each entry also posted to individual memorandum accounts in creditors ledger.

Sales returns day book	Dr Sales returns Cr Individual accounts in debtors ledger. Total returns also posted to the sales ledger control account.	Dr Sales returns Cr Sales ledger control account. Each entry also posted to individual memorandum accounts in debtors ledger.
Purchases returns day book	Dr Individual accounts in creditors ledger Cr Purchases returns. Total returns also posted to the purchases ledger control account.	Dr Purchases ledger control account Cr Purchase returns Each entry also posted to individual memorandum accounts in creditors ledger.

Expandable text

Format of the purchases day book

Date	Invoice #	Customer	Ledger Ref	£
4.1.X 6	1	Harry	PL3	2,700
4.1.X 6	2	Ron	PL18	145
4.1.X 6	3	Hermione	PL6	4,675
4.1.X 6	4	Neville	PL1	750
4.1.X 6	5	Draco	PL12	345
Total for 4.1.X 6				8,615

	£
Dr Purchases	8,615
Cr Purchases ledger control account	8,615

Individual purchases posted as credits to individual suppliers' accounts in creditors ledger.

Format of the sales returns day book

Date	Invoice #	Customer	Ledger Ref	£
4.1.X 6	1	Max	RL12	50
4.1.X 6	2	Ernie	RL2	450
4.1.X 6	3	Pat	RL20	390
4.1.X 6	4	Sam	RL27	670
4.1.X 6	5	Milo	RL1	2,300
Total for 4.1.X 6				3,860

	£
Dr Sales returns	3,860
Cr Sales ledger control account	3,860

Individual returns posted as credits to individual customers' accounts in debtors ledger.

Format of the purchases returns day book

Date	Invoice #	Customer	Ledger Ref	£
4.1.X 6	1	Harry	PL3	600
4.1.X 6	2	Cho	PL16	75
4.1.X 6	3	Fleur	PL2	800
4.1.X 6	4	Neville	PL1	50
4.1.X 6	5	Draco	PL12	100
Total for 4.1.X 6				1,625

	£
Dr Purchases ledger control account	8,615
Cr Purchases returns	8,615

Individual returns posted as debits to individual suppliers' accounts in creditors ledger.

Test Your Understanding 1

Mr Kipper-Ling runs a business providing equipment for bakeries. He always makes a note of sales and purchases on credit and associated returns, but he is not sure how they should be recorded for the purposes of his accounts.

Write up the following credit transactions arising in the first two weeks of August 20X6 into day books and advise Mr Kipper-Ling of the correct double entries assuming that control accounts are maintained as part of the double entry system.

1 August	Mrs Bakewell buys £500 worth of cake tins.
1 August	Mr Kipper-Ling purchases £2,000 worth of equipment from wholesalers TinPot Ltd.
2 August	Mr Kipper-Ling returns goods costing £150 to another supplier, I Cook.
3 August	Jack Flap buys £1,200 worth of equipment.
3 August	Mrs Bakewell returns £100 worth of the goods supplied to her.
4 August	Victoria Sand-Witch buys a new oven for £4,000.
5 August	Mr Kipper-Ling purchases £600 worth of baking trays from regular supplier TinTin Ltd.
8 August	Mr Kipper-Ling purchases ovens costing £10,000 from Hot Stuff Ltd.
8 August	Mr Kipper-Ling returns equipment costing £300 to TinPot Ltd.
9 August	Pavel Ova purchases goods costing £2,200.
11 August	Mrs Bakewell buys some oven-proof dishes costing £600.

5 VAT in day books

If a business is registered for VAT, the sales and purchases day books must include entries to record the tax.

Illustration 1 : VAT in day books

Sales day book

Date	Invoice	Customer	Ledger Ref	Gross	VAT	Net
				£	£	£
8.7.X6	1	Spencer	J1	587.50	87.50	500.00
10.7.X6	2	Archie	S5	705.00	105.00	600.00
				1,292.50	192.50	1,100.00

The double entry for the above transaction will be:

Dr	Sales ledger control account	£1,292.50
Cr	VAT	£192.50
Cr	Sales	£1,100.00

Purchases day book

Date	Supplier	Ledger Ref	Gross	VAT	Net
			£	£	£
8.7.X6	Peggy	Y1	1,762.50	262.50	1,500
10.7.X6	Zena	Z8	352.50	52.50	300
			2,115.00	315.00	1,800

The double entry for the above transaction will be:

Dr	VAT	£315
Dr	Purchases	£1,800
Cr	Purchases ledger control account	£2,115

Test Your Understanding 2

The following sales invoices have been issued by Quincy. in July:

Date	Customer	Inv No	Ledger ref.	
8 July	Simpson	1100	A8	£ 411.25 (including VAT)
10 July	Burns	1101	B5	£ 1,300 (excluding VAT)

Quincy is registered for VAT.

What double entry arises from the day book?

		Dr		Cr
A	Sales ledger control account	£1,711.25	Sales	£2,010.72
	VAT	£299.47		
B	Sales ledger control account	£2,010.72	Sales	£1,711.25
			VAT	£299.47
C	Sales ledger control account	£1,650.00	Sales	£1,938.75
	VAT	£288.75		
D	Sales ledger control account	£1,938.75	Sales	£1,650.00
			VAT	£288.75

6 Control accounts

Control accounts are ledger accounts that summarise a large number of transactions.

They do form part of the double entry system.

The sales ledger control account may include any of the following entries:

Sales ledger control account

Balance b/f	X	Balance b/f	X
Credit sales (SDB)	X	Sales returns (SRDB)	X
Bad debts recovered	X	Bank (CB)	X
Bank (CB) dishonoured cheques	X	Irrecoverable debts (journal)	X
Bank (CB) refunds of credit balances	X	Discounts allowed	X
		Contra	X
Balance c/f	X	Balance c/f	X
	X		X
Balance b/f	X	Balance b/f	X

The Purchases ledger control account may include any of the following entries:

Purchases ledger control account

Balance b/f	X	Balance b/f	X
Bank (CB)	X	Credit purchases (PDB)	X
Purchases returns (PRDB)	X	Bank (CB) refunds of debit balances	X
Discounts received	X		
Contra	X		
Balance c/f	X	Balance c/f	X
	X		X
Balance b/f	X	Balance b/f	X

SDB	Sales day book
PDB	Purchases day book
SRDB	Sales returns day book
PRDB	Purchases returns day book
CB	Cash book

Note that any entries to the control accounts must also be reflected in the individual accounts within the debtors and creditors ledgers.

Contra entries

The situation may arise where a customer is also a supplier. Instead of both owing each other money, it may be agreed that the balances are contra'd, i.e. cancelled.

The double entry for this type of contra is:

> Dr Purchases ledger control account

> Cr Sales ledger control account

The individual debtor and creditor accounts must also be updated to reflect this.

Credit balances on the sales ledger control account

Sometimes the sales ledger control account may show a credit balance, i.e. we owe the customer money. These amounts are usually small and arise when:

- The customer has overpaid.
- Credit notes have been issued for fully paid for goods.
- Payment is received in advance of raising invoices.

The purchases ledger control account may show a debit balance for similar reasons.

Test Your Understanding 3

Jones prepares monthly sales and purchase ledger control accounts. At 1 November 2005 the following balances existed in the company's records.

	Dr £	Cr £
Sales ledger control account	54,000	1,000
Purchases ledger control account	200	43,000

The following information is extracted in November 2005 from the company's records:

	£
Credit sales	251,000
Cash sales	34,000
Credit purchases	77,000
Cash purchases	29,000
Sales returns	11,000
Purchases returns	3,000
Amounts received from credit customers	242,000
Dishonoured cheques	500
Amounts paid to credit suppliers	74,000
Cash discounts allowed	3,000
Cash discounts received	2,000
Irrecoverable debts written off	1,000
Increase in allowance for debtors	1,200
Interest charged to customers	1,400
Contra settlements	800

At 30 November 2005 the balances in the sales and purchases ledgers, as extracted, totalled:

	Dr £	Cr £
Sales ledger balances	To be calculated	2,000
Purchases ledger balances	200	To be calculated

Prepare the sales ledger control account and the purchase ledger control account for the month of November 2005 to determine the closing debit and closing credit balances on the sales ledger control account and purchase ledger control account respectively.

7 The cash book

- All transactions involving cash at bank are recorded in the cash book.

- Many businesses have two distinct cash books – a **cash payments book** and a **cash receipts book**.

- A note of cash discounts given and received is also recorded in the cash book. This is to facilitate the recording of discounts in both the general and debtors/creditors ledgers.

- It is common for businesses to use a columnar format cash book in order to analyse types of cash payment and receipt.

Illustration 2 : The cash book

The cash payments book

The following is the cash payments book of a small print business.

Date	Detail	Bank received	Discount ledger	Creditors	Rent
		£	£	£	£
18.7.X6	Mr A	1,400	100	1,400	
18.7.X6	Office	3,000			3,000
18.7.X6	Mr B	210		210	
18.7.X6	Mr C	1,600	80	1,600	
18.7.X6	Shop	400			400
		6,610	180	3,210	3,400

What are the accounting entries arising from the totals in the cash book at the end of the day, assuming control accounts are kept?

Solution

The cash transactions are recorded in total as follows:

Dr Purchases ledger control account	£3,210
Dr Rent expense	£3,400
Cr Bank	£6,610

The discount is recorded as follows:

Dr Purchases ledger control account	£180
Cr Discounts received	£180

Entries must also be made to the individual accounts of Mr A, Mr B and Mr C in the creditors ledger in order to reflect the payments made and discounts received.

Test Your Understanding 4

The following is the cash receipts book of the SM Art Gallery.

Date	Detail	Bank received	Discount ledger	Debtors	Rent
		£	£	£	£
18.7.X6	C Monet	10,000	500	10,000	
18.7.X6	Interest	20			20
	Acc # 1			25,000	
18.7.X6	VV Gogh	25,000			
18.7.X6	Interest	100			100
	Acc # 2				
18.7.X6	P Picasso	13,700	300	13,700	
		48,820	800	48,700	120

What are the accounting entries arising from the totals in the cash book at the end of the day, assuming control accounts are kept?

8 Petty cash book

- All transactions involving small amounts of cash are recorded in the petty cash book.

- The petty cash system is usually designed to deal with sundry small payments in cash made by a business, e.g. paying the milkman, purchasing biscuits, buying stationery or reimbursing travel expenses

- The cash receipts will be recorded together with the payments which will be analysed in the same way as a cash book.

The imprest system

The best way of dealing with petty cash is by means of an imprest system, which works as follows.

Step 1

The business decides on the amount of cash to be held as a float.

Dr petty cash	X
Cr bank	X

This round sum amount will be referred to as the 'petty cash float'.

Step 2

As the petty cashier makes payments he records these in the petty cash book, which is not part of the double entry system. All expenditure must be evidenced by an expense receipt and the petty cashier will attach an expense voucher to each expense.

Step 3

When the petty cash runs low, a cheque is drawn to return the petty cash to the exact amount of the original float. At this stage the expense vouchers should be produced by the petty cashier to the cheque signatory which will exactly equal the cheque required.

This aspect of control is the essential feature of the petty cash system. At any stage:

Float = Cash in petty cash box + sum total of expense vouchers since last reimbursement

Controls over petty cash

The following controls and security over petty cash should be found in a business:

- Petty cash must be kept in a petty cash box.

- Petty cash box must be secured in a safe.

- Person responsible for petty cash must be reliable and know what he/she is doing.

- All petty cash must be supported by invoices.

- Petty cash vouchers must be signed by the claimant and the person responsible for running the petty cash.

- Regular spot checks must be carried out to ensure that the petty cash is accurate.

Illustration 3 : Controls over petty cash

The petty cash book

On 1 March 20X9 a petty cash float of £100 is introduced by Dialex. During March the following payments are made out of petty cash:

		£
2 March	Biscuits	10
8 March	Stationery	20
11 March	Bus fare	3
16 March	Train fare	5
25 March	Stationery	40

On 31 March the cash is reimbursed. Write up the petty cash book for the month and show the resulting entries to the general ledger.

Solution

Received	Date	Details	Voucher	Total	Stationery expenses	Sundry expenses	Travelling
£				£	£	£	£
100	1 Mar	Cash book					
	2 Mar	Gateway biscuits	1	10		10	
	8 Mar	Basildon Bond	2	20	20		
	11 Mar	Bus fares	3	3			3
			3				
	16 Mar	Rail fares	4	5			5
	25 Mar	Office International	5	40	40		
				78	60	10	8
78	31 Mar	Cash					
		Balance c/f		100			
178				178			
100	1 Apr	Balance b/f					

No double entry bookkeeping entries are made from the receipts side of the petty cash book – in a good system the only receipt should be the reimbursement of the float, the double entry of which is dealt with in the posting of the cash book.

As regards the payments, the double entry in the general ledger is performed as follows:

Stationery

20X9	£	20X9	£
Mar Petty cash book	60		

Sundry expenses			
20X9	£	20X9	£
Mar Petty cash book	10		

Travelling expenses			
20X9	£	20X9	£
Mar Petty cash book	8		

9 The journal

The journal is a book of prime entry which records transactions which are not routine (and not recorded in any other book of prime entry), for example:

- year-end adjustments
    - depreciation charge for the year
    - irrecoverable debt write-off
    - record movement in allowance for debtors
    - accruals and prepayments
    - closing stock
- acquisitions and disposals of fixed assets
- opening balances for balance sheet items
- correction of errors.

The journal is a clear and comprehensible way of setting out a bookkeeping double entry that is to be made.

Presentation of a journal

A journal should be laid out in the following way:

> Dr Fixed asset   x
>
> Cr Cash   x

to record the purchase of a new fixed asset.

A brief narrative should be given to explain the entry.

Test Your Understanding 5

Igor Romanov runs a Russian restaurant. He is a very good chef but not quite so good at accounting and needs help to record the following transactions:

(1) Closing stock of 250 bottles of vodka at a cost of £2,750 has not been recorded.

(2) Igor needs to charge depreciation on his restaurant. He holds a 25-year lease which cost him £150,000 ten years ago.

(3) A regular customer, V Shady, keeps a tab behind the bar. He currently owes £350 but was last seen buying a one-way ticket to Moscow. Igor has given up hope of payment and intends to write the debt off.

(4) On the last day of the year Igor bought two new sofas for cash for the bar area of the restaurant. They cost £600 each but the purchase has not been reflected in the accounts.

What journals should Igor post?

10 Chapter summary

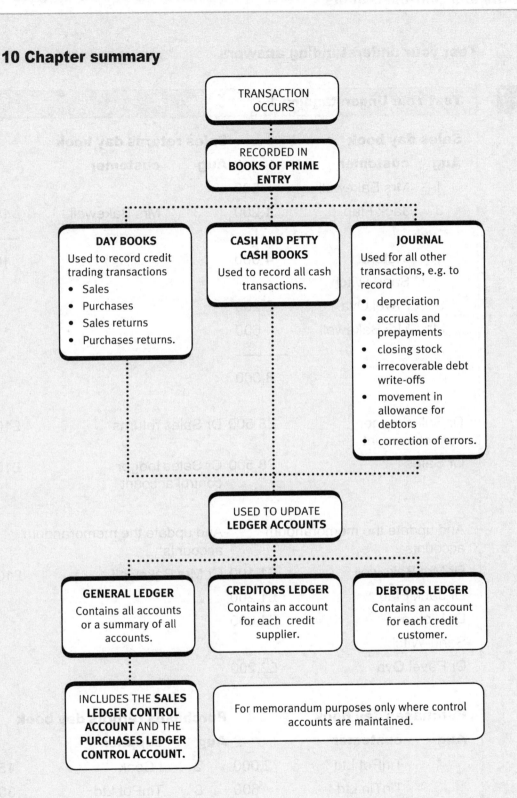

TRANSACTION OCCURS

RECORDED IN BOOKS OF PRIME ENTRY

DAY BOOKS

Used to record credit trading transactions

- Sales
- Purchases
- Sales returns
- Purchases returns.

CASH AND PETTY CASH BOOKS

Used to record all cash transactions.

JOURNAL

Used for all other transactions, e.g. to record

- depreciation
- accruals and prepayments
- closing stock
- irrecoverable debt write-offs
- movement in allowance for debtors
- correction of errors.

USED TO UPDATE LEDGER ACCOUNTS

GENERAL LEDGER

Contains all accounts or a summary of all accounts.

CREDITORS LEDGER

Contains an account for each credit supplier.

DEBTORS LEDGER

Contains an account for each credit customer.

INCLUDES THE SALES LEDGER CONTROL ACCOUNT AND THE PURCHASES LEDGER CONTROL ACCOUNT.

For memorandum purposes only where control accounts are maintained.

Test your understanding answers

Test Your Understanding 1

Sales day book			Sales returns day book		
Aug	**customer**	**£**	**Aug**	**customer**	**£**
1	Mrs Bakewell	500			
3	Jack Flap	1,200	3	Mrs Bakewell	100
					100
4	Victoria Sand-Witch	4,000			
9	Pavel Ova	2,200			
11	Mrs Bakewell	600			
		8,500			

Dr Sales ledger control account	£8,500		Dr Sales returns	£100	
Cr Sales	£8,500		Cr Sales ledger control account	£100	

And update the memorandum accounts:		And update the memorandum accounts:	
Dr Mrs Bakewell	£1,100	Cr Mrs Bakewell	£100
Dr Jack Flap	£1,200		
Dr Victoria Sand-Witch	£4,000		
Dr Pavel Ova	£2,200		

Purchases day book			Purchases returns day book		
Aug	**customer**	**£**	**Aug**	**supplier**	**£**
1	TinPot Ltd	2,000	2	I Cook	150
5	TinTin Ltd	600	8	TinPot Ltd	300
8	Hot Stuff	10,000			
		12,600			450

Dr Purchases	£12,600	Dr Purchases ledger control account	£450
Cr Purchases ledger control account	£12,600	Cr Purchases returns	£450

And update the memorandum accounts:

Cr TinPot Ltd   £2,000

Cr TinTin Ltd   £600

Cr Hot Stuff   £10,000

And update the memorandum accounts:

Dr I Cook   £150

Dr TinPot Ltd   £300

Test Your Understanding 2

The correct answer is D

Sales day book

Date	Customer	invoice	Ledger ref.	Gross £	VAT £	Net £
8 July	Simpson	1100	A8	411.25	61.25	350.00
10 July	Burns	1101	B5	1,527.50	227.50	1,300.00
				1,938.75	288.75	1,650.00

The double entry for the above transaction will be:

Dr	Sales ledger control account	£1,938.75
Cr	VAT	£288.75
Cr	Sales	£1,650.00

Test Your Understanding 3

Sales ledger control account

	£		£
Balance b/f	54,000	Balance b/f	1,000
Credit sales	251,000	Sales returns	11,000
Dishonoured cheques	500	Cash received	242,000
Interest charged	1,400	Discounts allowed	3,000
		Irrecoverable debts	1,000
		Contra	800
Balance c/f	2,000	Balance c/f	50,100
	308,900		308,900
Balance b/f	50,100	Balance b/f	2,000

Purchases ledger control account

	£		£
Balance b/f	200	Balance b/f	43,000
Purchases returns	3,000	Credit purchases	77,000
Cash paid	74,000		
Discounts received	2,000		
Contra	800		
Balance c/f	40,200	Balance c/f	200
	120,200		120,200
Balance b/f	200	Balance b/f	40,200

Test Your Understanding 4

The cash transactions are recorded in total as follows:

Dr Bank	£48,820
Cr Sales ledger control account	£48,700
Cr Interest income	£120

The discount is recorded as follows:

Dr Discounts allowed	£800
Cr Sales ledger control account	£800

Entries must also be made to the individual accounts of Monet, Gogh and Picasso in the debtors ledger in order to reflect the payments received and discounts allowed.

Test Your Understanding 5

1	Dr Closing stock (balance sheet)	£2,750
	Cr Closing stock (cost of sales)	£2,750

To record the closing stock of vodka.

2	Dr Depreciation expense (£150,000/25 yrs)	£6,000
	Cr Accumulated depreciation	£6,000

To record depreciation on the restaurant lease

3   Dr Irrecoverable debt expense   £350
         Cr Sales ledger control account   £350

To record the write-off of a debt outstanding from V Shady.

NB Igor must also remember to update V Shady's individual account in the debtors ledger.

4   Dr Fixtures and fittings cost   £1,200
         Cr Cash   £1,200

To record the purchase of two sofas for the bar.

Control account reconciliations

Chapter learning objectives

Upon completion of this chapter you will be able to:

- prepare, reconcile and understand the purpose of supplier statements

- identify errors which would be highlighted by performing a control account reconciliation

- perform basic control account reconciliations for debtors and creditors, identifying and correcting errors in control accounts and ledgers.

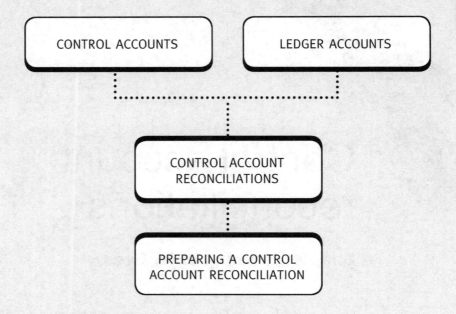

1 Control accounts

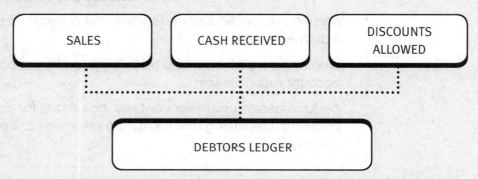

- Control accounts are a means of proving the accuracy of the ledger accounts, such as debtors and creditors.

- The diagram above shows the information that is included in the **debtors ledger**.

- If we wanted to check the accuracy of the accounts debtors ledger, one way we can do this is by getting the information from different sources:

  - The sales can be taken from the sales day book.

  - The cash received and discounts allowed are recorded in the cash book.

  - The opening balances can be taken from the prior month's closing balances.

- An alternative way to check the accuracy of the accounts debtors ledger is to compare the sum total of the individual debtors accounts to the balance on the sales ledger control account.

- Remember, the control account is normally part of the double entry system, whereas the ledger contains memorandum accounts which are not part of the double entry system. Nevertheless, both are updated using the same sources and therefore should agree.

2 Supplier statements

- These statements are issued to a business by suppliers to summarise the transactions that have taken during a given period, and also to show the balance outstanding at the end of the period.

- Their purpose is to ensure that the amount outstanding is accurate and agrees with underlying documentation.

- The purchases ledger control account and individual list of creditors balances should agree with the total of the supplier statements.

- As such, these are a further way to prove the accuracy of accounting records.

3 Control account reconciliations

The reconciliation is a working to ensure that the entries in the ledger accounts agree with the entries in the control account. The two should have the same closing balance as ideally they have had exactly the same entries in both accounts.

- A **sales ledger reconciliation** compares the total of the accounts in the debtors ledger with the balance on the sales ledger control account.

- A **purchase ledger reconciliation** compares the total of the accounts in the creditors ledger with the balance on the purchases ledger control account.

If there are differences between the control account and the ledger accounts, they must be identified and reconciled. Differences may arise due to errors in:

- the debtors or creditors ledger
- the sales or purchases ledger control accounts
- both the control account and ledger account.

It is also possible to reconcile a supplier statement to the control account.

The purpose for doing this is as follows:

- before any payments are made to suppliers it is important to ensure that the suppliers statement is correct – else we could make over or under payments.

- each invoice and credit note listed on the statement should be checked to the original documentation for accuracy.

- once accuracy has been established, it is then possible to decide which invoices need paying and when by.

Below is an example extract of a statement from a supplier:

STATEMENT					
Date	**Transaction**	**Total**	**Current**	**30+**	**60+**
		£	£	£	£
10 May 20X9	Invoice 100	94.50			94.50
1 June 20X9	CN 2008	(24.56)			(24.56)
4 July 20X9	Invoice 110	101.99		101.99	
15 July 20X9	Invoice 156	106.72	106.72		
	TOTALS	278.65	106.72	101.99	69.94
May I remind you that our credit terms are 30 days.					

Here is the creditors ledger which corresponds with this supplier:

Nino Ltd

	£		£
1 June 20X9 CN	24.56	10 May 20X9 Invoice 100	94.50
		4 July 20X9 Invoice 110	110.99
		15 July 20X9 Invoice 156	106.72

You can see that the invoice dated 4 July 20X9 in the ledger is of a total £110.99, however in the statement it appears as £101.99.

The purchase invoice itself should be reviewed to check which is the correct amount. If the suppliers statement is incorrect, then a polite telephone call to the supplier should be made or a letter sent explaining the problem.

If it is the ledger that is incorrect then it should be updated.

Test Your Understanding 1

Suggest reasons why there might be a difference between the balance on the sales ledger control account and the total of the list of debtors ledger balances.

KAPLAN PUBLISHING

4 Preparing a control account reconciliation

The format of a control account reconciliation, in this case for sales, is as follows:

Sales ledger control account

	£		£
Balance given by the examiner	X		
Adjustments for errors	X	Adjustments for errors	X
		Revised balance c/f	X
	___		___
	X		X
	___		___

Reconciliation of individual debtors balances with control account balance

	£
Balance as extracted from list of debtors	X
Adjustments for errors	X/(X)
	___
Revised total agreeing with balance c/f on control account	X
	___

- The examiner will provide details of the error(s).

- You must decide for each whether correction is required in the control account, the list of individual balances or both.

- When all errors have been corrected, the revised balance on the control account should agree with the revised total of the list of individual balances.

- Due to the nature of the F3 examination, you will not be asked to produce a full control account reconciliation. However, you may be asked for the revised balance on the control account/list of individual balances after one or two errors have been corrected.

Illustration 1 : Preparing a control account reconciliation

Alston's purchase ledger control account is an integral part of the double entry system. Individual ledger account balances are listed and totalled on a monthly basis, and reconciled to the control account balance. Information for the month of March is as follows:

(1) Individual ledger account balances at 31 March have been listed out and totalled £19,766.

(2) The purchases ledger control account balance at 31 March is £21,832 (net).

(3) On further examination the following errors are discovered:

   –   The total of discount received for the month, amounting to £1,715, has not been entered in the control account but has been entered in the individual ledger accounts.

   –   On listing-out, an individual credit balance of £205 has been incorrectly treated as a debit.

   –   A petty cash payment to a supplier amounting to £63 has been correctly treated in the control account, but no entry has been made in the supplier's individual ledger account.

   –   The purchases day book total for March has been undercast (understated) by £2,000.

   –   Contras (set-offs) with the debtors ledger, amounting in total to £2,004, have been correctly treated in the individual ledger accounts but no entry has been made in the control account.

Required:

(a) Prepare the part of the purchases ledger control account reflecting the above information.

(b) Prepare a statement reconciling the original total of the individual balances with the corrected balance on the control account.

Solution:

The best way to approach the question is to consider each of the three points above in turn and ask to what extent they affect (a) the purchases ledger control account and (b) the listing of creditors ledger balances.

Step 1

The total of discount received in the cash book should have been debited to the purchases ledger control account and credited to discount received. Thus, if the posting has not been entered in either double entry account it clearly should be. As this has already been entered into the individual ledger accounts, no adjustment is required.

Step 2

Individual credit balances are extracted from the creditors ledger. Here, this error affects the ledger accounts balance. No adjustment is required to the control account, only to the list of balances.

Step 3

The question clearly states that the error has been made in the **individual ledger accounts**. Amendments should be made to the list of balances. Again, no amendment is required to the control accounts.

Step 4

The total of the purchases day book is posted by debiting purchases and crediting purchases ledger control account. If the total is understated, the following bookkeeping entry must be made, posting the £2,000 understatement:

Dr Purchases

Cr Purchases ledger control account.

As the individual ledger accounts in the creditors ledger are posted individually from the purchases day book, the total of the day book being understated will not affect the listing of the balances in the creditors ledger.

Step 5

Here it is clear that the error affects the **control account**, not the creditors ledger. Correction should be made by the bookkeeping entry:

Dr Purchases ledger control account

Cr Sales ledger control account.

Purchases ledger control account

20X9	£	20X9	£
Discount received	1,715	31 Mar Balance	21,832
Sales receivable			
ledger control	2,004	Purchase	2,000
Balance c/f	20,113		
	─────		─────
	23,832		23,832
	─────		─────

Reconciliation of individual balances with control account balance

	Cr
	£
Balances as extracted	19,766
Credit balance incorrectly treated 2 x £205	410
Petty cash payment	(63)
	─────
Net total agreeing with control account	20,113
	─────

Test Your Understanding 2

Rayneydaze is a business selling umbrellas branded with corporate logos. The umbrellas are sold in bulk on credit. The accountant is carrying out a reconciliation of the sales ledger control account balance, which is £172,120 to the total of the balances on the individual accounts in the debtors ledger, which is £176,134.

The following has been found:

(1) A contra item of £1,500 has not been entered in the sales ledger control account.

(2) A cheque for £555 from a customer has been dishonoured. The correct double entry has been posted but the individual accounts have not been updated.

(3) A payment of £322 from a customer has incorrectly been entered in the debtors' ledger as £233.

(4) Discounts allowed totalling £120 have not been entered in the control account.

(5) Cash received of £800 has been debited to the individual customer's account in the debtors ledger.

(6) Total credit sales of £4,500 to a large accountancy firm, Close & Counter have been posted correctly to the ledger account but not recorded in the control account.

Correct the sales ledger control account and reconcile this to the sum total of the individual accounts in the debtors ledger.

Test Your Understanding 3

Tonga received a statement from a supplier, Cook, showing a balance of £14,810. Tonga's Creditors ledger shows a balance due to Cook of £10,000. Investigation reveals the following:

(1) Cash paid to Cook of £4,080 has not been allowed for by Cook.

(2) Tonga recorded the fact that a £40 cash discount was not allowed by Cook, but forgot to record this in the creditors ledger.

What discrepancy remains between the records of Tonga and Cook after allowing for these items?

A   £9,930

B   £9,850

C   £770

D   £690

5 Chapter summary

CONTROL ACCOUNTS

- Control accounts include a summary of transactions that have occurred in the period.
- They are a means of checking that the information in the ledger accounts is correct.
- They are part of the double entry system.

LEDGER ACCOUNTS

- Ledger accounts include a separate account for each credit customer/ credit supplier.
- They are memorandum accounts and not part of the double entry system.

CONTROL ACCOUNT RECONCILIATIONS

- These are a means of checking that the balance on the control account agrees with the balance on the ledger account.
- There may be errors in the ledger account, the control account or both.

PREPARING A CONTROL ACCOUNT RECONCILIATION

- Compare the balance on the ledger account with the control account.
- Review the list of errors to see which account needs amending.
- Set up a T account for the control accounts.
- Prepare a reconciliation for the ledger account.

Test your understanding answers

Test Your Understanding 1

The following are reasons why the sales control account may not agree with the debtors ledger account:

- The sales day book, sales returns day book or cash receipts book have been incorrectly totalled.

- A total from a book of prime entry has been transferred to the control account as a different figure.

- An individual entry from a book of prime entry has been transferred to the individual customer's account as a different figure.

- An entry in the control account or the individual customer's account has been omitted or posted to the wrong side of the account.

- The double entry for a day book total has been incorrectly made.

- An individual customer's account has been incorrectly balanced.

- The list of debtors ledger balances has been incorrectly totalled.

- An entry has been made in either the control account or the individual customer's account but not in both.

- An individual customer's balance has been omitted from the list of balances.

Test Your Understanding 2

Sales ledger control account

	£		£
Balance b/f	172,120		
Credit sales (6)	4,500	Contra (1)	1,500
		Discounts (4)	120
		Balance c/f	175,000
	176,620		176,620
Balance b/f	175,000		

Sales ledger reconciliation

	£
Balance per debtors ledger	176,134
Dishonoured cheque (2)	555
Misposting (3)	(89)
Cash received (5)	(1,600)
Revised balance	175,000

Test Your Understanding 3

The correct answer is D

	Cook	Tonga	
	£	£	
Difference			
Balance per question	14,810	10,000	
Adjustment	(4,080)	40	
Revised balance	10,730	10,040	690

12

Bank reconciliations

Chapter learning objectives

Upon completion of this chapter you will be able to:

- describe the purpose of bank reconciliations
- identify the main differences between the cash book and the bank statement
- identify the bank balance to be reported in the final accounts
- correct cash book errors or omissions
- prepare bank reconciliation statements
- derive bank statement and cash book balances from given information.

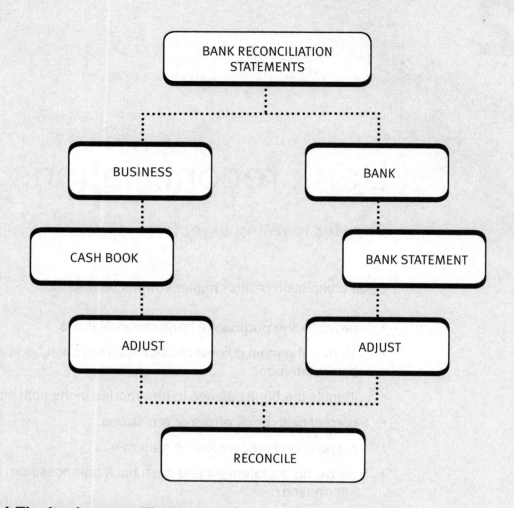

1 The bank reconciliation

The objective of a bank reconciliation is to reconcile the difference between:

- the cash book balance, i.e. the business' record of their bank account; and

- the bank statement balance, i.e. the bank's records of the bank account.

Note that debits and credits are reversed in bank statements because the bank will be recording the transaction from its point of view, in accordance with the business entity concept.

Nature and purpose of a bank reconciliation statement.

The **cash book** records all transactions with the bank. The **bank statement** records all the bank's transactions with the business.

The contents of the cash book should be exactly the same as the record provided by the bank in the form of a bank statement, and therefore our records should correspond with the bank statement.

This is in fact so, but with three important provisos:

(1) The ledger account maintained by the bank is the opposite way round to the cash book. This is because the bank records the balance in favour of an individual as a credit balance, i.e. a liability of the bank to the individual. From the individual's point of view it is, of course, an asset, i.e. a debit balance in his cash book.

(2) Timing differences must inevitably occur. A cheque payment is recorded in the cash book when the cheque is despatched. The bank only records such a cheque when it is paid by the bank, which may be several days later.

(3) Items such as interest may appear on the bank statement but are not recorded in the cash book as the cashier is unaware that they have arisen.

The existence of the bank statement provides an important check on the most vulnerable of a company's assets – cash. However, the differences referred to above make it essential to reconcile the balance on the ledger account with that of the bank statement.

The reconciliation is carried out frequently, usually at monthly intervals.

2 Differences between the bank statement and the cash book

When attempting to reconcile the cash book with the bank statement, three types of difference may be found:

- unrecorded items
- timing differences
- errors

Unrecorded items

These are items which arise in the bank statements before they are recorded in the cash book. Such 'unrecorded items' may include:

- interest
- bank charges
- dishonoured cheques.

They are not recorded in the cash book simply because the business does not know that these items have arisen until they see the bank statement.

The cash book must be adjusted to reflect these items.

Test Your Understanding 1

On which side of the cash book should the following unrecorded items be posted?

- bank charges
- direct debits/standing orders
- direct credits
- dishonoured cheques
- bank interest.

Timing differences

These items have been recorded in the cash book, but due to the bank clearing process have not yet been recorded in the bank statement:

- outstanding/unpresented cheques (cheques sent to suppliers but not yet cleared by the bank)
- outstanding/uncleared lodgements (cheques received by the business but not yet cleared by the bank).

The bank statement balance needs to be adjusted for these items:

	£
Balance per bank statement	X
Less:	
Outstanding/unpresented cheques	(X)
Add:	
Outstanding/uncleared lodgements	X
Balance per cash book (revised)	X

Errors in the cash book

The business may make a mistake in their cash book. The cash book balance will need to be adjusted for these items.

Errors in the bank statement

The bank may make a mistake, e.g. record a transaction relating to a different person within our business bank statement. The bank statement balance will need to be adjusted for these items.

Expandable text

Outstanding or unpresented cheques

Suppose a cheque relating to a payment to a supplier of Poorboy is written, signed and posted on 29 March. It is also entered in the cash book on the same day. By the time the supplier has received the cheque and paid it into his bank account, and by the time his bank has gone through the clearing system, the cheque does not appear on Poorboy's statement until, say, 6 April. Poorboy would regard the payment as being made on 29 March and its cash book balance as reflecting the true position at that date.

Outstanding deposits

In a similar way, a trader may receive cheques by post on 31 March, enter them in the cash book and pay them into the bank on the same day. Nevertheless, the cheques may not appear on the bank statement until 2 April. Again the cash book would be regarded as showing the true position. Outstanding deposits are also known as **outstanding lodgements**.

3 Pro forma bank reconciliation

Cash book

Bal b/f	X	Bal b/f	X
Adjustments	X	Adjustments	X
Revised bal c/f	X	Revised bal c/f	X
	—		—
	X		X
	—		—
Revised bal b/f	X	Revised bal b/f	X

Bank reconciliation statement as at .....

	£
Balance per bank statement	X
Outstanding cheques	(X)
Outstanding lodgements	X
Other adjustments to the bank statement	X/(X)
Balance per cash book (revised)	X

- Beware of overdrawn balances on the bank statement.
- Beware of debits/credits to bank statements.
- Beware of aggregation of deposits in a bank statement.
- **Beware that the bank balance on the balance sheet is always the balance per the revised cash book.**

Test Your Understanding 2

In preparing a company's bank reconciliation statement, the accountant finds that the following items are causing a difference between the cash book balance and bank statement balance:

(1) direct debit: £530

(2) lodgements not credited: £1,200

(3) cheque paid in by the company and dishonoured: £234

(4) outstanding cheques: £677

(5) bank charges: £100

(6) error by bank: £2,399 (cheque incorrectly credited to the account).

Which of these items will require an entry in the cash book?

A   3, 4 and 6

B   1, 3 and 5

C   1, 2 and 4

D   2, 5 and 6

Test Your Understanding 3

The following information has been extracted from the records of N Patel:

Bank account

		£			Chq. no.	£
1 Dec	Balance b/f	16,491	1 Dec	Alexander	782	857
2 Dec	Able	962	6 Dec	Burgess	783	221
	Baker	1,103	14 Dec	Barry	784	511
10 Dec	Charlie	2,312	17 Dec	Cook	785	97
14 Dec	Delta	419	24 Dec	Hay	786	343
21 Dec	Echo	327	29 Dec	Rent	787	260
23 Dec	Cash sales	529				
30 Dec	Fred	119	31 Dec	Balance c/f		19,97
		22,262				22,262

High Street Bank

Bank Statement – N Patel

Date		Details	Withdrawals	Deposits	Balance
			£	£	£
1	December	Balance b/f			17,478
2	December	780	426		
2	December	781	737		16,315
2	December	Deposit		176	16,491
5	December	782	857		
5	December	Bank charges	47		15,587
6	December	Deposit		2,065	17,652
10	December	Standing order (rates)	137		17,515
11	December	783	212		17,303
13	December	Deposit		2,312	19,615
17	December	784	511		19,104
17	December	Deposit		419	19,523
23	December	Deposit		327	19,850
24	December	Deposit		528	20,378
28	December	786	343		20,035
30	December	310923	297		19,738
31	December	Balance c/f			19,738

(a) **Prepare a bank reconciliation statement at 1 December.**

(b) **Update the cash book for December.**

(c) **Prepare a bank reconciliation statement at 31 December.**

Test Your Understanding 4

The following is a summary of Ami's cash book as presented to you for the month of December 20X6:

	£		£
Receipts	1,469	Balance b/f	761
Balance c/f	554	Payments	1,262
	_____		_____
	2,023		2,023
	_____		_____

All receipts are banked and payments made by cheque.

On investigation you discover:

(1) Bank charges of £136 entered on the bank statement had not been entered in the cash book.

(2) Cheques drawn amounting to £267 had not been presented to the bank for payment.

(3) A cheque for £22 had been entered as a receipt in the cash book instead of as a payment.

(4) A cheque drawn for £6 had been incorrectly entered in the cash book as £66.

What balance is shown on the bank statement at 31 December 20X6?

A   £913

B   £941 overdraft

C   £941

D   £407 overdraft

4 Chapter summary

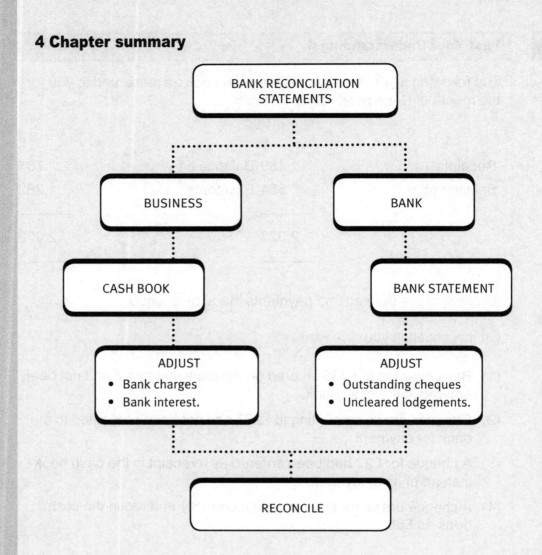

BANK RECONCILIATION STATEMENTS

BUSINESS — BANK

CASH BOOK — BANK STATEMENT

ADJUST
- Bank charges
- Bank interest.

ADJUST
- Outstanding cheques
- Uncleared lodgements.

RECONCILE

Test your understanding answers

Test Your Understanding 1

Cash book

	£		£
Bank interest	X	Bank charges	X
Direct credits	X	Direct debits/	
		standing orders	X
		Dishoured cheques	X

Test Your Understanding 2

The correct answer is B

Test Your Understanding 3

(a)   Bank reconciliation statement as at 1 December

	£
Balance per bank statement	17,478
Less: Outstanding cheques (426 + 737)	(1,163)
Add: Outstanding lodgements	176
Balance per cash book	16,491

(b)

Bank

	£		£
Balance b/f	19,973	Deposit difference	
		(529 – 528)	1
Error – cheque 783		Bank charges	47
(221 – 212)	9		
		Rates – s/order	137
		Revised balance c/f	19,797
	———		———
	19,982		19,982
	———		———
Revised balance b/f	19,797		

Bank reconciliation statement as at 31 December	£
Balance per bank statement	19,738
Less: Outstanding cheques (97 + 260)	(357)
Add: Outstanding lodgements (Fred)	119
Bank error (Cheque 310923)	297
	———
Balance per cash book	19,797
	———

Test Your Understanding 4

The correct answer is D

Cash book

	£		£
Adjustment re cheque (4)	60	Balance b/f	554
Balance c/f	674	Bank charges (1)	136
		Adjustment re paid cheque entered as receipt (3)	44
	734		734
		Balance b/f	674

Bank reconciliation statement as at 31 December 20X6

	£	£
Balance per bank statement at 31 December 20X6 (derived)		(407) O/D
Less: Cheques issued but not yet presented (2)		(267)
Balance per cash book at 31 Dec 20X6		(674) O/D

Correction of errors and suspense accounts

Chapter learning objectives

Upon completion of this chapter you will be able to:

- identify the types of error which may occur in bookkeeping systems

- identify errors which would not be highlighted by the extraction of a trial balance (TB)

- identify errors leading to the creation of a suspense account.

- describe the purpose of a suspense account

- prepare journal entries to correct errors and clear out a suspense account

- prepare statements correcting profit for errors discovered.

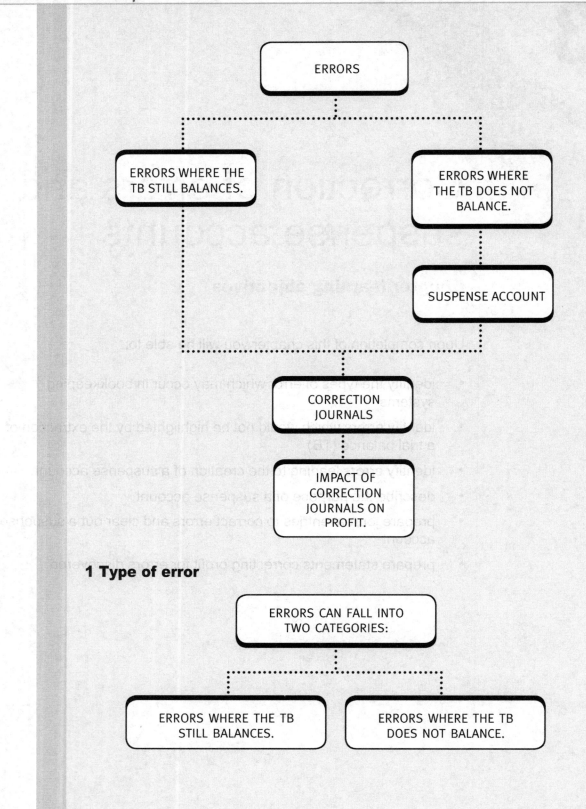

1 Type of error

Errors where the trial balance still balances

- **Error of omission**

  A transaction has been completely omitted from the accounting records, e.g. a cash sale of £100 was not recorded.

- **Error of commission**

  A transaction has been recorded in the wrong account, e.g. rates expense of £500 has been debited to the rent account in error.

- **Error of principle**

  A transaction has conceptually been recorded incorrectly, e.g. a fixed asset purchase of £1,000 has been debited to the repair expense account rather than an asset account.

- **Compensating error**

  Two different errors have been made which cancel each other out, e.g. a rent bill of £1,200 has been debited to the rent account as £1,400 and a casting error on the sales account has resulted in sales being overstated by £200.

- **Error of original entry**

  The correct double entry has been made but with the wrong amount, e.g. a cash sale of £76 has been recorded as £67.

- **Reversal of entries**

  The correct amount has been posted to the correct accounts but on the wrong side, e.g. a cash sale of £200 has been debited to sales and credited to bank.

When correcting these errors, a good approach is to consider:

(1) What was the double entry? ('did do').

(2) What should the double entry have been? ('should do').

(3) Therefore what correction is required? ('to correct').

Always assume that if one side of the double entry is not mentioned, it has been recorded correctly.

Test Your Understanding 1

Provide the journal to correct each of the following errors:

(1) A cash sale of £100 was not recorded.

(2) Rates expense of £500, paid in cash has been debited to the rent account in error.

(3) A fixed asset purchase of £1,000 on credit has been debited to the repairs expense account rather than an asset account.

> (4) A rent bill of £1,200 paid in cash has been debited to the rent account as £1,400 and a casting error on the sales account has resulted in sales being overstated by £200.
>
> (5) A cash sale of £76 has been recorded as £67.
>
> (6) A cash sale of £200 has been debited to sales and credited to cash.

Errors where the trial balance does not balance

- Single sided entry – a debit entry has been made but no corresponding credit entry or vice versa.

- Debit and credit entries have been made but at different values.

- Two entries have been made on the same side.

- There is an incorrect addition in any individual account, i.e. miscasting.

- Opening balance has not been brought down.

- Extraction error – the balance in the trial balance is different from the balance in the relevant account.

If there is a difference on the trial balance, then a suspense account is used to make the total debits equal the total credits.

	£	£
Fixed assets	5,000	
Debtors	550	
Stock	1,000	
Cash	200	
Creditors		600
Share capital		2,000
Accumulated profits		4,000
Suspense account		150
	———	———
	6,750	6,750

The balance on the suspense account must be cleared before final accounts can be prepared.

Corrections to any of the six errors mentioned above will affect the suspense account.

Approach to questions:

- Take the approach as before.
- Use the suspense account to make the 'did do' Dr = the 'did do' Cr and then part of the correction journal will be to reverse this suspense account entry.

E.g. The purchase of a fixed asset costing £100 has been recorded by debiting £10 to the fixed assets account and crediting £100 to cash.

What was the double entry? ('Did do')	What should the double entry have been? ('Should do')	Correcting journal
Dr Fixed assets £10 (Dr Suspense £90) Cr Cash £100	Dr Fixed assets £100 Cr Cash £100	Dr Fixed assets £90 Cr Suspense £90

- Where an opening balance has not been brought down, journal it in and send the opposite entry to suspense.
- The correction journal must always include an equal debit and credit.

A **suspense account** is an account in which debits or credits are held temporarily until sufficient information is available for them to be posted to the correct accounts.

Suspense accounts are often encountered and must be dealt with according to the usual rules of double entry bookkeeping.

There are two main reasons why suspense accounts may be created:

- On the extraction of a trial balance the debits are not equal to the credits and the difference is put to a suspense account.
- When a bookkeeper performing double entry is not sure where to post one side of an entry he may debit or credit a suspense account and leave the entry there until its ultimate destination is clarified.

Test Your Understanding 2

The debit side of a company's trial balance totals £1,200 more than the credit side. Which of the following errors would fully account for the difference?

A   The petty cash balance of £1,200 has been omitted from the trial balance.

B   A receipt of £1,200 for commission receivable has been omitted from the records.

C   £600 paid for plant maintenance has been correctly entered into the cash book and credited to the plant cost account.

D   Discount received of £600 has been debited to the discount allowed account.

Test Your Understanding 3

Bond's trial balance failed to agree and a suspense account was opened for the difference. Bond does not maintain control accounts for sales and purchases. The following errors were found in Bond's accounting records:

(1)   In recording the sale of a fixed asset, cash received of £33,000 was credited to the disposals account as £30,000

(2)   An opening accrual of £340 had been omitted from the trial balance

(3)   Cash of £8,900 paid for plant repairs was correctly accounted for in the cash book but was credited to the plant cost account

(4)   A cheque for £12,000 paid for the purchase of a machine was debited to the machinery account as £21,000

Which of the errors will require an entry to the suspense account to correct them?

A   1, 3 and 4 only

B   All

C   1 and 4 only

D   2 and 3 only

Illustration

Correction of errors

On extracting a trial balance, the accountant of ETT discovered a suspense account with a debit balance of £1,075 included therein; she also found that the debits exceeded the credits by £957. She posted this difference to the suspense account and then investigated the situation. She discovered:

(1) A debit balance of £75 on the postages account had been incorrectly extracted on the list of balances as £750 debit.

(2) A payment of £500 to a credit supplier, X, had been correctly entered in the cash book, but no entry had been made in the supplier's account.

(3) When a motor vehicle had been purchased during the year the bookkeeper did not know what to do with the debit entry so he made the entry Dr Suspense, Cr Bank £1,575.

(4) A credit balance of £81 in the sundry income account had been incorrectly extracted on the list of balances as a debit balance.

(5) A receipt of £5 from a credit customer, Y, had been correctly posted to his account but had been entered in the cash book as £625.

(6) The bookkeeper was not able to deal with the receipt of £500 from the owner's own bank account, and he made the entry Dr Bank and Cr Suspense.

(7) No entry has been made for a cheque of £120 received from a credit customer M.

(8) A receipt of £50 from a credit customer, N, had been entered into his account as £5 and into the cash book as £5.

What journals are required to correct the errors and eliminate the suspense account

Expandable Text

Solution:

Process of clearing a suspense account

The starting position we have is as follows (once we have posted our £957):

Suspense account

	£		£
Balance b/f	1,075	Trial balance difference	957

We now need to work our way through the information given in numbered points 1 to 8 to try and clear this suspense account.

You need to ask yourself the following questions for each point:

(a) what was the double entry that has been made?

(b) what should the double entry have been?

(c) what is the journal we need to correct this?

(1) (a) They have posted Dr postage 750, Cr bank 75, so the other Dr of 675 will auitomatically go to the suspense a/c.

   (b) It should have been : Dr postage 75, Cr bank 75

   (c) correction = Dr suspense a/c 675, Cr postage 675

(2) (a) They have posted Dr suspense a/c 500, Cr cash 500.

   (b) It should have been: Dr creditors (X) 500, Cr cash 500

   (c) correction = Dr creditors (X) 500, Cr suspense a/c 500

(3) (a) They have posted: Dr suspense a/c 1575, Cr cash 1575.

    (b) It should have been Dr Motor vehicles cost 1575, Cr bank 1575

    (c) correction = Dr motor vehicles 1575, Cr suspense a/c 1575

(4) (a) They have posted Dr sundry income 81, Dr bank 81 Cr suspense a/c 162

    (b) should have been: Dr bank/cash 81. Cr sundry income 81

    (c) Correction = Dr suspense a/c 162, Cr sundry income 162

(5) (a) They have posted Dr cash 625, Cr debtors 5, so Cr suspense a/c 620

    (b) Should have been Dr cash 5, Cr debtors 5

    (c) Correction = Dr suspense a/c 620, Cr cash 620

(6) (a) They have posted Dr bank 500, Cr suspense a/c 500

    (b) Should have been: Dr bank 500, Cr capital 500

    (c) correction = Dr suspense a/c 500, Cr capital 500

(7) (a) They have posted nothing

    (b) They should have posted Dr bank 120, Cr debtors (M) 120

    (c) Correction = Dr bank 120, Cr debtors (M) 120

(8) (a) They have posted Dr cash 5, Cr debtors 5

    (b) Should have been Dr cash 50, Cr debtors 50

    (c) Correction = Dr cash 45, Cr debtors 45

Now you can post all of the journals that you have listed under the c) corrections which affect the suspense a/c.

Then you can balance off your suspense a/c and it should balance on both the debit and credit sides. Hence, this will clear your suspense a/c and leave it with a nil balance.

Once you have done so, you should get the following result:

Suspense Account

	£		£
Balance b/f	1,075	Trial balance difference	957
Postage (1)	675	Creditor X (2)	500
Sundry income (4)	162	Motor vehicle cost (3)	1,575
Cash (5)	620		
Capital (6)	500		
	3,032		3,032

Adjustments to profit

The correction journal may result in a change in profit, depending on whether the journal debits or credits the profit and loss account:

Dr Balance sheet account Cr Balance sheet account	No impact to profit
Dr Profit and loss account Cr Profit and loss account	No impact to profit
Dr Profit and loss account Cr Balance sheet account	Profit decreases
Dr Balance sheet account Cr Profit and loss account	Profit increases

For this purpose the suspense account is defined as a balance sheet account.

Test Your Understanding 4

Adjustments to profit

The following correction journals have been posted by Boris Brokovitch, a self-employed plumber:

(1)	Dr Suspense	£4,000
	Cr Rent	£4,000
(2)	Dr Creditors	£2,500
	Cr Suspense	£2,500
(3)	Dr Loan interest	£1,000
	Cr Loan	£1,000
(4)	Dr Suspense	£650
	Cr Sundry income	£650
(5)	Dr Suspense	£6,000

Boris' draft profit figure prior to the posting of these journals is £355,000.

What is the revised profit figure?

A   £354,000

B   £358,650

C   £356,150

D   £358,000

What affect will these correction journals have on the balance sheet?

2 Chapter summary

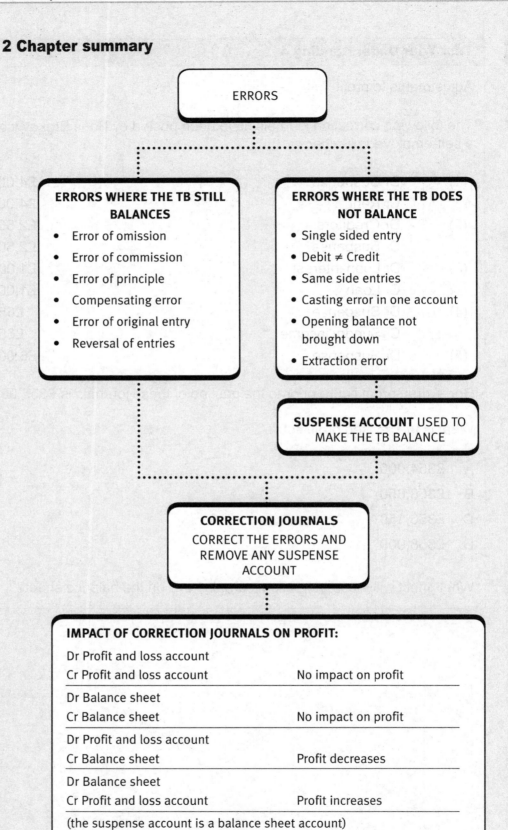

ERRORS

ERRORS WHERE THE TB STILL BALANCES

- Error of omission
- Error of commission
- Error of principle
- Compensating error
- Error of original entry
- Reversal of entries

ERRORS WHERE THE TB DOES NOT BALANCE

- Single sided entry
- Debit ≠ Credit
- Same side entries
- Casting error in one account
- Opening balance not brought down
- Extraction error

SUSPENSE ACCOUNT USED TO MAKE THE TB BALANCE

CORRECTION JOURNALS
CORRECT THE ERRORS AND REMOVE ANY SUSPENSE ACCOUNT

IMPACT OF CORRECTION JOURNALS ON PROFIT:

Dr Profit and loss account	
Cr Profit and loss account	No impact on profit
Dr Balance sheet	
Cr Balance sheet	No impact on profit
Dr Profit and loss account	
Cr Balance sheet	Profit decreases
Dr Balance sheet	
Cr Profit and loss account	Profit increases

(the suspense account is a balance sheet account)

Test your understanding answers

Test Your Understanding 1

	What was the double entry?	What should the double entry have been?	Correcting journal
1	–	Dr Cash £100 Cr Sales £100	Dr Cash £100 Cr Sales £100 To record both sides of the sale correctly.
2	Dr Rent £500 Cr Cash £500	Dr Rates £500 Cr Cash £500	Dr Rates £500 To record the rates expense correctly. Cr Rent £500 To reverse the incorrect debit to the rent account.
3	Dr Repairs £1,000 Cr Creditors £1,000	Dr Fixed Asset £1,000 Cr Creditors £1,000	Dr Fixed asset £1,000 To record the asset correctly. Cr Repairs £1,000 To reverse the incorrect debit to the repairs account.
4	Dr Rent £1,400 Cr Cash £1,200	Dr Rent £1,200 Cr Cash £1,200	Cr Rent £200 To reverse the extra £200 debited to the rent account. Dr Sales £200 To correct the casting error.

| 5 | Dr Cash £67

Cr Sales £67 | Dr Cash £76

Cr Sales £76 | Dr Cash £9

Cr Sales £9

To record the extra £9 sales not previously recorded. |
| 6 | Dr Sales £200

Cr Cash £200 | Dr Cash £200

Cr Sales £200 | Dr Cash £400

Cr Sales £400

First reverse the error of £200 and then record the sale of £200 correctly in both accounts. |

Test Your Understanding 2

The correct answer is D.

A and C would result in the credit side of the TB being £1,200 higher than the debit side.

B would have no effect on the trial balance since neither the debit nor the credit side of the transaction has been accounted for.

Test Your Understanding 3

The correct answer is B.

An entry to the suspense account arises wherever an account is missing from the trial balance or the initial incorrect entry did not include an equal debit and credit.

	What was the bouble entry?	What should the double entry have been?	Correcting journal
1	Dr Cash £33,000 Cr Disposals £30,000 (Cr suspense £3,000)	Dr Cash £33,000 Cr Disposals£33,000	Dr Suspense £3,000 Cr Disposals £3,000
2			Dr Suspense £340 Cr Accrual £340
3	(Dr Suspense£17,800) Cr Cash £8,900 Cr Plant cost £8,900	Dr Repairs £8,900 Cr Cash £8,900	Dr Repairs £8,900 Dr Plant cost £8,900 Cr Suspense £8,900
4	Dr Machinery cost £21,000 Cr Cash £12,000 (Cr Suspense £9,000)	Dr Machinery cost £12,000 Cr Cash £12,000	Dr Suspense £9,000 Cr Machinery cost £9,000

Test Your Understanding 4

Adjustments to profit

The correct answer is B.

	Increase	Decrease	
	£	£	£
Draft profit			355,000
1) Rent	4,000		
2) No impact			
3) Loan interest		1,000	
4) Sundry income	650		
5) No impact			
	————		
			3,650
Revised profit			358,650

Balance sheet

Journal 1.
The Dr entry would go towards clearing any suspense a/c balance.

Journal 2.
The Dr creditors would decrease the current liabilities. The Cr suspense a/c would go towards clearing the account balance.

Journal 3.
The Cr loan would increase the loan liability balance. It does not state whether it is current or long term.

Journal 4.
The Dr suspense a/c would work towards clearing any balance left.

Journal 5.
Dr suspense a/c would completely clear the balance in this account. The Cr cash would decrease the cash balance held, which is a current asset.

Applications of information technology

Chapter learning objectives

Upon completion of this chapter you will be able to:

- outline the form of accounting records in a typical computerised system
- compare manual and computerised accounting systems
- identify the advantages and disadvantages of computerised systems
- explain the use of integrated accounting packages
- explain the nature and use of microcomputers
- describe the main elements of a computerised accounting system
- describe typical data processing work
- explain other business uses of computers
- explain the nature and purpose of spreadsheets
- explain the nature and purpose of database systems.

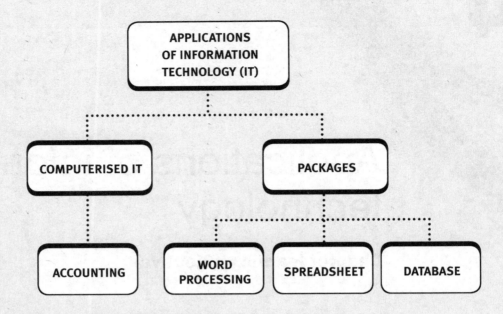

1 Manual accounting systems

A typical **manual system** consists of the following:

- separate **books of original entry**, which are the original accounting records of a business and are not part of the double entry

- **general ledger**, a book within which there is a page for each ledger account in the double entry system

- further ledgers, the main ones being the **debtors ledger**, **the creditors ledger** and the **cash book**.

Expandable text

Often these records are in the form of books but they are equally likely to be in some other form. For example, a debtors ledger may be a collection of individual cards with one or more cards for each customer. The advantage of cards lies in the ability to insert additional cards for customers with a lot of transactions or cards for new customers, and still retain the alphabetical order of customers.

Often the subsidiary ledgers may not be laid out as ledger accounts but as running totals of amounts owing. For example:

Sales ledger

Customer: J Bloggs

Date		Dr £	Cr £	Balance £
1 Mar	Brought forward			3,978.45
19 Mar	Invoice 2354	1,549.00		5,527.45
23 Mar	Cash receipt book		3,978.45	1,549.00

Whatever the format, the reasons for the types of records and the double entry principles remain the same no matter how the system is displayed.

2 Computerised accounting systems

Computerised accounting systems can vary in the form they take. They may be:

- completely computerised
- partially computerised.

For example, a business may have just the accounts receivable ledger on computer.

Expandable text

A fully-computerised system will operate under the same principles as a manual system except that all the records will be stored in one place, i.e. the hard disk of the computer. This does not necessarily mean that all accounting personnel have access to all records. The system will be broken down into sections in the same way as the manual system.

Another difference in a computerised system may be that when the data is printed out, the form of that information may look very different from a manual system, particularly with regard to the general ledger.

Whereas in a manual system the general ledger is a collection of 'T' accounts, the general ledger on a computer system will probably appear as an arithmetical listing of debits and credits. This does not mean, however, that the system is not performing double entry; it is.

3 Manual versus computerised accounting systems

Advantages of computers in a modern business environment include:

- speed
- stored program
- decision making
- file storage and processing, and
- accuracy and reliability.

Expandable text

The advantages of computerisation include:

(1) **Speed**. The computer is very fast – much faster than a clerk or any other type of office machine. This speed can be of value to the business in two ways:

- high volumes of work can be handled by a computer
- rapid turnaround and response can be achieved.

Thus, one company might value a computer primarily for its ability to cope with large numbers of orders; another might be more interested in speeding up its order processing.

(2) **Stored program**. Once the programs have been written and tested, the computer can perform large amounts of work with the minimum of labour costs. Only small teams of operators are needed for the largest machines. This is possible because the computer runs under the control of its stored program, and operator activity is limited to loading and unloading peripherals and indicating what work is to be done.

(3) **Decision making**. The computer can be programmed to undertake complicated decision-making processes. It can handle work to a much higher degree of complexity than other office machines – and often more than the manager.

(4) **File storage and processing**. Large files of data can be stored on magnetic media which require very little space. More importantly, files thus stored can be reviewed and updated at high speeds, and information can be retrieved from them very quickly.

(5) **Accuracy and reliability**. The computer is very accurate (provided always that its programs are free from faults) and generally reliable.

Disadvantages of computers in a modern business environment include:

- lack of intelligence
- quantifiable decisions
- initial costs
- inflexibility, and
- vulnerability.

Expandable text

Disadvantages of computers

(1) **Lack of intelligence**. The computer is a machine. It cannot recognise errors made in its program, or notice that data is incomplete or incorrect. Errors that would be detected by clerks in a manual system may go unnoticed in a computer-based system. It is therefore necessary to devote the utmost care to the development of computer-based systems, to foresee every contingency and to test every instruction. Thus, system development is often both prolonged and costly.

(2) **Quantifiable decisions**. The program can only take decisions that can be quantified, e.g. that can be expressed as two numbers or amounts that can be compared with each other. It cannot make value judgements of the type involved, in, e.g. selecting personnel, or deciding whether to take legal action if debts are overdue. The solution indicated by the program may have to be modified because of intangible factors known to the manager but incapable of being expressed in the program.

(3) **Initial costs**. Initial costs, e.g. hardware, software, site preparation and training, tend to be high. Note that today software costs often exceed hardware costs.

(4) **Inflexibility**. Because of the care and attention to detail needed in systems and program development and maintenance, computer systems tend to be inflexible. They take longer and cost more to alter than manual systems.

(5) **Vulnerability**. The more work an organisation transfers to a computer, the greater is its dependence on a single resource. If the machine breaks down or is damaged, or if computer staff take industrial action, many systems may be brought to a halt.

4 Integrated accounting packages

The usual pattern for financial accounting has been for computerisation on a piecemeal basis, tackling the aspects involving most work first, e.g.:

- debtors ledger
- creditors ledger
- payroll.

A number of integrated accounting packages exist which handle all parts of the process and ultimately produce the financial statements. Each package varies, but the broad groups are:

- cash book systems
- basic bookkeeping systems, and
- bookkeeping and accounting systems.

Expandable text

Cash book systems

This system emulates a manual cash book. Such a system might be suitable for a small business which does not sell on credit and which either

(i) provides a service or

(ii) buys its stock for cash or on credit from a small number of suppliers.

Basic bookkeeping systems

These might be suitable for the smaller business selling mainly on a cash basis, requiring basic bookkeeping. Such a system will normally offer basic facilities for maintaining a debtors ledger, a creditors ledger and a general ledger. There should be facilities for automatically producing a full printout of transactions and perhaps bank reconciliation statements. The package will also generate trial balances, profit and loss account and balance sheets.

Bookkeeping and accountancy systems

In addition to offering the basic facilities described above, these packages can cope with a greater number of customer and supplier accounts and offer more sophisticated credit control facilities. They can generate invoices, print out customers' statements and produce ageing schedules of debtors. They may be able to produce standard letters automatically to send to customers whose accounts are overdue or who have exceeded their agreed credit limit.

Within this group the more advanced packages may incorporate stock control facilities. Separate records are maintained for each stock item recording units purchased and sold and the balance of stock in hand.

5 Microcomputer packages

Most microcomputer accounting packages are used by people who are not computer programmers or systems analysts.

The users of such systems are normally accountants and their accounting staff.

To run an accounting package, the user will normally have the program on a hard disk. Data may be on separate disks. The program will probably operate on a 'menu system', i.e. the user will select the required options from a list of choices (the menu).

A typical **initial menu** would include the following options:

(1) create new accounts

(2) edit account data

(3) post transactions

(4) create report layouts

(5) print reports

(6) quit.

Expandable text

To select an option, the user will key in the appropriate number. For example, to create new accounts, number one would be keyed in.

Each of these options would involve another sub menu

The initial setup of a computerised accounting system is similar to a manual system, i.e. debtors and creditors ledgers and general ledger are set up and account codes allocated for each individual account.

In the majority of cases, the bank account is contained within the general ledger.

The computer program will have been set up to 'recognise' different transaction types, such as:

- sales invoices
- credit notes (re sales)
- purchase invoices
- credit notes (re purchases)
- receipts
- payments, and
- journals.

To post to the ledger, the user would batch up the appropriate source documents, e.g. sales invoices, and compute the batch total.

The user would then select the 'Post to ledger' option from the appropriate sub menu and key in the following data for each sales invoice:

- customer account code
- date
- invoice number
- description, and
- total value of goods sold.

Provided valid code numbers are used and the totals agree, the posting will be accepted; similarly, the batch total will need to be verified before the program will actually post the transactions to the ledgers. An additional security measure is that of passwords, e.g. the user would have to know the appropriate password to load the system in the first place and possibly different passwords for each ledger.

6 Database systems

A **database** is a collection of information that can be used for many different purposes, and by a number of business appplications.

For example supplier database contains the data relating to suppliers, and may use headings (fields) such as:

- supplier name
- supplier code, and
- supplier address.

The advantages of a database over a manual card index system would include:

- The amount of information held in each record/field can be much larger than a card index.
- Calculations can be performed automatically, e.g. return on capital employed.
- Records may be sorted, or those matching a certain criterion selected, automatically, and in a variety of sequences.
- Reports based on the information may be prepared and printed.

Expandable text

Database design

There are various ways of designing database systems so as to link the data together:

- A flat file database is a single file database. All records in this type of database are of a standard format. Data can be stored, accessed, sorted and updated.
- A relational database is one where files can be linked together and data can be accessed from any file.

- A programmable database is one with its own programming language which enables the database to be tailored to individual needs.

Database systems will continue to be a major area of expansion of computer applications in the future.

Database management system

The software that runs the database is known as the database management system. The database management system organises the data input into the database and allows various application programs to use the database.

7 Chapter summary

```
                    ┌─────────────────────┐
                    │  APPLICATIONS OF IT │
                    └─────────────────────┘
                  ┌──────────┴──────────┐
        ┌──────────────────┐      ┌──────────────┐
        │  COMPUTERISED    │      │  PACKAGES    │
        │  SYSTEMS         │      └──────────────┘
        └──────────────────┘
```

COMPUTERISED SYSTEMS

BENEFITS
- Speed
- Accuracy
- Storage
- Reliability
- Decision making.

PROBLEMS
- Lack of intelligence
- Initial costs
- Inflexibility.

ACCOUNTING SYSTEMS

COMPONENTS
- Cash book
- Basic bookkeeping
- Bookkeeping and accounting.

PACKAGES

WORD PROCESSING (WP)

SPREAD SHEET (S/S)

DATABASE (DB)

FUNCTIONALITY

WP
- Texting
- Text creation
- Text printing.

S/S
- 'What if?' analysis
- Budgeting
- Forecasting.

DB
- File storage
- File retrieval.

EASE OF USE

Incomplete records

Chapter learning objectives

Upon completion of this chapter you will be able to:

- explain and illustrate the calculation of profit or loss as the difference between opening and closing net assets

- explain techniques used in incomplete record situations:
    - calculation of opening capital
    - use of ledger total accounts to calculate missing figures.
    - use of cash and/or bank summaries
    - use of given gross profit percentage to calculate missing figures.

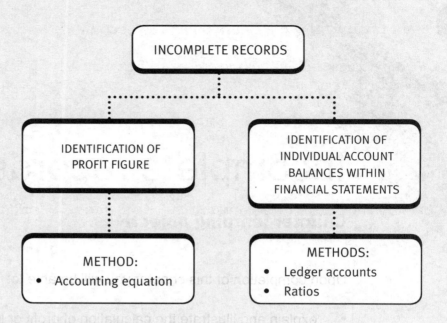

1 Incomplete records

When you are preparing a set of accounts, it is likely that you may not have all of the information available to you to complete a set of financial statements.

It is likely that you may have an incomplete ledger or control accounts system.

If this is the case, you will have to use the best information that it available to you and 'guestimate' any missing figures.

There are a number of different ways which we can use to calculate missing figures and balances, such as:

- Accounting equation method
- Opening capital calculations
- Balancing figure approach
- Ratios – mark up and margin
- Lost inventory methods

2 Identification of profit figure using the accounting equation

If a business has kept very little information on its transactions it may only be possible to calculate net profit for the year. This can be done using the accounting equation as follows:

Net assets = Capital + Profit – Drawings

Therefore:

Change in net assets = Capital introduced in period + Profit for the period – Drawings for the period

NB Net assets = Assets – Liabilities

Test Your Understanding 1

Andy Carp's balance sheet at 31 December 20X4 shows that his fishing business has net assets of £5,000. The balance sheet as at 31 December 20X5 shows that the business has net assets of £8,000. Andy's drawings for the year amounted to £2,500 and he didn't introduce any further capital in that year.

What profit is made by Andy Carp in the year ended 31 December 20X5?

A   £5,500

B   £500

C   £10,500

D   £7,500

---

3 Identification of individual account balances within financial statements

- In most cases a business will keep limited accounting records from which it is possible to prepare a full set of financial statements. You may be asked to calculate any of the balances within these financial statements.

- In these types of questions the opening asset and liability balances will be given along with details of transactions during the year.

- Opening capital can be calculated as:

  Opening assets – Opening liabilities

- Two further methods may be used to identify other missing figures:

(1) use of ledger accounts to find a balancing figure

(2) use of ratios

 ## 4 The balancing figure approach

The balancing figure approach, using ledger accounts is commonly used in the following way:

Ledger account	Missing figure
Debtors	Credit sales Money received from debtors
Creditors	Credit purchases Money paid to creditors
Cash at bank	Drawings Money stolen
Cash in hand	Cash sales Cash stolen

Cash at bank

	£		£
Cash received from customers	X	Cash paid to suppliers	X
Bankings from cash in hand	X	Expenses	X
Sundry income	X	Drawings	X
		Money stolen	X
		Balance c/f	X
	X		X
Balance b/f			

Cash in hand

	£		£
Cash sales	X	Cash purchases	X
Sundry income	X	Sundry Expenses	X
		Bankings	X
		Money stolen	X
		Balance c/f	X
	X		X
Balance b/f			

Note that in the case of debtors and creditors, you may need to use **total debtors** and **total creditors** accounts where information given cannot be split between cash and credit sales and purchases:

Total debtors

	£		£
Balance b/f	X	Total cash received in respect of sales(from cash and credit customers)	X
Total sales (cash and credit)	X		
		Balance c/f	X
	X		X
Balance b/f	X		

Total creditors

	£		£
		Balance b/f	X
Total cash paid in respect of purchases (cash purchases and payments to credit suppliers)	X	Total purchases (cash and credit)	X
Balance c/f	X		
	X		X
		Balance b/f	X

Test Your Understanding 2

Suppose that opening debtors for B Rubble's business are £30,000, there have been total receipts from customers of £55,000 of which £15,000 relates to cash sales and £40,000 relates to receipts from debtors, discounts allowed in the year totalled £3,000 and closing debtors was £37,000.

What are total sales for the year?

A   £65,000

B   £50,000

C   £47,000

D   £62,000

Test Your Understanding 3

The opening creditors of Dick Dastard-Lee's business are £15,000, total payments made to suppliers during the year was £14,000. Discounts received were £500 and closing creditors are £13,000.

What are total purchases for the year?

A   £16,500

B   £16,000

C   £12,000

D   £12,500

Questions may require you to calculate 'missing' income statement figures, for example rent and rates values, from a list of information including payments and opening/closing accruals and prepayments.

To calculate the missing value for each expense, use either:

*   T-accounts, or
*   Equations.

Test Your Understanding 4

The following information relates to Ivor Big-Head's business:

On 1 January	Electricity accrued	£250
	Rent prepaid	£300
Cash paid in the year	Electricity	£1,000
	Rent	£2,000
On 31 December	Electricity accrued	£300
	Rent prepaid	£400

What are the profit and loss account charges for electricity and rent for the year?

	Electricity	Rent
	£	£
A	1,050	2,100
B	1,050	1,900
C	950	1,900
D	950	2,100

Test Your Understanding 5

On 1 January, Elma Fudd's bank account is overdrawn by £1,367, payments in the year totalled £8,536 and on 31 December the closing balance is £2,227 (positive).

What are total receipts for the year?

A £4,942

B £7,676

C £9,396

D £12,130

Test Your Understanding 6

On 1 January, Daisee Chain's business had a cash float of £900. During the year cash of £10,000 was banked, £1,000 was paid out as drawings and wages of £2,000 was paid. On 31 December the float was £1,000.

How much cash was received from customers for the year?

A   £12,900

B   £14,900

C   £13,100

D   £6,900

5 Ratios – mark-up and margin

Gross profit can be expressed as a percentage of either sales or cost of sales:

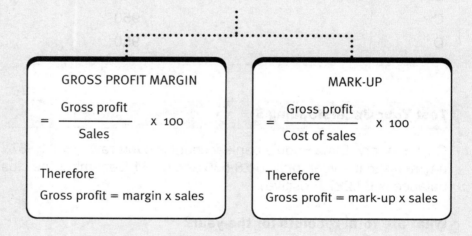

E.g.

	£
Sales	5,000
Cost of sales	(4,000)
Gross profit	1,000

- Gross profit margin $\quad = \quad \dfrac{1{,}000}{5{,}000} \quad X\,100 = 20\%$

- Mark-up $\quad = \quad \dfrac{1{,}000}{4{,}000} \quad X\,100 = 25\%$

Test Your Understanding 7

Padraig O'Flaherty has sales of £1,000. He makes a margin of 25%

What is the cost of sales figure?

A   £200

B   £800

C   £750

D   £250

Test Your Understanding 8

Lorna McDuff has cost of sales of £600 and a 25% mark up

What is her sales figure?

A   £750

B   £800

C   £250

D   £200

Using margin and mark-up

An examination question will often provide you with margin and cost of sales or mark-up and sales. You will then be required to calculate the remaining figures in the profit and loss account. This can be done using the following 'relationship' columns:

Margin 25%		Mark-up 25%	
Sales	2. 100%	Sales	3. Logic!
Cost of sales	3. Logic!	Cost of sales	2. 100%
Gross profit	1. Ratio	Gross profit	1. Ratio

Therefore, if we know the mark-up % or margin % and one of figures in the profit and loss account, we can calculate the remaining figures in the profit and loss account.

Test Your Understanding 9

Jethro Longhorn can tell you the following with regard to his business:

Margin	5%
Opening stock	£800
Closing stock	£600
Purchases	£2,840

Complete Jethro's profit and loss account with the above figures.

6 Cost of lost stock

- In incomplete record questions, stock may have been lost – probably due to a fire or flood.

- Closing stock that has not been lost is subtracted in cost of sales because by definition, the stock has not been sold in the year.

- Lost stock has also not been sold in the year and therefore also needs subtracting within cost of sales.

- Therefore, to work out the cost of lost stock, complete the trading account from the information given and then lost stock can be calculated as a balancing figure.

Test Your Understanding 10

Jack Spratt provides the following information about his business:

Margin	20%
Sales	£100,000
Opening stock	£10,000
Purchases	£82,000
Closing stock after fire	£3,000

What is the cost of stock lost in the fire?

A £12,000

B £9,000

C £69,000

D £5,667

Double entries for stock and lost stock

Actual closing stock is posted by:

Dr	Stock (B/S)	X
Cr	Profit and loss account	X

Lost stock will still be credited to the profit and loss account so that it is removed from cost of sales. However, the debit side of the entry will depend on whether or not the lost stock has been insured:

If insured	Dr	Insurance company (Current asset)
	Cr	Profit and loss account (Cost of sales)
If not insured	Dr	Profit and loss account (Expense)
	Cr	Profit and loss account (Cost of sales)

Test Your Understanding 11

Fred lost his entire stock in a fire. His unsigned insurance policy is still in the pocket of his good suit. Fred has supplied you with the following information:

Mark-up	25%
Sales	£10,000
Opening stock	£2,000
Purchases	£7,500

Prepare the profit and loss account of Fred and show the journal to record closing stock.

7 Reconstruction of full financial statements

Although you will not face an examination question of this length, the following illustration will help you to see how a full set of financial statements can be reconstructed using the methods within this chapter.

Illustration 1 : Reconstruction of full financial statements

Incomplete records – reconstruction of full financial statements

Malcolm is a retailer, selling stationery. He does not keep a full set of records. The following records have been extracted from his books.

	30 September 20X4	30 September 20X5
	£	£
Fixtures and fittings: Cost	20,000	To be determined
Accumulated depreciation	8,000	To be determined
Motor vehicles: Cost	22,000	To be determined
Accumulated depreciation	4,180	To be determined
Stock	18,000	33,900
Debtors	10,000	12,000
Allowance for debtors	500	To be determined
Prepayments – Rates	400	450
Bank	2,000	(15,500)
Cash	600	600
Creditors	4,000	4,600
Accruals – Light and heat	250	300

He also has the following transactions for his cash and bank transactions for the year ended 30 September 20X5.

	Cash £	Bank £
Balance b/f	600	2,000
Receipts:		
Cash sales	15,000	
From debtors		140,000
Loan received (long-term)		30,000
Sale proceeds of a motor vehicle sold during the year		8,200
Cash banked		15,000
	15,600	195,200
Payments:		
Creditors		110,000
Rates		9,000
Light and heat		2,000
Telephone		1,500
Loan interest		1,500
Insurance		1,000
Rent		20,000
Wages and salaries		25,000
Withdrawals		15,000
Purchase of fixtures		5,000
Purchase of new motor vehicle		20,000
Sundry expenses		700
Cash paid into bank	15,000	
Balance c/f	600	(15,500)

The following further information is available:

(1) The loan was received at the beginning of the year and is entitled to 5% interest pa.

(2) The motor vehicle disposed of during the year had cost £10,000 and the accumulated depreciation on it as at 30 September 2004 was £1,900.

(3) Discount received during the year amounted to £500.

(4) Goods amounting to £1,000 at cost were withdrawn by Malcolm during the year.

(5) The depreciation policy is as follows:

    (a) Fixtures and fittings, 20% pa on a straight-line basis.

    (b) Motor vehicles, 10% pa on a reducing-balance basis.

(6) The allowance for debtors is to be 5% of closing debtors.

Required:

(a) Prepare Malcolm's profit and loss account for the year ended 30 September 20X5.

(b) Prepare Malcolm's balance sheet as at 30 September 20X5.

Solution

(a) **Malcolm profit and loss account for the year ended 30 September 2005**

	£	£
Sales: Cash		15,000
Credit **(W1)**		142,000
		157,000
Less: Cost of sales		
Opening stock	18,000	
Purchases **(W2)**	111,100	
Goods withdrawn	(1,000)	
	128,100	
Less: Closing stock	(33,900)	
		(94,200)
Gross profit		62,800
Add: Discount received	500	
Profit on sale of motor vehicle **(W3)**	100	
		600
		63,400

	£	£
Less:		
Increase in allowance for debtors **(W4)**	(100)	
Rates (9,000 + 400 – 450)	(8,950)	
Light and heat (2,000 + 300 – 250)	(2,050)	
Telephone	(1,500)	
Loan interest	(1,500)	
Insurance	(1,000)	
Rent	(20,000)	
Wages and salaries	(25,000)	
Depreciation:		
Motor vehicles **(W6)**	(2,972)	
Fixtures and fittings **(W5)**	(5,000)	
Sundry expenses	(700)	
		(68,772)
Net loss		(5,372)

(b) Malcolm balance sheet as at 30 September 2005

	Cost	Accumulated depreciation	Net book value
	£	£	£
Fixed assets			
Fixtures and fittings **(W5)**	25,000	(13,000)	12,000
Motor vehicles **(W6)**	32,000	(5,252)	26,748
	57,000	(18,252)	38,748

Current assets

Stock		33,900
Debtors	12,000	
Less: allowance for debtors	(600)	
		11,400
Rates prepaid		450
Cash		600
		46,350

Current liabilities

Creditors	4,600	
Light and heat accrued	300	
Bank overdraft	15,500	
		(20,400)
		25,950

Long-term liabilities

Loan	(30,000)
	34,698

	Cost £	Accumulated depreciation £	Net book value £
Represented by			
Capital **(W7)**			56,070
Net loss			(5,372)
Drawings **(W8)**			(16,000)
			34,698

(W1) Debtors

	£		£
Balance b/f	10,000	Bank	140,000
Credit sales (derived)	142,000	Balance c/f	12,000
	_____		_____
	152,000		152,000
	_____		_____

(W2) Creditors

	£		£
Discount received	500	Balance b/f	4,000
Bank	110,000	Credit purchases (derived)	111,100
Balance c/f	4,600		
	_____		_____
	115,100		115,100
	_____		_____

(W3)

	£	£
Disposal proceeds		8,200
Less: Net book value:		
Cost	10,000	
Accumulated depreciation	(1,900)	
	_____	
		8,100
		_____
Profit on disposal		100
		_____

(W4)

	£
Allowance for debtors	
– Required (5% x £12,000)	600
– B/f	(500)
Increase in provision	100
	_____

(W5)

Fixtures and fittings

	Cost	Accumulated depreciation	Net book value
	£	£	£
Balance b/f	20,000	(8,000)	12,000
Additions	5,000	–	5,000
	25,000	(8,000)	17,000
Charge for the year: 20% x £25,000		(5,000)	(5,000)
	25,000	(13,000)	12,000

(W6)

Motor vehicles

	Cost	Accumulated depreciation	Net book value
	£	£	£
Balance b/f	22,000	(4,180)	17,820
Disposals	(10,000)	1,900	(8,100)
	12,000	(2,280)	9,720
Additions	20,000		20,000
	32,000	(2,280)	29,720
Charge for the year: 10% x £29,720		(2,972)	(2,972)
Balance c/f	32,000	(5,252)	26,748

(W7)

Capital as at 30 September 2004

	£	£
Fixtures and fittings (20,000 – 8,000)		12,000
Motor vehicles (22,000 – 4,180)		17,820
Stock		18,000
Debtors (10,000 – 500)		9,500
Rates prepaid		400
Bank		2,000
Cash		600
		60,320
Creditors	4,000	
Light and heat accrued	250	
		(4,250)
		56,070

(W8)

Drawings

	£
Bank	15,000
Goods Withdrawn	1,000
	16,000

8 Chapter summary

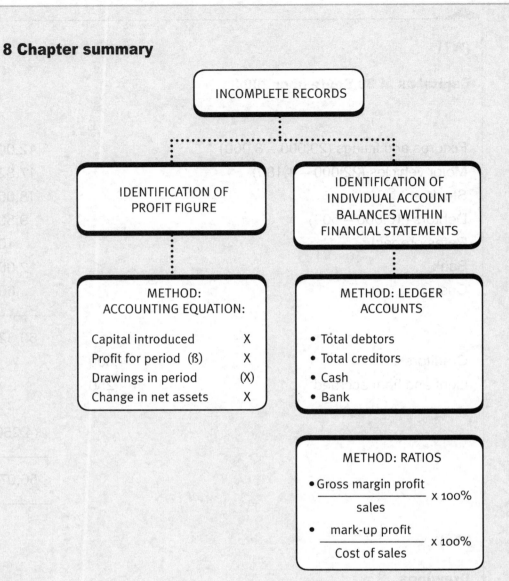

INCOMPLETE RECORDS

IDENTIFICATION OF PROFIT FIGURE

IDENTIFICATION OF INDIVIDUAL ACCOUNT BALANCES WITHIN FINANCIAL STATEMENTS

METHOD:
ACCOUNTING EQUATION:

Capital introduced	X
Profit for period (ß)	X
Drawings in period	(X)
Change in net assets	X

METHOD: LEDGER ACCOUNTS

- Total debtors
- Total creditors
- Cash
- Bank

METHOD: RATIOS

- $\dfrac{\text{Gross margin profit}}{\text{sales}} \times 100\%$

- $\dfrac{\text{mark-up profit}}{\text{Cost of sales}} \times 100\%$

Test your understanding answers

Test Your Understanding 1

The correct answer is A

Change in net assets introduced	= Capital the year	+ Profit for for the year	– Drawings
£8,000 – £5,000	= 0	+ Profit for the year	– £2,500
Profit	= £3,000	+ £ 2,500	
	= £5,500		

Test Your Understanding 2

The correct answer is A

Debtors

	£		£
Balance b/f	30,000	Bank	40,000
Credit Sales (ß)	50,000	Discount allowed	3,000
		Balance c/f	37,000
	80,000		80,000
Balance b/f	37,000		

Total sales = £50,000 + £15,000 = £65,000

or

Total debtors

	£		£
Balance b/f	30,000	Bank (total cash rec'd)	55,000
Credit Sales (ß)	65,000	Discount allowed	3,000
		Balance c/f	37,000
	95,000		95,000
Balance b/f	37,000		

Test Your Understanding 3

The correct answer is D

Total creditors

	£		£
Bank	14,000	Balance b/f	15,000
Discount received	500	Purchases (ß)	12,500
Balance c/f	13,000		
	27,500		27,500
		Balance b/f	13,000

Test Your Understanding 4

The correct answer is B

Profit and loss account (extracts)

	£
Expenses	
Electricity(−250 + 1,000 + 300)	1,050
Rent (300 + 2,000 − 400)	1,900

Test Your Understanding 5

The correct answer is D

Bank

	£		£
Receipts (ß)	12,130	Balance b/f	1,367
		Payments	8,536
		Balance c/f	2,227
	———		———
	12,130		12,130
	———		———
Balance c/f	2,227		

Test Your Understanding 6

The correct answer is C

Cash in till

	£		£
Balance b/f	900	Bank	10,000
Receipts	13,100	Drawings	1,000
		Wages	2,000
		Balance c/f	1,000
	———		———
	14,000		14,000
	———		———
Balance c/f	1,000		

Test Your Understanding 7

The correct answer is C

Gross profit: £1,000 x 25% = £250

Cost of sales

	£
Sales	1,000
Cost of sales (ß)	(750)
Gross profit	250

Test Your Understanding 8

The correct answer is A

Gross profit: £ 600 x 25% = £150

Sales:

	£
Sales (ß)	750
Cost of sales	(600)
Gross profit	150

Test Your Understanding 9

	£	£	%
Sales		3,200	100
Cost of sales			
Opening stock	800		
Purchases	2,840		
Closing stock	(600)		
	–––––		
		(3,040)	(95)
		–––––	–––––
Gross profit		160	5
		–––––	–––––

Test Your Understanding 10

The correct answer is B

	£	£	%
Sales		100,000	100
Cost of sales			
Opening stock	10,000		
Purchases	82,000		
Closing stock	(3,000)		
Stock lost (ß)	(9,000)		
	–––––		
		(80,000)	(80)
		–––––	–––––
Gross profit		20,000	20
		–––––	–––––

Test Your Understanding 11

	£	£
Sales		10,000
Cost of sales:		
Opening stock	2,000	
Purchases	7,500	
Stock lost (ß)	(1,500)	
		(8,000)
Gross profit		2,000
Dr P&L (expense)		1,500
Cr P&L (cost of sales)		1,500

Being the recording of uninsured stock destroyed by the fire.

16

Partnerships

Chapter learning objectives

Upon completion of this chapter you will be able to:

- define the circumstances creating a partnership

- explain the advantages and disadvantages of operating as a partnership compared with operating as a sole trader or limited liability company

- explain the typical contents of a partnership agreement, including profit-sharing terms

- explain the accounting differences between partnerships and sole traders:
  - capital accounts
  - current accounts
  - division of profits

- explain and illustrate how to record partners' shares of profits/losses and their drawings in the accounting records and financial statements

- explain and illustrate how to account for guaranteed minimum profit share

- explain how to account for loans from partners

- draft the profit and loss account, including division of profit, and balance sheet of a partnership from a given trial balance (TB)

- define goodwill in relation to partnership accounts

- identify the factors leading to the creation of goodwill in relation to partnership accounts

- calculate the value of goodwill from information given

- account for the effect of the admission of a new partner.

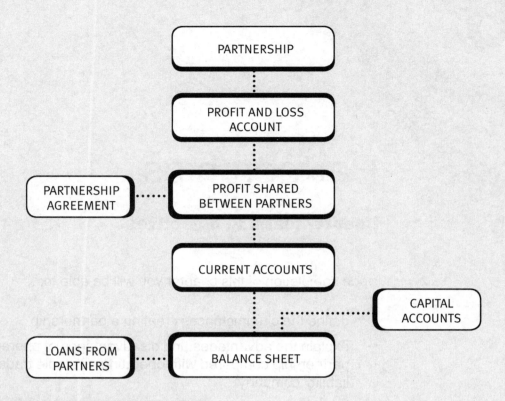

1 Definition of a partnership

- A **partnership** is 'the relationship which subsists between persons carrying on a business in common with a view of making profit'

- Therefore a partnership is a business which has two or more joint owners.

- As in the case of a sole trader, the profits of the business are owed to the owners.

- It is therefore necessary to share the profits of the business amongst the partners.

Expandable text

A partnership is a natural progression from a sole trader, the sole proprietor taking in one or more partners (co-proprietors) in common with a view to profit. In many countries a partnership is not a corporate entity, but a collection of individuals jointly carrying on business.

2 Advantages and disadvantages of partnerships

SOLE TRADER	VERSUS	PARTNERSHIP	VERSUS	LIMITED LIABILITY COMPANY

Advantages of a partnership over a sole trader

- A partnership shares business risks between more than one person.

- Each partner can develop special skills upon which the other partners can rely, whereas a sole trader has responsibility for everything.

- Greater resources will be available since more individuals will be contributing to the business.

Disadvantages of a partnership over a sole trader

- There may be disputes in the running of the business.

- Partners are jointly and severally liable for one another. Thus if one partner is being sued in relation to the business, all partners share the responsibility and potential liability.

Advantages of a partnership over a limited liability company

- The arrangement is less formal than setting up a company, which requires the issue of shares and the appointment of directors.

- If the partners wish to dissolve the business, this is easier to achieve by a partnership than by a company.

Disadvantage of a partnership over a limited liability company

- The partners are not protected from the creditors of the business. Unless the partnership is set up as a limited liability partnership, partners have unlimited liability.

3 The partnership agreement

A partnership will usually have a partnership agreement which will state how the profits are to be shared ('appropriated') amongst the partners.

The division of profit stated in the agreement may be quite complex in order to reflect the expected differing efforts and contributions of the partners.

Salaries	May be awarded to partners who take on extra responsibility within the business.
Interest on capital	May be provided at a set percentage to reflect the differing amounts of capital invested.
Interest on drawings	To penalise those partners who take out more drawings from the business, the partnership may charge interest on drawings. Interest may be charged on all drawings or only those above a certain level This results in a reduction in the amount of profit that the partner is allocated.
Profit share ratio (PSR)	This is the ratio in which any remaining profits should be shared amongst the partners after they have been allocated salaries, interest on capital and interest on drawings.

It is important to appreciate that the above examples are means of dividing the profits of the partnership and are not expenses of the business. **A partnership salary is merely a device for calculating the division of profit; it is not a salary in the normal meaning of the term.**

Expandable text

A partnership agreement, which need not necessarily be in written form, will govern the relationship between the partners. Important matters to be covered include:

*   name of firm, the type of business, and duration
*   capital to be introduced by partners
*   distribution of profits between partners
*   drawings by partners
*   arrangements for dissolution, or on the death or retirement of partners

- settling of disputes, and

- preparation and audit of accounts.

In the absence of a partnership agreement, the Partnership Act 1890 (PA 1890) states that profits should be shared as follows:

- No partner should receive a salary.

- No interest on capital should be allowed.

- Profits should be shared equally between the partners.

- Where a partner advances funds in excess of the agreed capital amount (possibly as a loan), they are entitled to interest on the excess at 5% pa.

4 Financial statements for a partnership

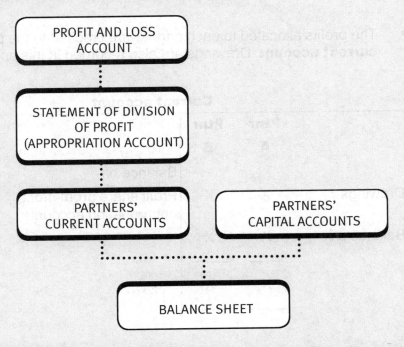

- The **profit and loss account** for a partnership is exactly the same as that for a sole trader.

- An extra statement is required in which the profit from the profit and loss account is shared between the partners. This is referred to as a **statement of division of profit** or **appropriation account**:

	Partner A	Partner B	Total
	£	£	£
Salaries	X		X
Interest on capital	X	X	X
Interest on drawings		(X)	(X)
Profit share ratio 3:2	X	X	ß
	—	—	—
Total profit share	X	X	
Net profit from profit and loss account			X

- The profits allocated to each partner are credited to the partners' **current account**. Drawings are also recorded in this account:

Current account

	Ptnr A	Ptnr B		Ptnr A	Ptnr B
			Balance b/f	X	X
Drawings	X	X	Profit share (from profit appropriation account)	X	X
Balance c/f	X	X			
	—	—		—	—
	X	X		X	X
	—	—		—	—

- The partners' **capital account** records the initial capital invested in the business by each partner. Transactions in this account are rare, being the injection of further capital or withdrawal of capital by a partner:

Capital account

	Ptnr A	Ptnr B		Ptnr A	Ptnr B
			Balance b/f	X	X
Withdrawals of long-term capital	X	X	Injection of long-term capital	X	X
Balance c/f	X	X			
	—	—		—	—
	X	X		X	X
	—	—		—	—
			Balance b/f	X	X

- The closing balances on the partners' **current** and **capital accounts** form the capital section of the **balance sheet**:

		£	£
Capital accounts	Partner A	X	
	Partner B	X	
		—	
			X
Current accounts	Partner A	X	
	Partner B	X	
		—	
			X
			—
			X

- The remainder of the balance sheet (assets and liabilities) is as for a sole trader.

Expandable text

Capital accounts

At the commencement of the partnership, an agreement will have to be reached as to the amount of capital to be introduced. This could be in the form of cash or other assets. Whatever the form of assets introduced and debited to asset accounts, it is normal to make the credit entry to fixed capital accounts. These are so-called because they are not then used to record drawings or shares of profits but only major changes in the relations between partners. In particular, fixed capital accounts are used to deal with:

- capital introduced or withdrawn by new or retiring partners
- revaluation adjustments.

The balances on fixed capital accounts do not necessarily bear any relation to the division of profits. However, to compensate partners who provide a larger share of the capital, it is common for interest on capital accounts to be paid to them.

This is dealt with in the calculations for the profit shares transferred from the profit and loss account.

Current accounts

Current accounts are used to deal with the regular transactions between the partners and the firm, i.e. matters other than those sufficiently fundamental to be dealt with through the capital accounts. Most commonly these are:

- share of profits, interest on capital and partners' salaries, usually computed annually
- monthly drawings against the annual share of profit.

Both accounts are presented in a columnar format. This is convenient for examination purposes and is quite common in a partnership set of books as each partner will have similar transactions during the year. A columnar format allows two (or more) separate accounts to be shown using the same narrative. It is important to remember that each partner's account is separate from the other partner(s).

Balance sheet presentation

One of the main differences between the capital section of the balance sheet of a sole trader and a partnership is that the partnership balance sheet will often only give the closing balances whereas the sole trader's movements in capital are shown. The main reason for the difference is simply one of space.

Movements in the capital and current accounts for a few partners cannot be easily accommodated on the face of the balance sheet.

Illustration

Parvati and Lavender run a business selling homemade potions and lotions. They have been very successful in their first year of trading and have made a profit of £48,000.

Their partnership agreement makes the following provisions:

- Parvati is to be allocated a salary of £11,000 to reflect her extensive potion knowledge.
- Interest on capital is to be provided at 7% pa.
- The balance of profits are to be split equally.

When they set the business up, Parvati injected capital of £8,000 and Lavender £12,000.

How much profit is allocated to Lavender?

A £18,360

B £24,140

C £18,640

D £29,360

Expandable Text

The correct answer is C

	Parvati	Lavender	Total
	£	£	£
Salaries	11,000		11,000
Interest on capital	560	840	1,400
Profit share ratio 1:1	17,800	17,800	35,600 (ß)
Total profit share	29,360	18,640	
Net profit from profit and loss account			48,000

Test Your Understanding 1

Britney, Justin and Cameron are in partnership selling CDs and DVDs via their website Bigstars.com. They haven't been very successful in the past year and in the year ended 30 June 20X6, recorded a loss of £120,000 Their partnership agreement states the following:

- interest on capital to be provided at 4% pa
- Cameron to be allocated a salary of £25,000, and Justin £14,000
- no interest to be charged on drawings
- balance of profits to be shared in the ratio 4:3:1.

Capital balances at the start of the year stood as follows:

Britney	£35,000
Justin	£26,000
Cameron	£40,000

How much profit or loss is allocated to Cameron?

A   £6,220

B   £36,220

C   (£34,540)

D   (£54,920)

Test Your Understanding 2

Hamish and Campbell started a business making and distributing haggis on 1 January 20X6. This was largely prompted by Hamish winning £40,000 at bingo just before Christmas. Hamish invested half his winnings in the business and Campbell borrowed £14,000 from his Uncle Hoolie to invest.

In the first year of trade, the business made £25,000 profit, with which both partners were rather pleased.

They have set up a partnership agreement, but even so are not sure how much profit they are each allocated. The agreement says the following:

- Neither partner receives a salary.

- Interest on capital is to be provided at 4%.

- Interest on drawings is to be charged at 2%.

- The balance of profit is to be split in the ratio 3:2.

Both Hamish and Campbell drew £5,000 from the business on 1July 20X6 to pay for their annual fishing holiday to Spain.

Show how this information appears in the partners' capital and current accounts and in the balance sheet.

5 Guaranteed minimum profit share

A partner may be guaranteed a minimum share of the profits.

If the partner has not received this guaranteed amount after allocating profits in the usual way, the shortfall should be given to the partner.

This amount is funded by the other partners in accordance with the profit share ratio.

Illustration

A partnership, organising European holidays, has four partners – Pierre, Wolfgang, Edwin and Carmen. In the year to 30 June 20X5 the partnership made profits of £106,250.

Pierre invested £100,000 in the partnership. He withdrew £30,000 from the business on 1 July 20X4.

Wolfgang invested £20,000 in the partnerhsip. He withdrew £30,000 on 30 June 20X5.

Edwin invested £50,000 in the business. He withdrew £25,000 on 1 July 2004 and a further £25,000 on 1 January 2005.

Carmen also invested £50,000 and withdrew £30,000 on 1 July 20X4.

Allocate the profits of the business in accordance with the following partnership agreement:

- **interest on capital at 5% pa**
- **Wolfgang is to receive £5,000 salary**
- **interest on drawings at 10% pa**
- **profit share ratio 2:1:3:4**
- **guaranteed minimum profit share of £42,500 for Carmen.**

Expandable Text

Working – interest on drawings

Pierre	£30,000 x 10%	£3,000
Wolfgang	No interest as drawings at year end	
Edwin	£25,000 x 10%	£2,500
	£25,000 x 10% x 6/12	£1,250
		————
		£3,750
Carmen	£30,000 x 10%	£3,000

	P	W	E	C	Total
	£	£	£	£	£
Salaries		5,000			5,000
Interest on capital	5,000	1,000	2,500	2,500	11,000
Interest on drawings	(3,000)	–	(3,750)	(3,000)	(9,750)
Profit share ratio 2:1:3:4	20,000	10,000	30,000	40,000	100,000 (ß)
	22,000	16,000	28,750	39,500	
Adjustment				3,000	
Pierre 2/6 x £3,000	(1,000)				
Wolfgang 1/6 x £3,000		(500)			
Edwin 3/6 x £3,000			(1,500)		
	21,000	15,500	27,250	42,500	106,250

6 Loans from partners

- A partner may loan the business some money and may then receive interest on this loan.

- The double entry when the loan is made is:

Dr Cash X

Cr Loan (liability) X

- The interest arising is treated as a business expense which is charged to profits before the profits are shared.

- The double entry for the loan interest is:

Dr loan interest expense X

Cr Bank (if paid) or X

Current account (if outstanding)

7 Full partnership accounts

The following illustrates the process of drawing up a full set of financial statements for a partnership. Although you will not face a question as long as this in your examination, it is useful to understand how full partnership accounts are produced from the trial balance and other information.

Illustration 1 : Full partnership accounts

Preparing partnership accounts

Ken and Barbie are in partnership making and selling gourmet pies. The TB of their business at 30 June 20X6 was:

	Dr	Cr
	£	£
Irrecoverable debts	2,350	
Rent and rates	35,000	
Motor expenses (including depreciation)	17,400	
Allowance for debtors		5,450
Motor vehicles – cost	32,750	
Motor vehicles – accumulated depreciation		15,578
Cash at bank	467	
Drawings – Ken	13,500	
Drawings – Barbie	15,000	
Stock	3,000	
Fixtures and fittings – cost	27,000	
Fixtures and fittings – accumulated depreciation		13,500
Sundry expenses	14,780	
Sales		157,000
Creditors		9,800
Debtors	16,000	

	£	£
Current account – Ken		7,655
Current account – Barbie		9,264
Capital account – Ken		35,000
Capital account – Barbie		20,000
	273,247	273,247

They provide the following further information which is not reflected in the TB:

- Stock held at the year end cost £4,500.

- Fixtures and fittings have not yet been depreciated – the applicable rate is 10% straight line.

- Prepayments at the year end were £2,500 in respect of rates.

- On the last day of the year, Ken paid £13,000 to the business bank account as a loan.

- Barbie is awarded a salary of £7,500.

- Interest on capital is provided at 8% pa.

- The balance of profits is split equally.

You are required to prepare a profit and loss account, statement of division of profits, partners' current accounts and a balance sheet at 30 June 20X6

Solution

Profit and loss account for Ken and Barbie Gourmet Pies for the year ended 30 June 20X6

	£	£
Sales		157,000
Cost of sales:		
Opening stock	3,000	
Purchases	96,000	
Closing stock	(4,500)	
		(94,500)
Gross profit		62,500
Irrecoverable debts	2,350	
Rent and Rates (35,000 – 2,500)	32,500	
Motor expenses	17,400	
Sundry expenses	14,780	
Depreciation expense		
(fixtures and fittings: 10% x 27,000)	2,700	
		(69,730)
Net loss		(7,230)

Balance sheet for Barbie and Ken Gourmet Pies   at 30 June 20X6

	Cost £	Acc'd Dep'n £	NBV £
Fixed assets			
Fixtures and Fittings (13,500+2,700)	27,000	(16,200)	10,800
Motor vehicles	32,750	(15,578)	17,172
			27,972
Current assets			
Stock		4,500	
Debtors	16,000		
Less: allowance for debtors	(5,450)		
		10,550	
Prepayments		2,500	
Cash (467 + 13,000)		13,467	
		31,017	
Current liabilities			
Creditors		(9,800)	
Net current assets			21,217
Long-term liabilities			
Loan			(13,000)
			36,189

Represented by:

	Ken	Barbie	
Capital accounts	35,000	20,000	55,000
Current accounts	(12,610)	(6,201)	(18,811)
			36,189

Current accounts

	Ken	Barbie		Ken	Barbie
	£	£		£	£
Share of loss	6,765	465	Balance b/f	7,655	9,264
Drawings	13,500	15,000	Balance c/f	12,610	6,201
	20,265	15,465		20,265	15,465
Balance b/f	12,610	6,201			

Appropriation account

	Ken	Barbie	Total
	£	£	£
Salary		7,500	7,500
Interest on capital	2,800	1,600	4,400
Profit share ratio (1:1)	(9,565)	(9,565)	(19,130) (ß)
	(6,765)	(465)	(7,230)

8 Partnership accounts and goodwill

Goodwill is the difference between the value of the partnership business as a whole and the aggregate of the fair values of the net assets:

Value of the business	X
Fair value of net assets	(X)
Goodwill	X

A number of factors will lead to the creation of goodwill in a partnership business:

- good reputation
- location
- technical know-how
- excellent profits over the past years
- good prospects in the future.

KAPLAN PUBLISHING

Goodwill 'belongs' to the partners in the same ratio as their profit share agreement, although attributing goodwill is only necessary when:

(1) The partners elect to change their PSR.

(2) A partner retires or dies.

(3) A new partner joins the partnership.

The calculation of goodwill

Partnership goodwill can be calculated in a number of ways:

(1) the difference between the fair value of purchase consideration and the fair value of the separable net assets; or

(2) a multiple of previous year's profit or any other mathematical formulae; or

(3) a share/percentage paid by an incoming partner for goodwill can be used to determine the total goodwill; or

(4) any other basis given in the question.

Test Your Understanding 3

Calculate the goodwill in each of these cases.

(1) The fair value of purchase consideration and fair value of the net assets are given as £750,000 and £500,000 respectively.

(2) Goodwill is to be valued at 4 times the profit of last year. Last year's profit is given as £25,000.

(3) The incoming partner introduces £6,000 in payment for his share of a quarter of the goodwill.

9 Adjustments to partnership accounts

If any of the following situations occur:

- the profit-share ratio is changed

- a partner retires or dies

- a new parter joins the business

then the profit-share ratio will change and so ownership of the goodwill also changes. Adjustments to the capital accounts of the partners are required before such a change takes place in order that partners retain their share of goodwill generated to date. This can be done with or without a goodwill account.

Use of a goodwill account

Calculate the goodwill in the business and then:

Dr	Goodwill account	X
Cr	Capital accounts in old ratio	X

Adjustment without a goodwill account

Calculate the goodwill in the business and then:

Dr	Capital accounts of partners in new ratio	X
Cr	Capital accounts of partners in old ratio	X

In order that partners now taking a smaller share of the profits are 'compensated' for the goodwill 'lost', this 'compensation' is funded by the partners now taking a larger share of the profits.

Note that the death of a partner is not examinable.

Illustration 2 : Goodwill on change of PSR

John, Lewis and Fraser have been partners in a delicatessen for 10 years. They share their profits in the ratio 3:4:2. As Lewis wishes to step back from the operational side of the business in order to spend more time with his family, it has been agreed that the profit share ratio will be changed to 3:1:2. The value of the goodwill in the business is £54,000.

What journals are required to account for this

(a) If a goodwill account is used

(b) without a goodwill account ?

Solution

(a) using a goodwill account

Dr	Goodwill	£54,000	
Cr	Capital (John)	£18,000	(3/9 x £54,000)
Cr	Capital (Lewis)	£24,000	(4/9 x £54,000)
Cr	Capital (Fraser)	£12,000	(2/9 x £54,000)

KAPLAN PUBLISHING

(b) without a goodwill account

Dr	Capital (John)	£27,000 (3/6 x £54,000)
Dr	Capital (Lewis)	£9,000 (1/6 x £54,000)
Dr	Capital (Fraser)	£18,000 (2/6 x £54,000)
Cr	Capital (John)	£18,000 (3/9 x £54,000)
Cr	Capital (Lewis)	£24,00 (4/9 x £54,000)
Cr	Capital (Fraser)	£12,000 (2/9 x £54,000)

Test Your Understanding 4

Harvey, Nichol and Selfridge have been in partnership for a number of years with a PSR of 1:1:4. They have agreed to change this ratio to 1:1:2. The value of goodwill in the business is £24,000.

How should this be accounted for?

10 Revaluation of assets on a change in partnership structure

- When there is a change in the structure of the partnership due to an admission, retirement or death of a partner, then the assets will generally be revalued.

- Any revaluation profits or losses are awarded to the partners in the old profit share ratio.

- This reflects the fact that the old partners have built up the business and they are therefore entitled to the gain or must bear the loss.

Illustration 3 : Revaluation of assets

Proper and Quibble are partners sharing profits and losses in the ratio of 4:1. On 1 January 20X6, when Proper and Quibble's capital balances stand at £27,000 and £12,000 respectively, a new partner Right joins the business, and the following take place:

- Right introduces capital of £10,000.

- Land and buildings are revalued upwards by £80,000.

- Goodwill is valued at £40,000.

- The profit share is revised to 2:2:1 (P:Q:R).

Write up the capital accounts of the partners to record the above, assuming that a goodwill account is used.

Solution

Capital accounts

	Proper £	Quibble £	Right £		Proper £	Quibble £	Right £
				Balance b/f	27,000	12,000	
				Revaluation Old ratio (4:1)			
				– Land and buildings	64,000	16,000	
				Goodwill	32,000	8,000	
				Bank			10,000
Balance c/f	123,000	36,000	10,000				
	123,000	36,000	10,000		123,000	36,000	10,000
				Bal b/f	123,000	36,000	10,000

Test Your Understanding 5

Miranda and Charlotte are partners sharing profits and losses equally. Capital account balances at 1 January 20X6 are £50,000 and £50,000 respectively. On this date, a new partner, Carrie joins the business, introducing capital of £30,000. Land and buildings are revalued by £100,000 and goodwill is valued at £20,000. After the admission of Carrie, the profit share is revised to 2:2:1 and goodwill is to be eliminated from the books.

What is the balance on Charlotte's capital account after this transaction has been accounted for?

A   £60,000

B   £102,000

C   £110,000

D   £52,000

11 Chapter summary

PARTNERSHIP
A business with two or more joint owners.

PROFIT AND LOSS ACCOUNT
As for a sole trader.

PARTNERSHIP AGREEMENT

PROFIT SHARED BETWEEN PARTNERS
in statement of division of profit (appropriation account)
- Salaries
- Interest on capital
- Interest on drawings
- Profit-share ratio
- Minimum guaranteed profit share.

CURRENT ACCOUNTS

Drawings	Balance b/f
	Profit share
	Interest on
	Loan
Balance c/f	

LOANS FROM PARTNERS
- Included in balance sheet as if a third party loan
- Interest expensed and accrued to current account.

BALANCE SHEET
Capital section includes balances on partners' capital and current accounts.

CAPITAL ACCOUNTS
- Show long-term capital invested in business
- Movements are rare.

Test your understanding answers

Test Your Understanding 1

The correct answer is A

	Britney	Justin	Cameron	Total
	£	£	£	£
Salaries		14,000	25,000	39,000
Interest on capital	1,400	1,040	1,600	4,040
Profit share ratio	(81,520)	(61,140)	(20,380)	(163,040) (ß)
Total profit share	(80,120)	(46,100)	6,220	
Net profit from profit and loss account				(120,000)

Test Your Understanding 2

Statement of division of profit

	Hamish	Campbell	Total
	£	£	£
Interest on capital	800	560	1,360
Interest on drawings (W)	(50)	(50)	(100)
Profit share ratio 3:2	14,244	9,496	23,740 (ß)
Total profit share	14,994	10,006	
Net profit from profit and loss account			25,000

Working – interest on drawings

£5,000 x 2% x 6/12 = 50

Capital account

	Hamish	Campbell		Hamish	Campbell
	£	£		£	£
Balance c/f	20,000	14,000	1.1.X6 injection	20,000	14,000
	14,000	20,000		14,000	20,000
			Balance b/f	14,000	20,000

Current account

	Hamish	Campbell		Hamish	Campbell
	£	£		£	£
Drawings	5,000	5,000	Profit Share	14,994	10,006
Balance c/f	9,994	5,006			
	14,994	10,006		14,994	10,006
			Balance b/f	9,994	5,006

Balance sheet presentation

		£	£
Capital accounts	Hamish	20,000	
	Campbell	14,000	
			34,000
Current accounts	Hamish	9,994	
	Campbell	5,006	
			15,000
			49,000

Test Your Understanding 3

(1) £250,000 (£750,000 – £500,000)

(2) £100,000 (4 x £25,000)

(3) £24,000 (4 x £6,000)

Test Your Understanding 4

Using goodwill account

		£
Dr	Goodwill	24,000
Cr	Capital (Harvey) 1/6 x £24,000	4,000
Cr	Capital (Nichol) 1/6 x £24,000	4,000
Cr	Capital (Selfridge) 4/6 x £24,000	16,000

Without goodwill account

	Harvey £	Nichol £	Selfridge £		Harvey £	Nichol £	Selfridge £
				Balance b/f	X	X	X
				Goodwill adjustment	4,000	4,000	16,000
Goodwill adjustment	6,000	6,000	12,000				
Balance c/f	X	X	X				
	X	X	X		X	X	X
				Balance c/f	X	X	X

Therefore the overall effect is to:

		£
Dr	Harvey Capital	2,000
Dr	Nichol Capital	2,000
Cr	Selfridge Capital	4,000

Thus Harvey and Nichol, who have a greater share of goodwill under the new profit-share ratio, are compensating Selfridge, who is entitles to a lesser share under the new profit-share ratio.

Test Your Understanding 5

The correct answer is B

Without goodwill account

	Miranda	Charlotte	Carrie		Miranda	Charlotte	Carrie
	£	£	£		£	£	£
				Balance b/f		50,000	
					50,000		
				Revaluation Old ratio (1:1)	50,000	50,000	
Goodwill adjustment (2:2:1)	8,000	8,000	4,000	Goodwill adjustment	10,000	10,000	
Balance c/f	102,000	102,000	26,000	Bank			30,000
	110,000	110,000	30,000		110,000	110,000	30,000
				Balance c/f	102,000	102,000	26,000

Company accounts

Chapter learning objectives

Upon completion of this chapter you will be able to:

- explain the difference between a sole trader and a limited liability company

- illustrate the required presentation of financial statements

- identify the components of the statement of movement in reserves

- identify the components of the statement of total recognised gains and losses

- identify items requiring separate disclosure on the face of the profit and loss account

- explain the capital structure of a limited liability company

- explain and illustrate the share premium account

- define a rights issue and its advantages and disadvantages

- record a rights issue in ledger accounts and show the effect in the balance sheet

- define a bonus (capitalisation) issue and its advantages and disadvantages

- record a bonus issue in ledger accounts and show the effect in the balance sheet

- explain and illustrate other reserves which may appear in a company balance sheet

- explain why the heading, retained earnings (profit and loss reserve), appears in a company balance sheet

- explain how finance is raised by borrowing rather than by the issue of shares

- calculate and record interest expense in the ledger accounts and the financial statements

- explain the requirements of Financial Reporting Standards (FRS) as regards current assets and liabilities

- explain the impact of corporation tax on company profits and illustrate the ledger account required to record it

- record corporation tax in the profit and loss account and balance sheet of a company

- explain and illustrate the recording of dividends.

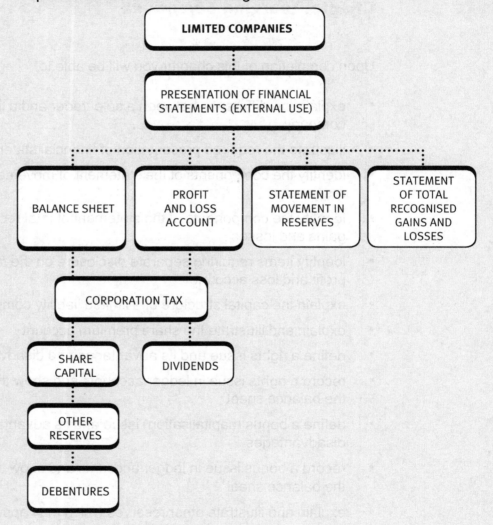

1 Characteristics of limited companies

	Limited liability company	Sole trader
Separate legal entity	A limited company is a separate legal entity, i.e. in the eyes of the law it is a person in its own right and is distinct from its owners.	A sole trader is legally not separate from his business even though he is treated as such for accounting purposes.
Liability	A company is fully liable for its own debts. This means that if the company goes into liquidation, the owners (shareholders) of the company are liable only for amounts that they have not yet paid for their shares. Thus the shareholders are said to have limited liability.	If a sole trader goes into liquidation then he is personally liable for any outstanding debts of his business.
Ownership and management	A company is owned by shareholders. The managers of the company are called directors and are appointed by the shareholders. The directors may or may not be shareholders in the company. Thus most shareholders do not play a part in the day-to-day running of the company.	A sole trader is generally both the owner and manager of his or her business.
Formalities	Financial statements are required to be made publicly available and require an annual audit by qualified aufitors.	No such formalities exist for sole traders.

Expandable text

The advantages of operation as a limited company rather than as a sole trader can be as follows:

- The liability of the shareholders is limited to the capital already introduced by them.

- There is a formal separation of the business from the owners of the business, which may be helpful to the running of the business. For example, if several members of a family are the shareholders in a company, but only two of the family are directors, it is clear to all concerned who is running the company.

- Ownership of the business can be shared between people more easily than in other forms of business organisation, e.g. a partnership.

- Shares in the business can be transferred relatively easily.

- There may be tax advantages.

The disadvantages of operation as a limited company rather than as a sole trader can be as follows:

- the costs of formation of the company

- costs of complying with companies' legislation, including the audit requirement

- directors of a company are subject to greater legislative duties than others running an unincorporated business

- it is difficult/expensive to return capital surplus to the business's requirements back to the shareholders

    there may be tax disadvantages.

2 Presentation of financial statements

(The accounts of a limited company are regulated by the Companies Act (CA 1985) and by self-regulation.

The self-regulatory body is the Accounting Standards Board (ASB). The ASB issue Financial reporting standards (FRSs) which provide guidance on acceptable methods of accounting.

CA 1985 (and subsequent additions and amendments in 1989) incorporates the recommended formats for company published accounts. The following financial summaries are required:

- balance sheet
- profit and loss account
- statement of movement in reserves
- notes to the accounts (the F3 syllabus does not require knowledge of these).

In addition, FRS 3 Reporting financial rerformance requires that a **Statement of Total Recognised Gains and Losses (STRGL)** is provided within the financial statements of a company.

3 Balance sheet

There are many similarities to the balance sheet of a sole trader, although some items (marked in bold) will require further explanation.

Balance Sheet for XYZ at 31 December XXXX

	£000	£000	£000
Fixed assets			
Intangible assets			
Goodwill		X	
Tangible assets			
Land and buildings	X		
Plant and machinery	X		
Motor vehicles	X		
	___	X	
Investments		X	
			X
Current assets			
Stock	X		
Debtors	X		
Prepayments and accrued income	X		
Investments	X		
Cash at bank and in hand	X		
	___		
		X	
Creditors: amounts falling due within one year			
Trade creditors	(X)		
Proposed dividends	(X)		
Taxation creditor	(X)		
Debenture interest payable	(X)		
Accruals and prepaid income	(X)		
	___	(X)	
		___	
Net current assets			X

Total assets less current liabilities		X
Creditors: amounts falling due after one year		
10% debentures		(X)
		———
Net assets		X
		———

	£000	£000	£000
Capital and reserves			
Ordinary share capital			X
Share premium account			X
Revaluation reserve			X
Profit and loss reserve			X
			———
			X
			———

Expandable text

CA 1985 requires that the balance sheet is presented in one of two formats:

- Format 1: vertical

- Format 2: horizontal.

The example shown above is the vertical format whereby the 'top half' of the balance sheet shows all assets less liabilities and the 'bottom half' of the balance sheet shows share capital and reserves.

This format is the most widely used within the United Kingdom.

The horizontal format requires all assets to be shown as the 'left-hand side' of the balance sheet and all liabilities including share capital and reserves to be shown as the 'right-hand side'.

Where a company has no need to use one of the headings within the balance sheet format, e.g. it has no fixed asset investments, it is normal for the company to ignore the heading altogether rather than to return a nil entry.

4 Profit and loss account

The suggested format, as laid down in the CA 1985, is as follows.

Note that all expenses are classified under one of three headings:

- **Cost of sales**

    This is calculated as for a sole trader and includes all production costs. The calculation should be shown in a note to the accounts rather than on the face of the profit and loss account.

- **Distribution costs**

    These are all expenses relating to selling or delivering products or services.

- **Administrative expenses**

    This includes all expenses not classified within cost of sales or distribution costs.

Some expenses such as depreciation will be split across all three expense categories.

Profit and loss account for XYZ Ltd for the year ended 31 December XXXX

	£000	£000
Turnover		X
Cost of sales		(X)
Gross profit		X
Distribution costs	X	
Administrative expenses	X	
		(X)
		X
Other operating income		X
		X
Income from other fixed asset investments	X	
Other interest receivable and similar income	X	
		X
		X
Interest payable and similar charges		(X)
		X
Tax on profit on ordinary activities		(X)
Profit after taxation		X
Dividends		(X)
Retained profit for the year		X

KAPLAN PUBLISHING

As a minimum, the CA 1985 requires the following items to be shown on the face of the profit and loss account:

- turnover
- operating profit
- profit before tax
- profit after tax – dividends paid and proposed.

Expandable text

The CA 1985 provides four permissible formats for the profit and loss account.

The example shown above is format 1; this is the most popular format in practice.

Format 2 classifies expenses differently and in more detail than format 1. Rather than including all expenses within one of three categories (cost of sales, distribution costs, administrative expenses), the following headings are used:

- Changes in stocks of finished goods and work-in-progress
- Raw materials and consumables
- Other external charges
- Staff costs:
  - Wages and salaries
  - Social security costs
  - Other pension costs
- Depreciation and other amounts written off tangible and intangible fixed assets
- Exceptional amounts written off current assets.

Formats 3 and 4 are very rarely used.

As with the balance sheet, if a company has no entry under a particular heading on the profit and loss account, it is common practice to omit the heading entirely.

Relationship between the profit and loss account and balance sheet

The link between the balance sheet and profit and loss account is shown below:

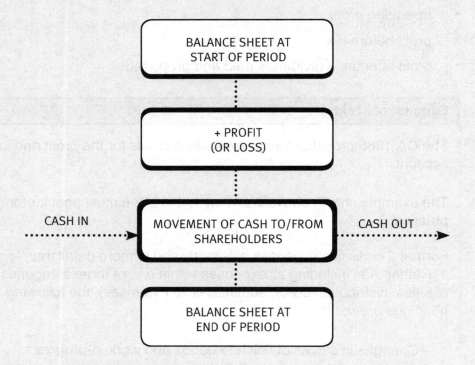

5 Statement of movement in reserves

This statement is included within the accounts to provide further information on reserves.

Statement of movement in reserves for XYZ Ltd

	Share premium account	Revaluation reserve	Profit and loss reserve	Total
	£m	£m	£m	£m
Balance at 1 January	X	X	X	X
Premium on issue of shares	X			X
Surplus on property revaluation		X		X
Transfer from profit and loss account of the year			X	X
	X	X	X	X

6 Statement of total recognised gains and losses (STRGL)

This is a requirement of FRS 3 Reporting Financial Performance. It shows gains and losses recognised in financial statements during the year, whether or not they have been shown in the profit and loss account.

Statement of total recognised gains and losses for XYZ Ltd

	£000
Profit for the financial year (before dividends)	X
Unrealised surplus on revaluation of properties	X
	—
Total recognised gains and losses relating to the year	X
	—

Illustration

The profit for the year of GoGo Ltd (before dividends) was £500,000. The surplus on revaluations was £200,000.

The STRGL for this situation is outlined below:

Statement of total recognised gains and losses for GoGo Ltd

	£000
Profit for the financial year (before dividends)	500
Unrealised surplus on revaluation of properties	200
	—
Total recognised gains and losses relating to the year	700
	—

7 Share capital

A company is owned via shares.

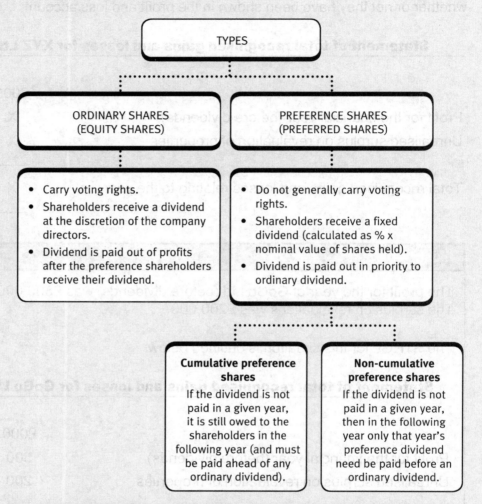

- Redeemable preference shares are preference shares which are repayable by the company at a specified future date. On this date the shares are cancelled and the shareholders repaid.

  These shares have the characteristics of debt. They are therefore classified as a **liability** on the balance sheet.

- Irredeemable preference shares are preference shares which are not redeemable. They remain in existence indefinitely.

  These shares are classified as **equity** on the balance sheet.

Expandable text

The **share capital** of a company may be divided into various classes. The company's internal regulations define the respective rights attached to the various shares, e.g. as regards dividend entitlement or voting at company meetings. In practice it is usually only larger companies which have different classes of share capital.

Ordinary shares are the normal shares issued by a company. The ordinary shareholders are the real owners of the business

Ordinary shareholders may receive dividends from the company from its profits. These dividends are often paid twice each year: an interim dividend during an accounting year and a final dividend after the balance sheet date when the company's profit for the year is known. Dividends will vary according to the company's level of profits and dividend policy. Ordinary dividends are often expressed in terms of pence (or pounds) per share. Sometimes in examination questions they are given as a percentage of the issued share capital.

No dividend may be paid on the ordinary shares until the preference share dividend has been paid in full.

Preference shares are shares carrying a fixed rate of dividend, the holders of which have a prior claim to any company profits available for distribution.

Special categories of preference shares include:

- **Participating preference shares** – where shareholders are entitled to participate together to a specified extent in distributable profits and surpluses on liquidation
- **Redeemable preference shares** – the terms of issue specify that they are repayable by the company.

Share capital values

- Each share has a **nominal** or **par value**, often £1, 50p or 25p. This value is often used as a means of calculating dividends to shareholders (paid as a percentage of the nominal value).

- Shares are issued by the company at an **issue price**. This is at least equal to the nominal value of the share, but often exceeds it.

- The **market value** of a share fluctuates according to the success and perceived expectations of a company. If a company is listed on the stock exchange, the value is determined by reference to recent transactions between buyers and sellers of shares. This value does not feature in the financial statements.

Share capital terminology

- **Authorised** share capital is the nominal value of the maximum number of shares that a company can have in issue at any particular point in time.

- **Issued** share capital is the share capital that has actually been issued to shareholders. The number of issued shares is used in the calculation of dividends.

- **Called-up** share capital is the amount of the nominal value paid by the shareholder plus any further amounts that they have agreed to pay in the future.

- **Paid-up** share capital is the amount of the nominal value which has been paid at the current date.

Accounting for the issue of shares

A company will generally issue shares at above par (nominal) value.

The double entry to record an ordinary or irredeemable preference share issue is:

Dr Cash	Issue price x no. shares
Cr Share capital (B/S)	Nominal value x no. shares
Cr Share premium account	ß

Both the share capital and share premium accounts are shown on the balance sheet within the 'Share capital and reserves' section.

The double entry to record a redeemable preference share issue is:

Dr Cash	issue price x no. shares
Cr Liability	issue price x no. shares

Test Your Understanding 1

Bourbon issues 200,000 25p shares at a price of £1.75 each.

Show this transaction using ledger accounts.

8 Rights issues

A **rights issue** is:

the offer of new shares to existing shareholders in proportion to their existing shareholding at a stated price (normally below market values).

The **advantages** are:

- a rights issue is the cheapest way for a company to raise finance through the issuing of further shares
- a rights issue to existing shareholders has a greater chance of success compared with a share issue to the public.

The **disadvantages** are:

- a rights issue is more expensive than issuing debt
- it may not be successful in raising the finance required.

A rights issue is accounted for in the same way as a normal share issue.

Test Your Understanding 2

Upon incorporation in 20X4, The Jammy Dodger, a limited liability company, issues 1,000 50p shares at nominal value. Needing further funds, in 20X5 it makes a rights issue of 1 for 5 at £0.75. This offer is fully taken up.

What accounting entries are required in 20X4 and 20X5? Illustrate the relevant section of the balance sheet at year end 20X5.

9 Bonus issues

A **bonus (or capitalisation or scrip)** issue is:

the issue of new shares to existing shareholders in proportion to their existing shareholding. No cash is received from a bonus issue.

The **advantages** are:

- issued share capital is divided into a larger number of shares, thus making the market value of each one less, and so more marketable
- issued share capital is brought more into line with assets employed in the company.

The disadvantages are:

- the administration costs of making the bonus issue
- Earnings per share (EPS), a key performance indicator for a company declines as earnings (profits) remain the same but the number of shares increases.

As no cash is received from a bonus issue, the issue must be funded from reserves. Any reserve can be used, though a non-distributable reserve such as the share premium account would be used in preference to reserves which can be distributed:

| Dr | Share premium (or other reserve) | Nominal value |
| Cr | Share capital | Nominal value |

Test Your Understanding 3

Ginger Knut, a limited liability company, has 20,000 50p shares in issue (each issued for £1.25) and makes a 1 for 4 bonus issue, capitalising the share premium account.

What are the balances on the share capital and share premium accounts after this transaction?

	SC	SPA
	£	£
A	15,000	10,000
B	12,500	12,500
C	25,000	Nil
D	22,500	2,500

Test Your Understanding 4

Rich T is a limited liability company with 200,000 25p shares in issue. At 1 January the balance on the share premium account is £75,000. The following transactions occur in the year ended 31 December 20X6:

| 31 January | There is a fully taken-up 2 for 5 rights issue. The issue price is £1.80. |
| 12 August | There is a 1 for 10 bonus issue made using the share premium account. |

What are the balances on the share capital and share premium accounts on 31 December 20X6?

	SC	SPA
	£000	£000
A	308	111
B	77	84
C	154	93
D	77	192

10 Other reserves

Any balances representing profits or surpluses owed to the shareholders are called reserves.

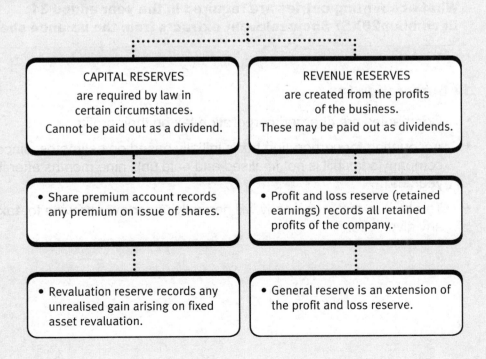

The profit and loss reserve (retained earnings) appears in the capital and reserves section of the balance sheet in the same way that the profits of a sole trader are added to capital.

Retained profits are due (although generally not paid out) to the shareholders of the company. It follows that they should be presented as part of the liability to the shareholders.

11 Debentures (loan stock)

- A limited company can raise funds by issuing debentures.

- A debenture is a document that is evidence of a debt.

- A person will buy a debenture for a set nominal value, e.g. £100. He or she is effectively loaning £100 to the company.

- The nominal value of the debenture will be repayable after a certain number of years.

- In the meantime, the debenture holder will receive an annual fixed amount of interest based on the nominal value.

- The interest incurred is included in 'interest payable' in the profit and loss account.

Test Your Understanding 5

Custard Creameries is an incorporated business which needs to raise funds to purchase plant and machinery. On 1 March 20X5 it issues £150,000 10% debentures, redeemable in 10 years' time. Interest is payable half-yearly at the end of August and February.

What accounting entries are required in the year ended 31 December 20X5? Show relevant extracts from the balance sheet.

12 Corporation tax

- Companies are charged corporation tax on their profits.

- Accounting for corporation tax is initially based on estimates, since a company's tax bill is not finalised and paid until nine months after its year end.

- This means that a company will normally under/over-provide for tax in any given year

- Tax will therefore appear in the year-end financial statements as:
    - A charge to profits in the profit and loss account being:
        - current year estimated tax + previous year's under provision or
        - current year estimated tax – previous year's over-provision.
    - A year-end liability in the balance sheet being the current year's estimated tax.

Test Your Understanding 6

Garry Baldy Ltd commenced trade on 1 January 20X4 and estimates that the corporation tax payable for the year ended 31 December 20X4 is £150,000.

In September 20X5, the accountant of Garry Baldy receives and pays a tax demand for £163,000 for the year ended 31 December 20X4. At 31 December 20X5 he estimates that the company owes £165,000 for corporation tax in relation to the year ended 31 December 20X5.

Draw up the tax charge and corporation tax creditor accounts for the years ended 31 December 20X4 and 20X5 and detail the amounts shown in the balance sheet and profit and loss account in both years.

Test Your Understanding 7

Choccychip Ltd estimated last year's tax charge to be £230,000. As it happened, their tax advisor settled with the tax authorities at £222,000.

This year, Choccychip estimate their tax bill to be £265,000, but they are a little confused as to how this should be reflected in the financial statements.

Which of the following is correct?

	Balance sheet liability (£)	Profit and loss account (£)
A	257,000	265,000
B	273,000	265,000
C	265,000	257,000
D	265,000	273,000

13 Dividends

- Dividends are the share of profits paid out to shareholders.
- Dividends on preference shares are a fixed amount.
- Dividends on ordinary shares are expressed as an amount per share, e.g 10p per share or 10% of nominal value.

Preference dividends

In line with the balance sheet presentation of preference shares:

- redeemable preference share dividends are classified as interest payable
- irredeemable preference share dividends are classified as dividends

These are calculated as a percentage of the nominal value of the preference share capital. If, at the year-end, the company has not paid all of the dividends due to preference share-holders, the company will show the amount owing as a current liability on the balance sheet under the heading 'proposed dividends'.

Ordinary dividends

A company may pay a mid-year or interim dividend. The double entry is:

Dr Dividends – (profit and loss account)	X
Cr Bank	X

At the end of the year companies may propose a dividend to the ordinary shareholders (i.e. tell the shareholders the amount of a dividend to be paid after the year end). This is a final dividend. It is not recorded unless it has been declared (or confirmed) prior to the year end. If this is the case, the double entry is:

Dr Dividends – (profit and loss account)	X
Cr Dividends payable (B/S)	X

The balance on the dividends payable account is shown as a current liability on the balance sheet.

Test Your Understanding 8

Cracker, a company, has share capital as follows:

Ordinary share capital (50p shares)	£200,000
8% Iredeemable preference share capital	£50,000

The company pays an interim dividend of 12.5p per share to its ordinary shareholders and pays the preference shareholders their fixed dividend. Before the year end the company declares a final dividend of 36.5p per share to its ordinary shareholders.

Calculate the amounts shown in the profit and loss account (P&L) and balance sheet (B/S) in relation to dividends for the year.

	P&L	B/S
	£000	£000
A	200	150
B	54	nil
C	200	146
D	101	72

14 Preparation of company accounts

You will not be asked to produce a full set of accounts in the F3 examination, although you may be required to provide certain balances.

The following example will, however, help you to fully understand the preparation of company accounts.

Test Your Understanding 9

The trial balance of Penguin, a company, as at 31 December 20X5 was as follows:

	Dr £	Cr £
Sales and purchases	20,000	50,000
Stock	8,000	
Distribution costs	8,000	
Administration expenses	15,550	
Debtors and creditors	10,000	20,000
Fundamental reorganisation costs	2,400	
Cash at bank	8,100	
Ordinary shares 50p		8,000
10% irredeemable preference shares £1		9,000
10% debentures		8,000
Fixed assets at NBV	35,000	
Share premium		3,000
Profit and loss reserve at 1 January 20X5		3,000
Debentures' interest	400	
Preference dividend	450	
Interim ordinary dividend	1,600	
Corporation tax		500
Suspense		8,000
	109,500	109,500

The following is to be taken into account.

(1) A building whose NBV is currently £5,000 is to be revalued to £11,000.

(2) A final ordinary dividend of 10p per share is to be proposed.

(3) The balance on the corporation tax account represents an over-provision of tax for the previous year. Corporation tax for the current year is estimated at £3,000.

(4) Closing stock is £12,000.

(5) The balance on the suspense account represents the proceeds from the issue of 4,000 ordinary shares.

Prepare the following statements for the year ended 31 December 20X5:

(1) Profit and loss account

(2) Balance sheet

(3) Statement of movement in reserves

(4) STRGL.

15 Chapter summary

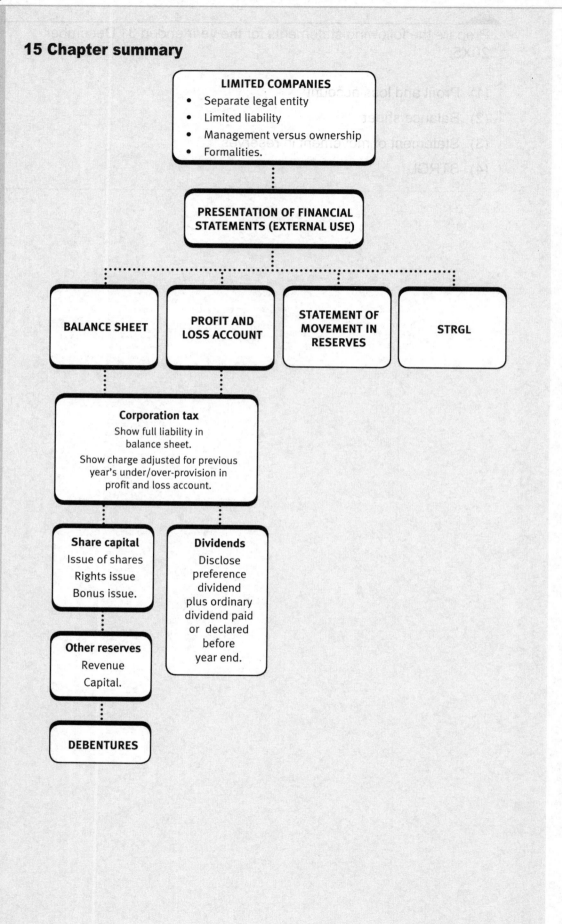

LIMITED COMPANIES
- Separate legal entity
- Limited liability
- Management versus ownership
- Formalities.

PRESENTATION OF FINANCIAL STATEMENTS (EXTERNAL USE)

BALANCE SHEET

PROFIT AND LOSS ACCOUNT

STATEMENT OF MOVEMENT IN RESERVES

STRGL

Corporation tax
Show full liability in balance sheet.
Show charge adjusted for previous year's under/over-provision in profit and loss account.

Share capital
Issue of shares
Rights issue
Bonus issue.

Dividends
Disclose preference dividend plus ordinary dividend paid or declared before year end.

Other reserves
Revenue
Capital.

DEBENTURES

Test your understanding answers

Test Your Understanding 1

Cash

	£		£
Share capital/ share premium account	350,000		

Share capital

	£		£
		Cash	50,000

Share premium

	£		£
		Cash	300,000

Working:

Nominal value: 200,000 x 25p = £50,000

Funds raised: 200,000 x £1.75 = £350,000

Test Your Understanding 2

| 20X4 | Dr | Cash | £500 |
| | Cr | Share capital | £500 |

20X5   For every five shares a shareholder owns, he or she is are entitled to buy another one. The offer is fully taken up, meaning that 200 new shares are issued.

	Dr	Cash (200 X 75)	£150
	Cr	Share capital (200 x 50p)	£100
	Cr	Share premium account	£50

Balance sheet

Capital and reserves:

	£
Share capital – 50p ordinary shares	600
Share premium account	50
Profit and loss reserve	X

Test Your Understanding 3

The correct answer is B

- For every four shares held, a new share is issued.
- Therefore 5,000 new shares are issued

| Dr Share premium account 5,000 X 50p | £2,500 |
| Cr Share capital | £2,500 |

Balance sheet

Capital and reserves:

	£
Share capital – 50p ordinary shares	12,500
(20,000 x 50p) + £2,500	
Share premium account	12,500
(20,000 x 75p) – £2,500	
Profit and loss reserve	X

Test Your Understanding 4

The correct answer is D

Share capital

	£		£
		Balance b/f	50,000
		Rights issue (cash)	20,000
Balance c/f	77,000	Bonus issue	7,000
	———		———
	77,000		77,000
	———		———
		Balance b/f	77,000

Share premium account

	£		£
		Balance b/f	75,000
Bonus issue (SC)	7,000	Rights issue (cash)	124,000
Balance c/f	192,000		
	———		———
	199,000		199,000
	———		———
		Balance b/f	192,000

Balance sheet

Capital and reserves:

	£
Share capital – 25p ordinary shares	77,000
Share premium account	192,000
Profit and loss reserve	X

Workings:

Rights issue: $\dfrac{200,000}{2}$ X 2 = 80,000 new shares

Proceeds: 80,000 x £1.80 = £144,000
Nominal value: 80,000 x 25p = £20,000

Bonus issue: $\dfrac{280,000}{10}$ X 1 = 28,000 new shares

Nominal value: 28,000 x 25p = £7,000

Test Your Understanding 5

1 March 20X5	Dr Cash	£150,000
	Cr 10% debentures	£150,000
31 August 20X5	Dr Interest payable	£7,500
	Cr Cash	£7,500
	£150,000 x 10% x 6/12 =	£7,500
31 December 20X5	Dr Interest payable	£5,000
	Cr Interest accrual	£5,000
	£150,000 x 10% x 4/12 =	£5,000

Balance sheet

	£
Creditors: amounts due over one year	
10% debentures	150,000
Creditors: amounts due within one year	
Trade creditors	X
Debenture interest creditor	5,000

Test Your Understanding 6

Corporation tax creditor (balance sheet)

	£		£
		20X4	
		Profit and loss account	150,000
September X5 Bank	163,000	Balance c/f	13,000
	163,000		163,000
Balance b/f (underprovision)	13,000	20X5 profit and	
Balance c/f	165,000	loss account (ß)	178,000
	178,000		178,000
		Balance b/f	165,000

Tax charge (profit and loss account)

	£		£
20X4 tax creditor	150,000	Profit and loss account	150,000
20X5 tax creditor	178,000	Profit and loss account	178,000

The profit and loss account tax charge in 20X5 is increased to reflect the underprovision made in 20X4.

Balance sheet

	20X4 £000	20X5 £000
Corporation tax creditor	150	165

Profit and loss account

Corporation tax expense	150	178

Test Your Understanding 7

The correct answer is C

- The liability in the balance sheet = the estimated amount payable for the current year.

- The tax charge in the profit and loss account = the estimated amount payable for the current year – last year's over-provision.

Test Your Understanding 8

The correct answer is C

No. of ordinary shares = £200,000/50p = 400,000

Ordinary dividend

Interim	400,000	x	12.5p	=	£50,000
Final	400,000	x	36.5p	=	£146,000
					£196,000

Preference dividend

50,000	x	8%	=	£4,000

Profit and loss account

	£
Profit after tax	X
dividends (£196,000 + £4,000)	(200,000)
Retained profit	X

Balance sheet

Balance sheet

	£
Creditors: amounts due within one year	
Proposed dividend	146,000

Penguin

Profit and loss account
for the year ended 31 December 20X5

	£
Turnover	50,000
Cost of sales (£8,000 1 20,000 – 12,000)	(16,000)
Gross profit	34,000
Distribution costs	(8,000)
Administrative expenses	(15,550)
Operating profit	10,450
Fundamental reorganisation costs	(2,400)
	8,050
Interest payable (10% x 8,000)	(800)
Profit before taxation	7,250
Taxation (3,000 – 500)	(2,500)
Profit after taxation	4,750
Dividends (450 + 1,600 + 450 due)	(2,500)
Retained profit	2,250

Balance sheet as at 31 December 20X5

	£	£	£
Tangible fixed assets (35,000 + 6,000)		41,000	
Current assets			
Stock	12,000		
Debtors	10,000		
Cash at bank and in hand	8,100		
	———		
		30,100	
Creditors: amounts due within one year			
Creditors	(20,000)		
Preference dividend due (900 – 450)	(450)		
Taxation	(3,000)		
Debenture interest	(400)		
	———		
		(23,850)	
		———	
Net current assets			6,250
			———
Total assets less current liabilities			47,250
Creditors: amounts due over one year			
10% debentures (8,000)			
			———
			39,250
			———
Share capital and reserves			
Ordinary share capital (8,000 + 2,000)			10,000
10% preference share capital			9,000
Share premium account (3,000 + 6,000)			9,000
Revaluation reserve			6,000
Profit and loss reserve			5,250
			———
			37,250
			———

Statement of movement in reserves for the year ended 31 December 20X5

	Share premium account	Reval- uation reserve	Profit and loss reserve	Total
	£	£	£	£
Balance at 1 January 20X5	3,000	–	3,000	6,000
Surplus on revaluation of building		6,000		6,000
Net profit for the year		2,250	250	
Issue of share capital (4,000 shares = £8,000 thus issue price is £2 which is made up the nominal value of £0.50 and share premiumof £1.50)	6,000			6,000
Balance at 31 December 20X5	9,000	6,000	5,250	20,250

Statement of total recognised gains and losses for the year ended 31 December 20X5

	£
Profit for the financial year	4,750
Unrealised surplus on revaluation of properties (11,000 – 5,000)	6,000
Total recognised gains and losses relating to the year	10,750

KAPLAN PUBLISHING

18

Accounting standards

Chapter learning objectives

Upon completion of this chapter you will be able to:

- recognise the difference between tangible fixed assets and intangible fixed assets
- identify types of intangible fixed assets.
- define research and development (R&D)
- explain the accounting treatment of R&D costs in accordance with SSAP 13
- calculate the amounts to be capitalised as development expenditure or expensed from given information.
- explain the purpose of amortisation
- calculate the amortisation charge and account for it correctly
- define an event after the balance sheet date in accordance with FRS 21
- account for both adjusting and non-adjusting events correctly in the financial statements
- classify events as adjusting or non-adjusting.
- define provision, contingent liability and contingent asset.
- classify items as provision, contingent asset or contingent liability from information given
- account for provisions, contingent liabilities and contingent assets correctly
- calculate provisions and changes in provisions and account for these changes correctly
- report provisions in the final accounts

- explain what is meant by an accounting policy and the provisions of FRS 18 regarding changes in accounting policy

- identify the appropriate accounting treatment for a change in a material accounting policy according to FRS 18

- describe the provisions of FRS 3 which govern financial statements regarding material errors which result in prior period adjustments.

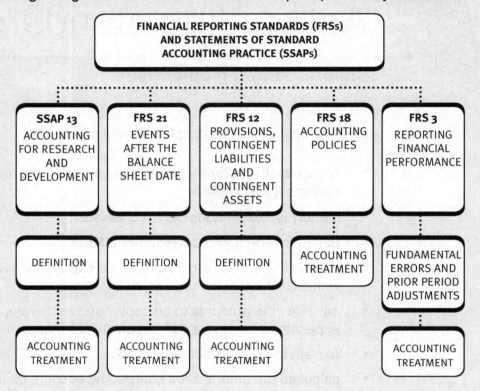

1 Intangible fixed assets

Fixed assets are assets used within the business on an ongoing basis in order to generate income.

They can be split into two distinct types:

Tangible fixed assets

Normally have physical substance, e.g. land and buildings.

Normally involve expenditure being incurred.

Cost of the tangible fixed asset is capitalised.

Depreciation is a reflection of the wearing out of the asset.

Intangible fixed assets

Do not normally have physical substance, e.g. copyright.

Can be purchased or may be created within a business without any expenditure being incurred, i.e. internally generated, e.g. brands.

Purchased intangible fixed assets are capitalised. Generally, internally-generated assets may not be capitalised.

Amortisation is a reflection of the wearing out of the (capitalised) asset.

Examples:
- Development costs
- Goodwill
- Trade marks
- Licences
- Patents
- Copyrights
- Franchises

2 Research and development (SSAP 13)

Research can be categorised as pure or applied and defined as:

- Pure research: experimental or theoretical work undertaken primarily to acquire new scientific or technical knowledge for its own sake rather than directed towards any specific aim or application.

- Applied research: original or critical investigation undertaken in order to gain new scientific or technical knowledge and directed towards a specific practical aim or objective.

Development can be defined as:

The use of scientific or technical knowledge in order to produce new or substantially improved materials, devices, products or services, to install new processes or systems prior to the commencement of commerical production or commercial applications, or to improving substantially those already produced or installed.

Test Your Understanding 1

Which of the following should be classified as development?

(1) Braynee Ltd has spent £300,000 investigating whether a particular substance, flubber, found in the Amazon rainforest is resistant to heat.

(2) Cleverclogs Ltd has incurred £120,000 expenses in the course of making a new waterproof and windproof material with the idea that it may be used for ski-wear.

(3) Ayplus Ltd has found that a chemical compound, known as XYX, is not harmful to the human body.

(4) Braynee Ltd has incurred a further £450,000 using flubber in creating prototypes of a new heat-resistant suit for stuntmen.

A   All of them

B   1 and 3

C   2 and 4

D   2 only

Accounting treatment of research and development

Where a company undertakes research and development, expenditure is being incurred with the intention of producing future benefits.

The accounting issue is therefore whether these costs should be expensed to the profit and loss account or capitalised as an intangible asset on the balance sheet to match future benefits arising.

Research

- All pure and applied research expenditure should be written off to the profit and loss account as it is incurred. This is in compliance with the prudence concept.

- Research expenditure does not directly lead to future benefits and therefore it is not possible to follow the matching concept.

- Any capital expenditure on research equipment should be capitalised and depreciated as normal.

Development

- Development expenditure may be capitalised as an intangible asset provided that certain criteria are met:
  - Separate project
  - Expenditure identifiable and reliably measured
  - Commercially viable
  - Technically feasible
  - Overall profitable
  - Resources available to complete

- Note that if these criteria are met, capitalisation of development expenditure is not a requirement, but a choice. A company may instead opt to write the expenditure off to the profit and loss account.

- The company must be consistent in its treatment of any development projects which meet the criteria.

- If the above criteria are not met, development expenditure must be written off to the profit and loss account as it is incurred.

- Once expenditure has been treated as an expense, it cannot be reinstated as an asset.

Subsequent treatment of capitalised development expenditure

- The asset should be amortised over the period that is expected to benefit. This ensures that costs are matched to the income in the profit and loss account.

- Amortisation should commence with commercial production.

- Each project should be reviewed at the year end to ensure that the 'SECTOR' criteria are still met. If they are no longer met, the previously capitalised expenditure must be written off to the profit and loss account immediately.

Expandable text

Development

An intangible asset arising from development (or from the development phase of an internal project) should be recognised if, and only if, an entity can demonstrate all of the following:

- there is a clearly defined project, and

- the related expenditure is separately identifiable, and

- the outcome of such a project has been assessed with reasonable certainty as to :

(1) its technical feasibility, and

(2) its ultimate commercial viability considered in the light of factors such as likely market conditions, public opinions and legislation, and

- further development costs to be incurred on the same project, together with related production, selling and administrative costs, will be more than covered by related revenues, and

- adequate resources exist, or are reasonably expected to be available, to enable the project to be completed and to provide any consequential increases in working capital.

The amount to be included is the cost of the development. Note that expenditure once treated as an expense cannot be reinstated as an asset.

Amortisation

If the useful economic life of an intangible asset is finite, its capitalised development costs must be amortised once commercial exploitation begins.

The amortisation method used should reflect the pattern in which the asset's economic benefits are consumed by the entity. If that pattern cannot be determined reliably, the straight-line method should be used.

An intangible asset with an indefinite useful economic life should not be amortised. An asset has an indefinite useful economic life if there is no foreseeable limit to the period over which the asset is expected to generate net cash inflows for the business.

KAPLAN PUBLISHING

Illustration 1 : Accounting for development costs

Brightspark Ltd is developing a new product, the widget. This is expected to be sold over a three-year period starting in 20X6. The forecast data is as follows:

	20X5 £000	20X6 £000	20X7 £000	20X8 £000
Net income from other activities	400	500	450	400
Net income from widgets	–	450	600	400
Development costs of widgets	(900)			

Show how the development costs should be treated if:

(a) the costs do not qualify for capitalisation

(b) the costs do qualify for capitalisation and Brightspark adopts a capitalisation policy

Solution

(a) **Profit treating development costs as expenses when incurred**

	20X5 £000	20X6 £000	20X7 £000	20X8 £000
Other activities – Net income	400	500	450	400
Widgets – Net income	–	450	600	400
Development costs	(900)	–	–	–
Net profit/(loss)	(500)	950	1,050	800

(b) **Net profit amortising development costs over life of widgets**

	20X5 £000	20X6 £000	20X7 £000	20X8 £000
Other activities – Net income	400	500	450	400
Widgets – Net income	–	450	600	400
Development costs of widgets **(W)**	–	(279.3)	(372.4)	(248.3)
Net profit	400	670.7	677.6	551.7

Amortisation working:

20X6: 450/1450 x £900,000 = £279,300

20X7: 600/1450 x £900,000 = £372,400

20X8: 400/1450 x £900,000 = £248,300

Test Your Understanding 2

This year, Deep Blue Sea Ltd has developed a new material from which the next generation of wetsuits will be made. This special material will ensure that swimmers are kept warmer than ever. The costs incurred meet the capitalisation criteria and by the 31 December 20X5 year end £250,000 has been capitalised.

The wetsuits are expected to generate income for five years from the date that commercial production commences on 1 January 20X6.

What amount is charged to the profit and loss account in the year ended 31 December 20X6?

A	nil
B	£250,000
C	£100,000
D	£50,000

Disclosure

The financial statements should disclose the following for capitalised development costs:

- a statement of the accounting policy on research and development expenditure

- the total amount of research and development expenditure charged in the profit and loss account, analysed between:
    - the current year's expenditure
    - amortisation charge on previously capitalised costs

- movements on deferred development expenditure and the amount carried forward at the beginning and end of the period.

3 Events after the balance sheet date (FRS 21)

Events after the balance sheet date can be defined as those material events which occur between the balance sheet date and the date on which the financial statements are approved.

4 Adjusting and non-adjusting events

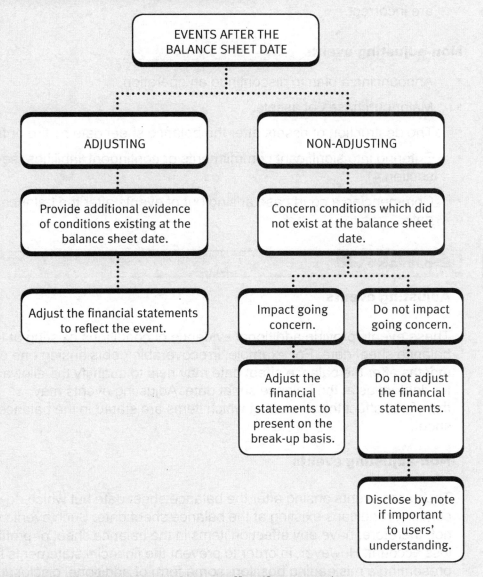

Examples of adjusting and non-adjusting events

The following examples are taken from FRS 21:

Adjusting events

* The settlement after the balance sheet date of a court case which confirms a year end obligation.

* The receipt of information after the balance sheet date that indicates that an asset was impaired at the balance sheet date.

- The bankruptcy of a customer after the balance sheet date that confirms that a year-end debt is irrecoverable.

- The sale of stock after the balance sheet at a price lower than cost.

- The determination after the balance sheet date of the cost of assets purchased or proceeds from assets sold before the balance sheet date.

- The discovery of fraud or errors showing that the financial statements are incorrect.

Non-adjusting events

- Announcing a plan to discontinue an operation.

- Major purchases of assets.

- The destruction of assets after the balance sheet date by fire or flood.

- Entering into significant commitments or contingent liabilities (see section 4).

- Commencing a court case arising out of events after the balance sheet date.

Expandable text

Adjusting events

These events provide additional evidence of conditions existing at the balance sheet date. For example, irrecoverable debts arising one or two months after the balance sheet date may help to quantify the allowance for debtors as at the balance sheet date. Adjusting events may, therefore, affect the amount at which items are stated in the balance sheet.

Non-adjusting events

These are events arising after the balance sheet date but which do not concern conditions existing at the balance sheet date. Such events will not, therefore, have any effect on items in the balance sheet or profit and loss account. However, in order to prevent the financial statements from presenting a misleading position, some form of additional disclosure is required if the events are material, by way of a note to the financial statements giving details of the event.

Proposed dividends

It is not acceptable to include dividends declared after the balance sheet date as liabilities at the year end. They should however be disclosed in a note to the accounts.

If dividends are declared before the year end, they must be accrued for in the balance sheet.

Test Your Understanding 3

Which of the following are adjusting events for BigCo Ltd? The year end is 30 June 20X6 and the accounts are approved on 18 August 20X6.

(1) Sales of year-end stock on 2 July 20X6 at less than cost.

(2) The issue of new ordinary shares on 4 July 20X6.

(3) A fire in the main warehouse occurred on 8 July 20X6. All stock was destroyed

(4) A major credit customer was declared bankrupt on 10 July 20X6

(5) All of the share capital of a competitor, TeenyCo Ltd, was acquired on 21 July 20X6

(6) On 1 August 20X6, £500,000 was received in respect of an insurance claim dated 13 February 20X6

A	1, 4 and 6.
B	1, 2, 4 and 6.
C	1, 2, 5 and 6.
D	1, 4, 5 and 6.

Disclosure

Where there are material non-adjusting events, a note to the financial statements should explain:

* the nature of the event
* an estimate of the financial effect.

Expandable text

A material event after the balance sheet date should be disclosed where it is a non-adjusting event of such materiality that its non-disclosure would affect the ability of the users of financial statements to reach a proper understanding of the financial position.

In respect of each event after the balance sheet date that must be disclosed as above, the following information should be stated by way of notes in the financial statements:

(a) the nature of the event

(b) an estimate of the financial effect, or a statement that such an estimate cannot be made.

The date on which the financial statements were authorised for issue, and who gave the authorisation, should be disclosed in the financial statements.

If the owners or others have the power to amend the financial statements after issue, that fact should be disclosed.

5 Provisions, contingent liabilities and assets (FRS 12)

A **provision** can be defined as a liability of uncertain timing or amount.

A **contingent liability** can be defined as a possible obligation that arises from past events.

A **contingent asset** can be defined as a possible asset arising from past events.

Expandable text

A contingent liability is:

(1) a possible obligation that arises from past events and whose existence will be confirmed only by the occurrence or non-occurrence of one or more uncertain future events not wholly within the control of the entity; or

(2) a present obligation that arises from past events but is not recognised because:

- it is not probable that an outflow of resources embodying economic benefits will be required to settle the obligation; or

- the amount of the obligation cannot be measured with sufficient reliability.

A **contingent asset** is a possible asset that arises from past events and whose existence will be confirmed only by the occurrence or non-occurrence of one or more uncertain future events not wholly within the control of the entity.

Accounting for contingent liabilities and assets

The requirements of FRS 12 as regards contingent liabilities and assets are summarised in the following table:

Probability of occurence	Contingent liabilities	Contingent assets
Virtually certain	Provide	Recognise
Probable	Provide	Disclose in note
Possible	Disclose in note	Ignore
Remote	Ignore	Ignore

- Note that the standard gives no guidance as to the meaning of the terms in the left-hand column. One possible interpretation is as follows:

Virtually certain	> 95%
Probable	51% – 95%
Possible	5% – 50%
Remote	< 5%

- For a contingent liability to be recorded as a provision, the following conditions must be met:

  - A present obligation exists as the result of a past event.

  - There is a probable transfer of economic benefits.

  - A reliable estimate of the amount can be made.

Expandable text

A provision is made where all of the following conditions are met:

- A present obligation (legal or constructive) exists as the result of a past event.

- There is a probable transfer of economic benefits.

- A reliable estimate of the amount can be made.

A **legal** present obligation is an obligation that derives from:

- the terms of a contract

- legislation

- any other operation of law.

A **constructive** obligation is an obligation that derives from an entity's actions where:

- the entity has in some way indicated that it will accept certain responsibilities
- the entity has created an expectation on the part of other parties that it will meet those responsibilities.

Illustration

A retail store has a policy of refunding purchases by dissatisfied customers, even though it is under no legal obligation to do so. Its policy of making refunds is generally known.

Should a provision be made at the year end?

Expandable Text

The policy is well known and creates a valid expectation.

There is a constructive obligation.

It is probable some refunds will be made.

These can be measured using expected values.

Conclusion: A provision is required.

Test Your Understanding 4

The draft financial statements of Madras, a limited liability company, for the year ended 31 December 20X6 are currently under review. The following points have been raised:

(i) An ex-employee has started an action against the company for wrongful dismissal. The company's legal team have stated that the ex-employee is not likely to succeed. The following estimates have been given by the lawyers relating to the case:

	£
(a) Legal costs (to be incurred whether the claim is successful or not)	5,000
(b) Settlement of claim if successful	15,000
Total	20,000

Currently no provision has been made by the company in the financial statements.

(ii) The company has a policy of refunding the cost of any goods returned by dissatisfied customers, even though it is under no legal obligation to do so. This policy of making refunds is generally known. At the year end returns totalling £4,800 have been made.

(iii) A claim has been made against a company for injury suffered by a pedestrian in connection with building work by the company. Legal advisers have confirmed that the company will probably have to pay damages of £100,000 but that a counter-claim made against the building subcontractors for £50,000 would probably be successful.

State with reasons what adjustments, if any, should be made by the company in the financial statements.

Accounting entries for provisions

A provision should initially be accounted for at the best estimate of the probable outflow:

Dr relevant expense account

Cr provision

Movement in provisions

Provisions should be reviewed at each balance sheet date and adjusted to reflect the current best estimate.

Increase in provision	Dr Relevant expense account
	Cr Provision
Decrease in provision	Dr Provision
	Cr Relevant expense account

Reporting provisions in the final accounts

Provisions are reported as a liability.

They may be classed as current or non-current, depending upon the subject matter of the provision.

Disclosure

- Where the requirement is to provide for a contingent liability, the liability is reflected in the financial statements, but called a provision in order to highlight the uncertainty surrounding it.
- The movement in this provision is recorded in the financial statements each year.
- When disclosure is made by note, the note should state:
  - the nature of the contingency
  - the uncertain factors that may affect the future outcome
  - an estimate of the financial effect, or a statement that such an estimate cannot be made.

6 Accounting policies (FRS 18)

The main issues covered by this standard are:

- selection of accounting policies
- changes in accounting estimates
- changes in accounting policy.

Selection of accounting policies

Accounting policies are the principles, bases, conventions, rules and practices applied by an entity that specify how the effects of transactions and other events are to be reflected in its financial statements.

FRS 18 states that two accounting concepts play an important role in the selection of accounting policies:

Going concern

FRS 18 states that an entity should prepare its financial statements on a going concern basis unless the entity has ceased or will cease trading. Thus the financial statements are prepared on the assumption that the entity will trade for the foreseeable future.

Accruals

Other than cash flow information, the financial statements of an entity should be prepared using the accruals basis of accounting.

The objectives against which an entity should then judge the appropriateness of accounting policies are:

- relevance
- reliability
- comparability
- understandability.

Changes in accounting estimates

Accounting estimates may be required in order to enable an accounting policy to be applied.

For example, the accounting policy to depreciate fixed assets will require estimation of:

- the most appropriate method (straight line or reducing balance)
- useful economic life
- residual value of the asset.

Where estimates are revised, the change should be accounted for prospectively, i.e. it should be accounted for in the current profit and loss account, but no adjustment should be made to previous years' financial statements.

Changes in accounting policy

An entity's accounting policies should be reviewed regularly to ensure that they remain the most appropriate to its particular circumstances for the purpose of giving a true and fair view.

The consistency theory means that an entity's accounting policies will generally remain the same from year to year.

Where they do change, the change is applied by way of an FRS 3 prior period adjustment (see next section)

Comparative information for previous years is also restated.

A change in accounting policy occurs if there has been a change in:

- recognition, e.g. an expense is now recognised rather than an asset
- presentation, e.g. depreciation is now included in cost of sales rather than administrative expenses, or
- measurement basis, e.g. stating assets at replacement cost rather than historical cost.

7 Fundamental errors and prior period adjustments (FRS3)

FRS 3 Reporting financial performance is concerned with a number of issues including:

- format of the profit and loss account
- profit and loss account disclosures
- errors and prior period adjustments.

The last of these three issues is examinable within the F3 syllabus (as is one of the profit and loss account disclosures – the Statement of Total Recognised Gains and Losses (STRGL), seen in the last chapter).

Fundamental errors

Fundamental errors are those which are of such significance that they mean the accounts do not provide a true and fair view.

Where these errors relate to the current accounting period, they are easily corrected.

Where they relate to previous accounting periods, e.g. discovery of a major fraud which occurred last year, they are corrected by way of a prior period adjustment.

Prior period adjustments

Prior period adjustments arise from:

- the correction of a fundamental error made in a prior period
- a change in an accounting policy.

These adjustments should not affect the results of the current period and they are therefore not included in arriving at the result for the current year.

KAPLAN PUBLISHING

Instead, they are accounted for by restating prior periods. This requires that the opening balance of the profit and loss reserve is adjusted to reflect the balance as if:

- the error had never been made, or
- the new accounting policy had always been in place.

The prior period adjustment is disclosed within the Statement of Movement of Reserves and the STRGL.

Where practical, comparative information for the prior year is also restated.

8 Chapter summary

```
┌─────────────────────────────────────┐
│ FINANCIAL REPORTING STANDARDS (FRSs) │
│     AND STATEMENTS OF STANDARD       │
│     ACCOUNTING PRACTICE (SSAPs)      │
└─────────────────────────────────────┘
```

| SSAP 13 ACCOUNTING FOR RESEARCH AND DEVELOPMENT | FRS 21 EVENTS AFTER THE BALANCE SHEET DATE | FRS 12 PROVISIONS, CONTINGENT LIABILITIES AND CONTINGENT ASSETS | FRS 18 ACCOUNTING POLICIES | FRS 3 REPORTING FINANCIAL PERFORMANCE |

SSAP 13 — ACCOUNTING FOR RESEARCH AND DEVELOPMENT

Pure research: experimental/ theoretical work to acquire new knowledge for its own sake.

Applied research: investigation undertaken in order to gain new knowledge and directed towards a practical aim.

Development: use of knowledge to produce new/ improved items prior to the commencement of commercial production.

FRS 21 — EVENTS AFTER THE BALANCE SHEET DATE

Those material events which occur between the balance sheet date and the date on which the financial statements are approved.

Adjusting event: amend financial statements to reflect event.

Non-adjusting event: do not amend financial statements unless event impacts going concern. Disclose non-adjusting event if material.

FRS 12 — PROVISIONS, CONTINGENT LIABILITIES AND CONTINGENT ASSETS

Provision: a liability of uncertain timing or amount.

Contingent liability: a possible obligation that arises from past events.

Contingent asset: possible assets arising from past events.

FRS 18 — ACCOUNTING POLICIES

Change to accounting policy applied retrospectively by way of prior period adjustment.

Change to accounting estimates accounted for prospectively (i.e. previous years' results not amended).

FRS 3 — REPORTING FINANCIAL PERFORMANCE

Fundamental errors and prior period adjustments.

Prior period adjustments accounted for retrospectively by restating the opening balance on the profit and loss reserve.

Research costs expensed to profit and loss account.

Development costs may be capitalised on balance sheet if SECTOR criteria met = CHOICE.

Development costs expensed to income statement if SECTOR criteria not met.

	Cont. liability	Cont. asset
Virtually certain	Provide	Recognise
Probable	Provide	Disclose
Possible	Disclose	Ignore
Remote	Ignore	Ignore

Test your understanding answers

Test Your Understanding 1

The correct answer is C

Both 1 and 3 involve researching materials, without any form of commercial production in mind.

Test Your Understanding 2

The correct answer is D

Amortisation will be charged for each of the five years that income is generated.

As there is no reliable pattern of this income, amortisation will be charged on the straight-line basis.

Therefore the amortisation charge for each of the years ended 31 December 20X6 – 20Y0 will be:

$$\frac{£250,000}{5 \text{ years}} = £50,000$$

Test Your Understanding 3

The correct answer is A

1	Sales of year-end stock at less than cost	Adjusting	Closing stock must be valued at the lower of cost and net realisable value (NRV). The post-year-end sale provides evidence of the NRV therefore closing stock must be adjusted to reflect the reduction in value.
2	Share issue	Non-adjusting	
3	Fire in warehouse	Non-adjusting	If this is BigCo's only or main warehouse and the fire affects going concern, the event will be reclassified as adjusting.
4	Bankruptcy of major customer	Adjusting	The bankruptcy of the customer provides evidence of their inability to pay their debt at the year-end. The amount outstanding from the customer at 30 June 20X6 should therefore be written off in the year end accounts.
5	Acquisition of TeenyCo Ltd	Non-adjusting	
6	Receipt of insurance monies	Adjusting	The receipt of insurance monies provides evidence of a year-end asset. The amount subsequently received should be reflected as such in the year-end accounts.

Test Your Understanding 4

(i) FRS 12 defines a contingency as an obligation or an asset that arises from past events whose existence will be confirmed only by the occurrence or non-occurrence of one or more uncertain future events not wholly within the control of the enterprise. A provision should be made if:

    (a) There is an obligation.

    (b) A transfer is probable.

    (c) There is a reliable estimate.

    The legal costs of £5,000 should therefore be provided for since they will have to be paid whatever the outcome of the case. However, the claim is not likely to succeed and so no provision should be made. A disclosure note should be made for the potential loss of £15,000.

(ii) FRS 12 states that an obligation can be legal or constructive. In this case the policy of refunds has created a constructive obligation. A provision for £4,800 should therefore be made.

(iii) As the success of the claim for damages of £100,000 is probable, it constitutes a present obligation as a result of a past obligating event, and would therefore be accounted for as a provision. The success of the counter-claim for £50,000 is also considered probable and would therefore need to be disclosed as a contingent asset (reimbursement). Only if it were considered virtually certain would the counter-claim be recognised as an asset in the balance sheet.

19

Cash flow statements

Chapter learning objectives

Upon completion of this chapter you will be able to:

- explain the differences between profit and cash flow

- explain the need for management to control cash flow

- explain the value of a cash flow statement to users of financial statements

- explain the inward and outward flows of cash in a typical company

- calculate cash flows from operating activities using the indirect method

- calculate cash flows from operating activities using the direct method

- calculate the cash flows from returns on investments and servicing of finance

- calculate the taxation cash flow

- calculate the capital expenditure cash flows

- calculate equity dividends paid

- calculate the management of liquid reseources cash flows

- calculate the financing cash flows

- prepare extracts from cash flow statements from given information.

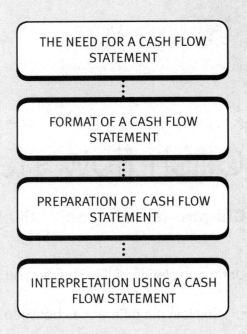

THE NEED FOR A CASH FLOW
STATEMENT

FORMAT OF A CASH FLOW
STATEMENT

PREPARATION OF CASH FLOW
STATEMENT

INTERPRETATION USING A CASH
FLOW STATEMENT

1 The need for a cash flow statement

Profit and liquidity

The accounting concepts of accruals and matching are used to compute a profit figure which shows the additional wealth created for the owners of a business during an accounting period. However, it is important for a business to generate cash as well as make profits. The two do not necessarily go hand in hand.

Profit represents the increase in net assets in a business during an accounting period. This increase can be in cash or it may be 'tied up' in other assets, for example:

- fixed assets may have been purchased

- there may be an increased amount of debtors

- there may be increased investment in stock

- the liabilities of the business may have decreased, i.e. more cash has been spent this year in paying off suppliers more quickly than was the case last year.

The benefits of a cash flow statement

A cash flow statement is needed as a consequence of the above differences between profits and cash. It helps to:

- provide additional information on business activities

- assess the current liquidity of the business

- allow the user to see the major types of cash flows into and out of the business

- estimate future cash flows

- determine cash flows generated from trading transactions rather than other cash flows.

The drawbacks of a cash flow statement

- the cash flow statement is backward looking. Users of the accounts are particularly interested in the future.

- no interpretation of the cash flow statement is provided within the accounts. Users are required to draw their own conclusions as to the relevance of the figures contained within it.

- Non-cash transactions, e.g. a bonus issue of shares are not highlighted on the face of the cash flow statement (although they are disclosed in a note elsewhere in the accounts). These are of interest to users as they will impact future cash flows.

2 Format of a cash flow statement

FRS 1 Cash flow statements requires companies to prepare a cash flow statement within their financial statements. The cash flow must be presented using standard headings.

Cash flow statement for the period ended ...

	£000	£000
Net cash inflow from operating activities (note)		6,889
Returns on investments and servicing of finance		
Interest received	2,911	
Dividends received	100	
Interest paid	(12)	
		2,999
Taxation		(2,922)
Capital expenditure		
Payments to acquire fixed assets	(1,567)	
Proceeds from sale of fixed assets	42	
		(1,525)
Equity dividends paid		(2,417)
Management of liquid resources		
Purchase of current asset investment		(450)
Financing		
Issue of ordinary share capital	206	
Redemption of debentures	(149)	
		57
Increase in cash		2,631

Key points:

- **Cash flows from operating activities** are the cash flows associated with the main revenue-earning activities of the business.

- **Returns on investments and servicing of finance** includes interest paid and received and also preference dividends paid. Note that equity or ordinary dividends paid appear later in the statement.

- **Taxation** includes tax paid in the year. It is therefore likely to include last year's tax liability.

- **Capital expenditure** is the cash paid out during the year to purchase both tangible and intangible assets. The cash inflow from the sale of fixed assets also appears here.

- **Equity dividends paid** are likely to be last year's final dividend plus this year's interim dividend.

- **Management of liquid resources** includes cash flows associated with the purchase and sale of current asset investments.

- **Financing** includes the proceeds of any share issue in the year together with any repayments or issue of loans or debentures.

- **Increase (or decrease) in cash** is the final balance on the cash flow statement and shows the movement in cash balance during the period covered by the cash flow statement. Cash balances and overdrafts repayable on demand are included within the definition of 'cash'.

- Note that the cash flow statement is presented in such a way that the first cash flows covered are mandatory, e.g. interest and taxation. Cash flows shown later in the statement are more discretionary. This is the reason why preference dividends are shown earlier than equity dividends.

3 Net cash inflow from operating activities

There are two methods to calculate cash from operating activities – the direct or indirect method. The method used will depend upon the information provided within the question.

Direct method

This method uses information contained in the ledger accounts of the company to calculate the cash from operations figure as follows:

	£	£
Cash sales		X
Cash received from debtors		X
		X
Less:		
Cash purchases	X	
Cash paid to credit suppliers	X	
Cash expenses	X	
		(X)

Expandable text

Example of calculations using direct method

The gross cash flows necessary for the direct method can be derived:

(1) from the accounting records of the entity by totalling the cash receipts and payments directly, or

(2) from the opening and closing balance sheets and profit and loss account for the year by constructing summary control accounts for:

  – sales (to derive cash received from customers)

  – purchases (to derive cash payments to suppliers)

  – wages (to derive cash paid to and on behalf of employees).

Example using control accounts

The balance sheets of a business are:

	Last year £	This year £
Fixed assets	153,364	149,364
Debtors	265,840	346,000
Cash		165,166
Creditors	(219,204)	(318,890)
	200,000	341,640
Share capital	200,000	200,000
Reserves		141,640
	200,000	341,640

Extracts from the profit and loss account for the year are:

	£	£
Sales		1,589,447
Cost of sales		
Purchases (no stock)	1,105,830	
Wages and salaries	145,900	
		(1,251,730)
Administration		
Purchases	96,077	
Salaries	100,000	
		(196,077)
Operating profit and retained profit for the year		141,640

Additional information

(1) Creditors consist of:

	Last year	This year
	£	£
Re fixed assets		46,000
Other	210,564	258,240
Wages accrued	8,640	14,650

(2) Purchase invoices relating to the acquisition of fixed assets totalling £80,000 have been posted to the creditors ledger during the year.

Calculate the net cash flow from operating activities using the direct method.

Solution

	£
Operating activities	
Cash received from customers **(W1)**	1,509,287
Cash payments to suppliers **(W2)**	(1,154,231)
Cash paid to and on behalf of employees **(W3)**	(239,890)
Net cash inflow from operating activities	115,166

Workings

(W1)

Sales ledger control account

	£		£
Balance b/f	265,840	Cash receipts (ß)	1,509,287
Sales	1,589,447	Balance c/f	346,000
	1,855,287		1,855,287

(W2)

Purchases ledger control account (excluding fixed asset purchases)

	£		£
Cash paid (ß)	1,154,231	Balance b/f	210,564
Balance c/f	258,240	Purchases	
		– Cost of sales	1,105,830
		– Administration	96,077
	————		————
	1,412,471		1,412,471
	————		————

Tutorial note: information relating to fixed assets is not included in the purchases ledger control account above in order to compute cash paid to suppliers of operating costs.

(W3)

Wages control

	£		£
Net wages paid (ß)	239,890	Balance b/f	8,640
Balance c/f	14,650	Cost of sales	145,900
		Administration	100,000
	————		————
	254,540		254,540
	————		————

Indirect method

This method reconciles between operating profit (as reported in the profit and loss account) and cash generated from operations as follows:

	£
Operating profit	X
Depreciation charge	X
Loss/(profit) on disposal of fixed assets	X/(X)
(Increase)/decrease in stock	(X)/X
(Increase)/decrease in trade debtors	(X)/X
Increase/(decrease) in trade creditors	X/(X)
Net cash inflow from operating activities	X

In order to prepare a cash flow statement, information from the current and prior year balance sheet and the current year profit and loss account is used. The following financial statements provide the source data for the requirements of test your understanding 1-7 below:

Expandable text

This working begins with the operating profit as shown in the profit and loss account. The remaining figures are the adjustments necessary to convert the profit figure to the cash flow for the period.

Depreciation	Added back to profit because it is a non-cash expense.
Increase in trade debtors	Deducted because this is part of the profit not yet realised into cash but tied up in debtors.
Decrease in stock	Added on because the decrease in inventories liberates extra cash.
Decrease in trade creditors	Deducted because the reduction in creditors must reduce cash

Test Your Understanding 1

Cash Flow statement source data

Balance sheet of Geronimo at 31 December

	20X6	20X5
	£000	£000
Fixed assets	1,048	750
Accumulated depreciation	(190)	(120)
	858	630
Current assets		
Stock	98	105
Trade debtors	102	86
Dividend receivable	57	50
Cash	42	18
	299	259
Current liabilities		
Trade creditors	(47)	(52)
Dividend payable	(30)	(27)
Interest accrual	(3)	(5)
Tax	(76)	(67)
	(156)	(151)
Net current assets	143	108
Long-term liabilities: Loan	(200)	(300)
Net assets	801	438
Capital and reserves		
Ordinary share capital	200	120
Share premium	106	80
Revaluation reserve	212	12
Profit and loss reserve	283	226
	801	438

Profit and loss account of Geronimo at 31 December 20X6

	£000
Sales	1,100
Cost of sales	(678)
Gross profit	422
Operating expenses	(309)
Operating profit	113
Interest receivable	15
Dividends receivable	57
Interest payable	(22)
Tax	(71)
Dividends	(35)
Net profit for year	57

- Operating expenses include a loss on disposal of fixed assets of £5,000.

- During the year plant which originally cost £80,000 and with depreciation of £15,000 was disposed of.

Calculate the cash generated from operations using the indirect method.

4 Return on investments and servicing of finance

Cash inflows may include:

- interest received
- dividends received.

Cash outflows may include

- interest paid
- preference dividends paid.

Calculation of interest/dividends received

The cash flow should be calculated by reference to:

(1) the charge to profits for the item (shown in the profit and loss account) and

(2) any opening or closing debtor balance shown on the balance sheet.

A T account working may be useful, e.g.:

Interest receivable

	£		£
Interest debtor b/f	X	Cash received (ß)	X
Interest receivable(P&L account)	X	Interest debtor c/f	X
	X		X

If there is no opening or closing balance sheet debtor, it follows that the interest receivable shown in the profit and loss account is the cash inflow.

Calculation of interest/preference dividends paid

Again the cash flow can be calculated by reference to the relevant balances included in the opening and closing balance sheets and profit and loss account.

The format of the T account working is as follows, e.g.:

Preference dividend creditor

	£		£
		Preference dividend creditor b/f	X
Cash paid (ß)	X	Preference dividend payable (P&L account)	X
Preference dividend creditor c/f	X		
	X		X

Test Your Understanding 2

Identify and calculate the amounts to be shown under the heading 'Return on investments and servicing of finance' within Geronimo's cash flow statement.

5 Taxation

A cash outflow will arise, being tax paid in the period.

This will be calculated in the same way as interest or dividends paid, i.e. by reference to the profit and loss account tax charge and the opening and closing tax creditors.

Test Your Understanding 3

Calculate the tax paid by Geronimo.

6 Capital expenditure

This section of the cash flow statement may include:

(a) cash outflows, being payments to acquire fixed assets

(b) cash inflows, being the proceeds of the sale of fixed assets

These amounts are often the trickiest to calculate within a cash flow statement. It is therefore recommended that T account workings are used.

The following T accounts will be required for each class of assets:

*   cost account

*   accumulated depreciation account

*   disposals account (where relevant).

Data provided in the source financial statements should then be entered into these T accounts and the required cash flows found, often as balancing figures.

NB if there is evidence of a revaluation, remember to include the uplift in value on the debit side of the cost T account.

In some cases, insufficient detail is provided to produce separate cost and accumulated depreciation accounts. Instead a net book value (NBV) account should be used:

NBV

	£		£
NBV b/f	X		
Additions at NBV (= cash to purchase fixed assets)	X	Disposals at NBV	X
Revaluation	X	Depreciation charge for year	X
		NBV c/f	X
	___		___
	X		X
	___		___

Test Your Understanding 4

Identify and calculate the cash outflow to purchase fixed assets and the proceeds from the sale of fixed assets to be shown under the heading 'Capital expenditure' within Geronimo's cash flow statement.

7 Equity dividends paid

If any equity dividend has been paid in the period, a cash outflow will arise.

This is calculated in the same way as a preference dividend paid.

Test Your Understanding 5

Calculate the equity dividend paid by Geronimo.

Management of liquid resources

This section of the cash flow statement may include:

*   cash outflows, being payments to acquire current asset investments
*   cash inflows, being the proceeds of the sale of current asset investments.

As current asset investments are not depreciated, the easiest way to calculate the cash flows in the period is by simple comparison of the opening and closing current asset investment balance, e.g.

	20X4	20X3
	£	£
Current asset investment	2,000	1,500

This would indicate that £500 has been spent during the period to acquire current asset investments. In the absence of any related year-end creditor, £500 is therefore the cash outflow.

8 Financing

Cash inflows may include:

- proceeds of issue of shares
- proceeds of issue of loans/debentures.

Cash outflows may include:

- repayment of loans/debentures.

Calculation of proceeds of issue of shares

This cash inflow is derived by comparison of the sum brought forward and the sum carried forward balances on two accounts:

- share capital
- share premium.

Calculation of proceeds of issue of loans/repayment of loans

This cash flow is derived by simply subtracting the brought forward balance from the carried forward.

Test Your Understanding 6

Identify and calculate each of the amounts to be shown under the heading 'Financing' within Geronimo's cash flow statement.

Test Your Understanding 7

Complete the following proforma cash flow statement for Geronimo using your answers to test your understanding.

Cash flow statement for Geronimo for year ended 31 December 20X6

	£000	£000
Net cash inflow from operating activities		
Return on investments and servicing of finance		
Interest paid		
Interest received		
Dividends received	————	
Taxation		
Capital expenditure		
Proceeds of sale of fixed assets		
Payments to acquire fixed assets	————	
Equity dividends paid		
Financing		
Proceeds of issue of shares		
Repayment of loans	————	————
Increase in cash		

Test Your Understanding 8

You are given below, in summarised form, the accounts of Algernon, a limited company, for 20X6 and 20X7.

	20X6 Balance sheet			20X7 Balance sheet		
	Cost £	Dep'n £	Net £	Cost £	Dep'n £	Net £
Plant	10,000	4,000	6,000	11,000	5,000	6,000
Buildings	50,000	10,000	40,000	90,000	11,000	79,000
			46,000			85,000
Investments at cost			50,000			80,000
Land			43,000			63,000
Stock			55,000			65,000
Debtors			40,000			50,000
Bank			3,000			
Creditors			(40,000)			(60,000)
Overdraft			–			(4,000)
			197,000			279,000
Ordinary shares of £1 each			40,000			50,000
Share premium			12,000			14,000
Revaluation reserve (land)			–			20,000
Profit and loss reserve			45,000			45,000
10% Loan notes			100,000			150,000
			197,000			279,000

Profit and loss accounts

	20X6	20X7
	£	£
Sales	200,000	200,000
Cost of sales	(100,000)	(120,000)
	100,000	80,000
Expenses	(50,000)	(47,000)
	50,000	33,000
Interest	(10,000)	(13,000)
Net profit for year (before dividends)	40,000	20,000

Notes:

A £20,000 dividend has been paid in the year.

(a) **Prepare a cash flow statement for Algernon for 20X7, to explain as far as possible the movement in the bank balance. The cash flow statement should be prepared using the direct method.**

(b) **Using the summarised accounts given, and the statement you have just prepared, comment on the position, progress and direction of Algernon.**

Test Your Understanding 9

Part of a company's cash flow statement is shown below:

	£000
Operating profit	1,255
Loss on disposal	(455)
Increase in debtors	(198)
Increase in creditors	340

The following criticisms of the extract have been made:

(1) The loss on disposal should have been added, not deducted.

(2) Increase in debtors should have been added, not deducted.

(3) Increase in creditors should have been deducted, not added.

Which of the criticisms are valid?

A   1, 2 and 3.

B   1 only.

C   2 and 3 only.

D   none of them.

Test Your Understanding 10

Which of the following could appear in a company's cash flow statement?

(1) Proposed dividend

(2) Dividends received

(3) Bonus issue of shares

(4) Surplus on revaluation of fixed assets

A   1 and 2.

B   1, 2 and 3.

C   2 only.

D   2 and 3.

Test Your Understanding 11

The following details are provided to the accountant of Caddyshack Ltd, which has an operating profit of £469,850 in the year ended 31 December 20X6:

(1) Depreciation of £37,400 has been charged to the profit and loss account; this included an amount of £7,600 which was the loss on disposal of a fixed asset.

(2) The following extract of the balance sheets at 31 December 20X5 and 20X6 have been provided:

	31 December 20X6	31 December 20X5
	£000	£000
Stock	145	167
Trade debtors	202	203
Prepayments	27	16
Trade creditors	196	212
Interest accrual	6	28

What is the net cash flow from operating activities?

A   £511,250

B   £510,850

C   £501,250

D   £503,250

9 Chapter summary

THE NEED FOR A CASH FLOW STATEMENT

- Helps to assess liquidity of a company.
- Helps to assess future cash flows.
- User can see cash flows in and out of the business.

FORMAT OF A CASH FLOW STATEMENT

FRS 1 requires the cash flow statement to have following headings:

- Net cash flow from operating activities
- Returns on investments and servicing of finance
- Taxation
- Capital expenditure
- Equity dividends
- Management of liquid resources
- Financing.

PREPARATION OF A CASH FLOW STATEMENT

The cash movement is simply the movement between the current and previous year balance in the balance sheet.

Watch out for trickier areas such as taxation, and fixed assets where a working will need to be done.

INTERPRETATION USING A CASH FLOW STATEMENT

The cash flow provides useful information including:

- how a business spends and receives cash,
- whether operating activities yield a positive cash flow
- whether the business has the ability to generate cash in the future.

Test your understanding answers

Test Your Understanding 1

	£000
Operating profit	113
Depreciation **(W1)**	85
Loss on disposal of plant	5
Decrease in stock	7
Increase in trade debtors	(16)
Decrease in trade creditors	(5)
	___
Net cash inflow from operating activities	189
	___

(W1)

Accumulated depreciation

	£000		£000
Disposals	15	balance b/f	120
Balance c/f	190	Depreciation charge (ß)	85
	___		___
	205		205
	___		___

Test Your Understanding 2

Interest paid

Interest payable

	£000		£000
Cash paid (ß)	24	Interest accrual b/f	5
Interest accrual c/f	3	Interest payable	
		(P&L account)	22
	27		27

Interest received

There is no balance for an interest debtor at the start or end of the year; therefore interest received must equal interest receivable in the profit and loss account

Interest received £15,000

Dividends received

Dividends receivable

	£000		£000
Dividend debtor b/f	50	Cash received (ß)	50
Profit and loss account		Dividend debtor c/f	57
dividends receivable	57		
	X		X

Test Your Understanding 3

Income tax payable

	£000		£000
		Tax creditor b/f	67
Cash paid (ß)	62	Profit and loss account	
		tax charge	71
Tax creditor c/f	76		
	___		___
	138		138
	___		___

Test Your Understanding 4

(See solution to test your understanding 1 for accumulated depreciation account.)

Fixed asset cost

	£000		£000
balance b/f	750		
Additions (= Cash to purchase fixed assets)	178	Disposals	80
Revaluation	200	balance c/f	1,048
	___		___
	1,128		1,128
	___		___

Disposals

	£000		£000
Cost	80	Accumulated depreciation	15
		Loss on disposal	5
		Proceeds (ß)	60
	___		___

Test Your Understanding 5

Equity dividend payable

	£000		£000
		Dividend creditor b/f	27
Cash paid (ß)	32	Dividend (P&L account)	35
Dividend creditor c/f	30		
	___		___
	62		62
	___		___

Test Your Understanding 6

Proceeds of share issue

	20X6	20X5	
	£000	£000	£000
Share capital	200	120	
Share premium	106	80	
	___	___	
	306	200	
	___	___	
Proceeds of share issue			106

Repayment of loan

- balance on loan account was £300,000 in 20X5; in 20X6 it is £200,000
- therefore £100,000 has been repaid.

Test Your Understanding 7

Cash flow statement for Geronimo for year ended 31 December 20X6

	£000	£000
Net cash inflow from operating activities		189
Return on investments and servicing of finance		
Interest paid	(24)	
Interest received	15	
Dividends received	50	
	———	
		41
Taxation		(62)
Capital expenditure		
Proceeds of sale of fixed assets	60	
Payments to acquire fixed assets	(178)	
	———	
		(118)
Equity dividends paid		(32)
Financing		
Proceeds of issue of shares	106	
Repayment of loans	(100)	
	———	
		6
		———
Increase in cash		24
		———

Test Your Understanding 8

(a)

Cash flow statement for the year ended 31 December 20X7

	£	£
Net cash inflow from operating activities		35,000
Return on investments and servicing of finance		
Interest paid		(13,000)
Capital expenditure		
Payments to acquire fixed assets (1,000 + 40,000)		(41,000)
Equity dividends paid		(20,000)
Management of liquid resources		
Payments to acquire investments		(30,000)
Financing		
Proceeds of issue of shares (10,000 + 2,000)	12,000	
Issue of loan notes	50,000	
		62,000
Decrease in cash		(7,000)

Note: net cash inflow from operating activities

	£
Cash receipts from customers **(W1)**	190,000
Cash paid to suppliersand employees **(W2)**	(155,000)
	35,000

Workings

(W1) Receipts from sales

Debtors

	£		£
Balance b/f	40,000	Cash receipts (ß)	190,000
Sales	200,000	Balance c/f	50,000
	240,000		240,000

(W2) Creditors and wages

	£		£
Cash paid (ß)	155,000	Balance b/f	40,000
Depreciation	2,000	Purchases re cost	130,000
Balance c/f	60,000	of sales (W3)	
		Expenses	47,000
	217,000		217,000

(W3) Cost of sales

	£		£
Opening stock	55,000	Cost of sales	120,000
Purchases and wages (ß)	130,000	Closing stock	65,000
	185,000		185,000

Tutorial note: Little information has been given as to the nature of the costs of the company, e.g. no information is supplied on wages and salaries. The payments figure thus includes all cash outflows relating to trading activities. Depreciation would have been charged in either cost of sales or expenses and this needs to be adjusted for. It does not matter whether the adjustment is shown in the creditors or the cost of sales accounts.

(b) Algernon has invested substantially in buildings, investments, stock and debtors in the year. The finance has come from new share capital in part but mainly from loans. The equity to assets ratio of the company has thus decreased. The working capital has been financed by an equal increase in trade creditors.

The profits have been fully distributed as dividends despite the halving of profits from last year. It might have been wiser to cut back on dividends in the period of expansion until the benefits of the expansion are seen in the form of higher profits.

Test Your Understanding 9

The correct answer is B

A loss on disposal should be added back to profit as it is a non-cash expense.

Test Your Understanding 10

The correct answer is C

Dividends received involve a cash receipt. The other transactions do not involve a movement of cash.

Test Your Understanding 11

The correct answer is D

	£
Operating profit	469,850
Depreciation and loss on disposal	37,400
Decrease in stock	22,000
Decrease in trade debtors	1,000
Increase in prepayments	(11,000)
Decrease in trade creditors	(16,000)
	503,250

Note that the movement in the interest accrual is not part of the reconciliation as this is dealt with within the Interest paid line of the cash flow statement.

The regulatory and conceptual framework

Chapter learning objectives

Upon completion of this chapter you will be able to:

- explain the regulatory system in the UK and the roles of the:
  - Financial Reporting Council (FRC)
  - Financial Reporting Review Panel (FRRP)
  - Accounting Standards Board (ASB)
  - Urgent Issues Task Force (UITF)

- explain how Financial Reporting Standards (FRSs) affect the financial reporting process

- explain the meaning of the qualitative characteristics of financial reporting and define and apply each of the following:
  - relevance (including materiality)
  - reliability (including faithful representation, substance over form, neutrality, prudence and completeness)
  - comparability
  - understandability

- illustrate the problems of achieving a balance between the qualitative characteristics

- explain the meaning of accounting concepts and define and apply each of the following:
  - going concern
  - accruals
  - consistency
  - materiality
  - substance over form
  - prudence
- explain the advantages and disadvantages of historic cost accounting (HCA) in times of changing prices
- explain in principle the main alternatives to HCA:
  - replacement cost
  - net realisable value (NRV)
  - economic value.

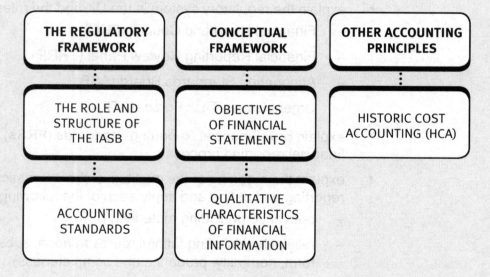

1 The regulatory framework

The need for regulation

- Regulation ensures that accounts are sufficiently reliable and useful, and prepared without unnecessary delay.

- Financial accounts are used as the starting point for calculating taxable profits.

- The annual report and accounts is the main document used for reporting to shareholders on the condition and performance of a company.

- The stock markets rely on the financial statements published by companies.

- International investors prefer information to be presented in a similar and comparable way, no matter where the company is based.

The role of accounting standards

There are two main sets of rules that companies must follow when preparing their financial statements:

- The Companies Act 1985 (CA 1985), updated in 1989 (developed by the parliamentary process)

- Accounting standards:
    - Statements of Standard Accounting Practice (SSAPs) issued by the Accounting Standards Committee (ASC) and later adopted by the ASB
    - FRSs issued by the ASB.

The CA 1985 requires that financial statements give a true and fair view. In order to achieve this true and fair view companies will normally have to follow the provisions of accounting standards.

The CA 1985 mostly provides rules on disclosure within the financial statements whereas SSAPs and FRSs provide guidance on the treatment of particular items within the financial statements.

In many cases the relevant UK accounting standards have been adapted in order to be consistent with International Financial Reporting Standards (IFRSs).

2 The role and structure of the Financial Reporting Council (FRC)

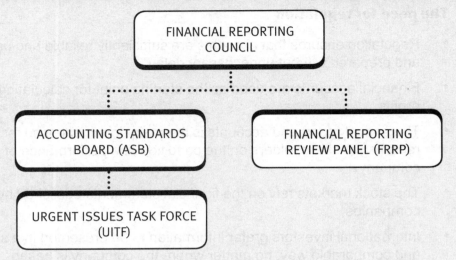

The **FRC Foundation** is the supervisory body. Its objective is to:

- guide the ASB on work programmes and issues of public concern
- guide the ASB on work programmes and issues of public concern
- see that work on accounting standards is properly financed
- act as a proactive public influence for securing good accounting practice.

- The **ASB** is responsible for developing, issuing and withdrawing accounting standards.
- The **UITF** issue rapid guidance where there are differing interpretations of SSAPs/FRSs.
- The **FRRP** enquires into annual accounts where it appears that the requirements of the CA 1985 may have been breached.

Expandable text

The Financial Reporting Council (FRC)

The FRC oversees the other regulatory bodies and their purpose is to:

- promote good financial reporting
- guide the ASB on programmes and policy issues
- verify financial reporting is conducted with efficiency and economy
- review funding of ASB and FRRP
- select members of ASB and FRRP.

The Accounting Standards Board (ASB)

The aim of the ASB is to establish and improve standards for financial reporting.

This aim is achieved by:

- developing a statement of principles for the future development of standards
- issuing new standards and amending existing standards
- addressing urgent issues promptly (delegated to the UITF).

The Urgent Issues Task Force (UITF)

The UITF are responsible for tackling urgent issues that may arise due to there being currently either no guidance or where existing guidance is conflicting and where the normal standard-setting process is not appropriate because it would take too long.

The UITF issues 'abstracts' which are rulings on controversial issues. Compliance with abstracts is normally necessary in order for the financial statements to show a 'true and fair view'.

The Financial Reporting Review Panel (FRRP)

The FRRP are concerned with examining departures from the accounting standards made by large companies.

The FRRP will review financial statements to make sure that they comply with CA 1985, accounting standards and best practice. If the FRRP feel that any departures from the accounting standards are not justified they will try to persuade the company to amend their financial statements. If the company cannot be persuaded to change their financial statements the FRRP will take the company to court to enforce their decision.

3 The conceptual framework

The ASB has produced a Statement of Principles for Financial Reporting. This is not an accounting standard, but sets out the concepts that the ASB believes should underpin financial statements for external users. The purpose of the statement is to:

- assist the board of the ASB in developing new standards and reviewing existing ones
- assist in harmonising accounting standards and procedures

- assist preparers of financial statements in applying SSAPs/FRSs and in dealing with topics not yet covered by SSAPs/FRSs

- assist auditors in forming an opinion as to whether financial statements conform with SSAPs/FRSs

- assist users of financial statements in interpreting financial statements

- provide those interested in the work of the ASB with information about its approach to the formulation of FRSs.

The scope of the framework

The framework deals with:

- the objective of financial statements

- the qualitative characteristics that determine the usefulness of information in financial statements

- the definition, recognition and measurement of the elements from which financial statements are constructed.

Underlying assumptions of the framework

The framework identifies two underlying assumptions:

1. the accruals basis of accounting

The accruals basis of accounting means that the effects of transactions and other events are recognised as they occur and not as cash or its equivalent is received or paid.

2. the going concern basis.

The going concern basis assumes that the entity has neither the need nor the intention to liquidate or curtail materially the scale of its operations.

Fair presentation/true and fair view

There is no absolute definition of fair presentation (also known as the true and fair view). It is felt that its meaning evolves over time and with changes in generally accepted accounting practice (GAAP).

When do financial statements show fair presentation?

Financial statements will generally show a fair presentation when:

they conform with accounting standards
they conform with the any relevant legal requirements
they have applied the qualitative characteristics from the Framework.

True and fair override

FRS's state that an entity whose financial statements comply with FRSs should disclose that fact.

However in extremely rare circumstances management may conclude that compliance with an FRS's or interpretation would be misleading.

In this case an entity should depart from the requirement of the standard provided the relevant regulatory framework permits such departure.

4 Objectives of financial statements

The objective of financial statements is to provide information about:

- the financial position of an entity (provided mainly in the balance sheet)
- the financial performance (provided mainly in the profit and loss account) and
- changes in the financial position of an entity (provided in the cash flow statement)

that is useful to a wide range of users in making economic decisions.

User groups

- equity investors (existing and potential)
- existing lenders and potential lenders
- employees
- stock market analysts and advisers
- business contacts including customers, suppliers and competitors
- the government, including the tax authorities
- the general public.

5 Qualitative characteristics of financial statements

The qualitative characteristics of financial statements are a set of attributes which together make the information in the financial statements useful to users.

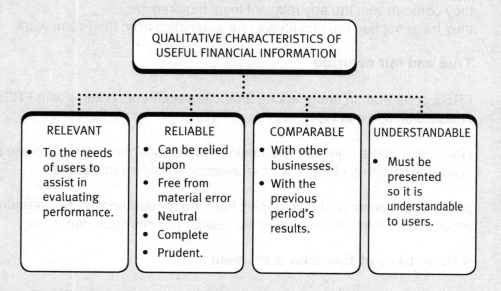

Problems of achieving a balance between the qualitative characteristics

At any given point in time it is unlikely that all of the qualitative characteristics can be satisfied, and therefore there will be conflicts between them. Examples are as follows:

- **Relevance and timeliness**

If financial statements are to be tailored to the needs of each individual user, then they will take longer to prepare.

- **Understandability and completeness**

If all aspects of the business are to be shown, this may make the financial statements less comprehensible.

- **Relevance and reliability**

Sometimes the information that is most relevant is not the most reliable or vice versa. In such conflicts, the information that is most relevant of the information that is reliable should be used.

This conflict might also arise over the timeliness of information, e.g. a delay in providing information can make it out of date and so affect its relevance, but reporting on transactions before uncertainties are resolved may affect the reliability of the information. Information should not be provided until it is reliable.

- **Neutrality and prudence**

Neutrality requires information to be free of deliberate or systematic bias while prudence is a potentially-biased concept towards not overstating gains or assets or understating losses or liabilities. Neutrality and prudence are reconciled by finding a balance that ensures that the deliberate and systematic overstatement of assets and gains and understatement of losses and liabilities do not occur.

Expandable text

Qualitative characteristics of financial statements

The qualitative characteristics are a set of attributes which together make the information in financial statements useful to users. The following diagram showing these characteristics may help by providing a summary of them.

The qualitative characteristics of financial information

The characteristics of useful financial information are briefly considered below:

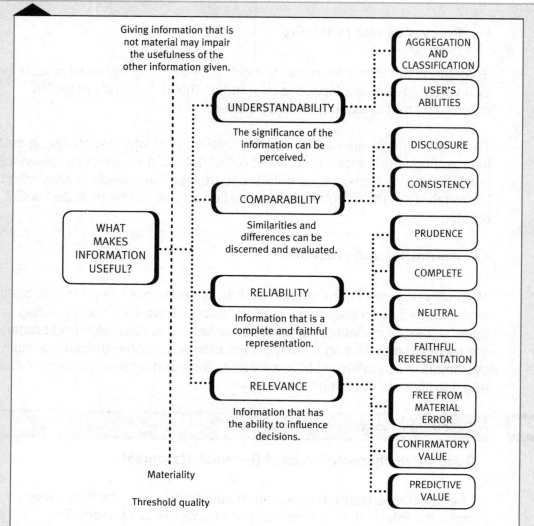

Giving information that is
not material may impair
the usefulness of the
other information given.

AGGREGATION
AND
CLASSIFICATION

USER'S
ABILITIES

UNDERSTANDABILITY

The significance of the
information can be
perceived.

DISCLOSURE

CONSISTENCY

COMPARABILITY

WHAT
MAKES
INFORMATION
USEFUL?

Similarities and
differences can be
discerned and evaluated.

PRUDENCE

COMPLETE

RELIABILITY

NEUTRAL

Information that is a
complete and faithful
representation.

FAITHFUL
RERESENTATION

RELEVANCE

FREE FROM
MATERIAL
ERROR

Information that has
the ability to influence
decisions.

CONFIRMATORY
VALUE

Materiality

PREDICTIVE
VALUE

Threshold quality

Materiality

This is described as a 'threshold' quality. If information could influence users' decisions taken on the basis of financial statements, it is material. In the profit and loss account an item is normally regarded as material, and therefore disclosable, if it is more than 5% of the normal level of pre-tax profit, though materiality cannot be measured in percentage terms alone.

Relevance

Relevance is one of the two basic requirements that financial information must have (the other is reliability). Financial information is relevant if it can assist users' decision making by helping them to evaluate past, present or future events or by confirming, or correcting, their existing evaluations. Relevant information may have predictive value or confirmatory value. That is, it helps users in assessing the future of the business or confirming past predictions.

KAPLAN PUBLISHING

Reliability

Information is obviously of limited use if it is unreliable. To be reliable, it must be free from bias and error. Some contingent items may by their nature be bound to be unreliable. FRS 12 gives guidance as to the extent to which such items should be recognised or disclosed. The subsidiary qualities that make information reliable are:

- **Faithful representation**

Information must faithfully represent the effects of transactions and other events.

- **Substance over form**

Some transactions have a real nature (substance) that differs from their legal form. An example is a hire-purchase transaction. Ownership in an asset being acquired on hire purchase does not pass until the last instalment is paid, but it could be misleading to present a balance sheet in which such assets did not appear until the end of the contract.

Whenever it is legally possible then, the real substance prevails over the legal form.

- **Neutrality**

Judgement is necessary in arriving at many items in the financial statements. Judgement is involved in fixing depreciation rates, valuing stock, determining the level of allowances for receivables and many others. Neutrality means that these judgements are made without bias.

- **Prudence**

Caution must be exercised in preparing financial statements and in estimating the outcome of uncertain events. This does not mean, however, that the approach should be over-cautious. The aim should be to report the most likely outcome, with a slight element of caution, not to prepare financial statements on the most pessimistic basis. That could be seriously misleading.

- **Completeness**

Information presented in financial statements should be complete, subject to the constraints of materiality and cost.

Comparability

Comparability means that the financial statements should be comparable with the financial statements of other companies and with the financial statements of the same company for earlier periods. To achieve comparability we need consistency and disclosure of accounting policies. Accounting standards contribute to comparability by reducing the options available to enterprises in their treatment of transactions. The requirement that companies disclose their accounting policies helps with adjustments to allow for differences between companies. Also, if a company changes its accounting policies there must be full disclosure of the effect of the change.

Understandability

Companies differ greatly in the extent of the efforts they make to enable users to understand their financial statements. Understandability is dependent upon users' abilities, and the Framework suggests that a reasonable knowledge of business and accounting has to be assumed here.

Limiting factors

You can see that some of the characteristics discussed above conflict to some extent with others. Information that is more reliable can be less relevant and vice versa. In other words a balance between characteristics needs to be achieved. Timeliness is another limiting factor. Financial statements may have to be prepared before all aspects of a transaction are known. A balance has to be struck between timeliness and reliability to achieve the best compromise to satisfy the economic decision-making needs of users.

Finally, benefit and cost have to be considered. As far as possible, the benefits from presenting the information should exceed the cost of providing it.

The elements of financial statements

For the Financial Accounting syllabus you do not need to be concerned with the detail of this section of Statement of Principles. However, it does contain three important definitions that you need to know: definitions of assets, liabilities and equity.

An asset is a resource controlled by an entity as a result of past events and from which future economic benefits are expected to flow to the entity.

This very general definition requires some explanation. The first point to note is that ownership is not required. As long as the item is controlled by the entity it can be recognised as an asset, provided its cost or value can be measured with reliability.

Secondly, there is the reference to future economic benefits. If an item does not yield benefits of some kind in the future (profit, for example) it has no value as an asset.

Finally, the definition refers to past events. The most common past event giving rise to an asset is the purchase of that asset.

A **liability** is a present obligation of the entity arising from past events, the settlement of which is expected to result in an outflow from the entity of resources embodying economic benefits.

Equity is the residual interest in the assets of the entity after deducting all its liabilities. In the terms used in earlier chapters, it is the proprietor's capital. When we come to study company accounting in later chapters, it will be the shareholders' interest in a company.

6 Other accounting principles

These generally-recognised principles underlie accounting and financial statements.

Going concern	The assumption that the business will continue in operation for the foreseeable future without significantly curtailing its activity
Accrual	To calculate the profit for the period, one must include all the income and expenditure relating to the period, whether or not the cash has been received or paid. This concept also states that income and expenses should be matched against each other within an accounting period as far as possible
Consistency	Items should be treated in the same way year on year. This will enable valid comparisons to be made. However, if circumstances change then a business is allowed to change policies to give a fairer representation of the financial statements.

| Materiality | Materiality is a threshold quality that is demanded of all information given in the financial statements, i.e. information that is material should be given in the financial statements but information that is not material need not be given.

Information is material if its omission or misstatement might reasonably be expected to influence the economic decisions of users.

Whether or not information is material will depend on the size and nature of the item and the size of the business |
|---|---|
| **Substance over form** | The economic substance of a trans action should be recorded rather than simply its legal form.

E.g. a fixed asset acquired under a hire-purchase agreement should be accounted for as an owned asset. This is the commercial substance of such a situation, even though it is not the case legally. |
| **Prudence** | Prudence is the inclusion of a degree of caution when making estimates under conditions of uncertainty.

It ensures that assets and income are not overstated and liabilities or expenses are not understated. |

Test Your Understanding 1

Which of the following statements are correct?

(1) Materiality means that only tangible items may be recognised as assets.

(2) Substance over form means that the commercial effect of a transaction must always be shown in the financial statements even if this differs from legal form.

(3) A business may only change an accounting policy to achieve a fairer representation.

A   2 and 3 only.

B   All of them.

C   1 and 2 only.

D   1 and 3 only.

7 Historic cost

The limitations of HCA

Under HCA, assets are recorded at the amount of cash or cash equivalents paid, or the fair value of the consideration given for them.

Liabilities are recorded at the amount of proceeds received in exchange for the obligation. This method of accounting has advantages, but it also has serious disadvantages.

Advantages of HCA

(1) Records are based on objectively verifiable amounts.

(2) It is simple and cheap.

(3) The profit concept is well understood.

(4) Within limits, historical cost figures provide a basis for comparison with the results of other companies, with the results of the same company for previous periods and with budgets.

(5) Lack of acceptable alternatives.

Disadvantages of HCA

(1) It overstates profits when prices are rising through inflation.

(2) It maintains financial capital but does not maintain physical capital.

(3) The balance sheet does not show the value of the entity.

(4) It provides a poor basis for assessing performance.

(5) It does not recognise the loss suffered through holding monetary assets while prices are rising.

Alternatives to HCA

- **Replacement cost** involves recording assets at the cost of replacing them. An advantage is that the replacement cost is more up-to-date than the historical cost.

- **Net Realisable Value (NRV)** assets and liabilities are carried at the amount which could currently be obtained by an orderly disposal. Assets are recorded at the amount after deducting the actual/expected disposal costs. Liabilities are recorded at their settlement values.

- **Economic value** involves recording assets at the value of keeping them in the business, i.e. not disposing of them. Assets recorded in this way are normally carried at the present value of the future discounted net cash flows. Liabilities are recorded at their discounted net present values.

Expandable text

The limitations of HCA

Introduction

Virtually everything you have studied so far in this book has been based on HCA. Under HCA, assets are recorded at the amount of cash or cash equivalents paid, or the fair value of the consideration given for them.

Liabilities are recorded at the amount of proceeds received in exchange for the obligation. This method of accounting has advantages, but it also has serious disadvantages.

Advantages of HCA

(1) Records are based on objectively verifiable amounts (actual cost of assets, etc.).

(2) It is simple and cheap.

(3) The profit concept is well understood.

(4) Within limits, historical cost figures provide a basis for comparison with the results of other companies for the same period or similar periods, with the results of the same company for previous periods and with budgets.

(5) Lack of acceptable alternatives.

Disadvantages of HCA

(1) It overstates profits when prices are rising through inflation. Several factors contribute to this. For example, if assets are retained at their original cost, depreciation is based on that cost. As inflation pushes prices up, the true value to the enterprise of the use of the asset becomes progressively more than the depreciation charge.

This disadvantage can be overcome by revaluing fixed assets. FRS 15 then requires depreciation to be based on the revalued amount.

(2) It maintains financial capital but does not maintain physical capital.

If an entity makes a profit it must necessarily have more net assets. If the whole of that profit is distributed as dividend by a company, or withdrawn by a sole trader, the entity has the same capital at the end of the year as it had at the beginning. In other words, it has maintained its financial capital. However, it will not have maintained its physical capital if prices have risen through inflation during the year, because the financial capital will not buy the same stock and other assets to enable the entity to continue operating at the same level.

(3) The balance sheet does not show the value of the entity. A balance sheet summarises the assets and liabilities of the entity, but there are several reasons why it does not represent the true value of the entity. One reason for this could be that the use of historic cost accounting means that assets are included at cost less depreciation based on that cost rather than at current value. (Another reason is, of course, that not all the assets are included in the balance sheet – internally-generated goodwill does not appear.)

(4) It provides a poor basis for assessing performance. The profit is overstated as explained in (1), while assets are understated as discussed in (3) above. The result is that return on capital employed is doubly distorted and exaggerated.

(5) It does not recognise the loss suffered through holding monetary assets while prices are rising. An entity holding cash or receivables through a period of inflation suffers a loss as their purchasing power declines.

The impact of changing prices

When prices are not changing, HCA does accurately and fairly show profits made by the entity and the value of the assets less liabilities to the entity. When prices are changing, however, there are problems.

Depreciation

Under a system of HCA, the purpose of depreciation is simply to allocate the original cost (less estimated residual value) of a fixed asset over its estimated useful economic life. If depreciation is charged in the profit and loss account, then by reducing the amount which can be paid out as a dividend, funds are retained within the company rather than paid to the shareholders. When the time comes to replace the asset, management must ensure that those funds are available in a sufficiently liquid form.

When inflation is taken into account, we can note that:

(1) The depreciation charge is based on the original cost of the asset measured in terms of historical £s, whereas the incomes against which depreciation is matched are measured in terms of current £s. The profit figure we calculate is not meaningful as it ignores price changes which have taken place since the asset was purchased.

(2) Although the concept of depreciation ensures that the capital of the entity is maintained intact in money terms, it does not ensure that the capital of the entity is maintained intact in real terms (see examples below).

The accumulated depreciation at the end of the asset's useful life will fall short of its replacement cost.

Example 1

An entity starts off with £1,000 cash and buys two machines at a cost of £500 each. All profits are distributed to the owners. At the end of ten years the company has no machines and £1,000 cash. Thus the capital of the entity has been maintained intact in money terms. Suppose at the end of ten years the current replacement cost of one machine is £1,000. Therefore the £1,000 cash at the end of the ten years will buy only one machine. In real terms, the capital at the end of the period is half that at the beginning of the period.

Profit has been over-distributed. If profit is a true surplus, the owners should be able to withdraw all the profit and be in exactly the same position as before in real terms.

Stock and cost of sales

Assume a company values stock on a historical cost basis using the first in first out (FIFO) method. During a period of inflation the effect of this method is to overstate the real profit of the entity, since sales (in current terms) are matched with cost of sales (in historical terms). If the company distributed the whole of its historical cost profit, it would not be maintaining the capital of the entity intact in real terms.

Example 2

An entity starts off on 1 January 20X7 with £1,000 cash (contributed by the proprietor). On the same day it purchases 500 motors at £2 each. These are sold on 31 March 20X7 for proceeds of £1,650. At this date the replacement cost of an identical motor is £2.20.

Under HCA the profit for the three months is £650 (£1,650 – £1,000). If the proprietor withdraws this profit, the closing balance sheet at 31 March would show capital account £1,000 represented by cash of £1,000.

Although capital has been maintained intact in money terms (it was £1,000 at 1 January), it has not been maintained intact in real terms. At 31 March, £1,000 cash will buy only 455 (approximately!) motors.

Comparability of data over time

Example 3

We saw earlier a need for users of accounts to be able to compare the results of the entity over a number of years so that trends could be identified. Thus, if sales were £100,000 four years ago and £130,000 in the current year, we could conclude that sales have increased by 30%. However, in real terms the increase may not be this amount, as price levels may have changed in the previous four years. If price levels have risen by 40% in the last four years, then the sales should be £140,000 in the current year in order to maintain the real value of sales. There has therefore been a real decline.

Test Your Understanding 2

In a time of rising prices, what effect does the use of the historical cost concept have on an entity's profit and asset values?

A   Both profit and asset values are understated.

B   Profit is understated and asset values overstated.

C   Profit is overstated and asset values understated.

D   Both profit and asset values are overstated.

8 Chapter summary

REGULATORY AND CONCEPTUAL FRAMEWORK

The regulatory framework:
- ASB produce accounting standards.
- UITF issues guidance on the interpretation of standards
- FRRP investigates accounts which may be in breach of the CA 1985.

The conceptual framework
- The framework for the preparation and presentation of accounts.

Other accounting principles
- Going concern
- Accruals
- Consistency
- Materiality
- Substance over form
- Prudence.

Objective of financial statements
- Aim to provide information about financial position and performance of an entity.

HCA
- Advantages
- Disadvantages
- Alternatives.

Qualitative characteristics
- Relevant
- Reliable
- Comparable
- Understandable.

Test your understanding answers

Test Your Understanding 1

The correct answer is A

Test Your Understanding 2

The correct answer is C

Questions

Chapter 1: Practice questions

Q 1. A sole trader business is:

A a business owned and operated by two or more people.

B a business owned by shareholders.

C a business run by directors.

D a business owned and operated by one person.

Q 2 Financial accounting is:

A the production of annual financial statements for external users.

B the production of monthly accounts.

C where managers use the accounts to plan and control on a daily basis.

D where it includes budgets and forecast information.

Chapter 2: Balance sheet and profit and loss account

Q 1 Which of the following is the accounting equation

A Assets – Liabilities – Capital = Drawings + Profit.

B Assets = Liabilities – Capital + Profit – Drawings.

C Assets – Liabilities – Capital = Profit – Drawings.

D Assets + Liabilities = Capital + Profit – Drawings.

(1 mark)

Q 2 Which of the following statements is true?

A The profit and loss account illustrates a business' financial position.

B The profit and loss account includes dividends paid.

C The profit and loss account illustrates the business' financial performance.

D The profit and loss account has to show the results for one year.

(1 mark)

Q 3 What is included in the balance sheet of a business?

A Capital, drawings, assets and liabilities.

B Capital, dividends paid, sales and assets.

C Assets, liabilities, profit on disposals of fixed assets and introduced capital.

D Dividends paid, assets, discounts and liabilities.

(1 mark)

Q **4** **Which of the following is incorrect?**

  A The balance sheet and profit and loss account form part of the financial statements of a business.

  B The balance sheet illustrates the accounting equation.

  C The profit and loss account illustrates the accounting equation.

  D The balance sheet and profit and loss account illustrate the financial position and performance of the business.

  (1 mark)

Q **5** **Which statement is not true?**

  A Stock is shown on the profit and loss account and in the balance sheet.

  B Expenses should be included on the profit and loss account.

  C Stock should be included on the balance sheet only.

  D Debtors are included in current assets on the balance sheet.

  (1 mark)

Chapter 3: Double entry bookkeeping

Q **6** **Which of the following is correct?**

  A A debit entry will increase fixed assets.
  A debit entry will increase drawings.
  A debit entry will increase profit.

  B A credit entry will increase a bank overdraft.
  A debit entry will increase creditors.
  A credit entry will increase debtors.

  C A debit entry will increase profit.
  A debit entry will increase debtors.
  A debit entry will decrease creditors.

  D A debit entry will increase debtors.
  A credit entry will decrease fixed assets.
  A credit entry will increase profit.

  (1 mark)

Q **7** **A credit balance on a ledger account indicates:**

  A an asset or an expense

  B a liability or an expense

  C an amount owing to the organisation

  D a liability or revenue

  (1 mark)

Q 8 The double entry system of bookkeeping normally results in which of the following balances on the ledger accounts?

Debit balances	Credit balances
A Assets and revenues	Liabilities, capital and expenses
B Revenues, capital and liabilities	Assets and expenses
C Assets and expenses	Liabilities, capital and revenues
D Assets, expenses and capital	Liabilities and revenues

(1 mark)

Q 9 The main aim of accounting is to:

A maintain ledger accounts for every asset and liability

B provide financial information to users of such information

C produce a trial balance

D record every financial transaction individually

(1 mark)

Q 10 A debit entry could lead to:

A an increase in assets or a decrease in expenses

B an increase in sales or an increase in liabilities

C a decrease in sales or a decrease in assets

D a decrease in liabilities or an increase in expenses

(1 mark)

Q 11 A credit entry could lead to:

A an increase in assets or increase in liabilities

B an increase in expense or an increase in share capital

C an increase in liabilities or an increase in share capital

D an increase in liabilities and a decrease in sales

(1 mark)

Chapter 4: Stock

12 **Tracey's business sells three products – A, B and C. The following information was available at the year end:**

	A £ per unit	B £ per unit	C £ per unit
Original cost	7	10	19
Estimated selling price	15	13	20
Selling and distribution costs	2	5	6
Units of stock	20	25	15

The value of stock at the year end should be:

A £675

B £670

C £795

D £550

(2 marks)

13 **A stock record card shows the following details:**

January 1   50 units in stock at a cost of £10 per unit

        4   90 units purchased at a cost of £15 per unit

     10   65 units sold

     20   30 units purchased at a cost of £20 per unit

     26   40 units sold

What is the value of stock at 31 January using the FIFO method?

A £1,125

B   £725

C   £975

D £1,000

(2 marks)

14 **What would be the effect on a business' profit, which has been calculated including stock at cost, of discovering that one of its stock items which cost £7,500 has a net realisable value of £8,500?**

A an increase of £8,500

B an increase of £1,000

C no effect at all

D a decrease of £1,000

(1 mark)

Q 15 According to SSAP9 stock and long term contracts, which of the following costs should be included in valuing the stocks of a manufacturing company?

1) Carriage outwards

2) Depreciation of factory plant

3) Carriage inwards

4) General administrative overheads

A All four items

B 1, 3 and 4 only

C 1 and 2 only

D 2 and 3 only

(1 mark)

Q 16 The closing stock of X amounted to £116,400 excluding the following two stock lines:

- 400 items which had cost £4 each. All were sold after the balance sheet date for £3 each, with selling expenses of £200 for the batch.

- 200 different items which had cost £30 each. These items were found to be defective at the balance sheet date. Rectification work after the balance sheet amounted to £1,200, after which they were sold for £35 each, with selling expenses totalling £300.

Which of the following total figures should appear in the balance sheet of X for stock?

A £122,300

B £121,900

C £122,900

D £123,300

(2 marks)

Chapter 5: Value added tax (VAT)

Q 17 All the sales of Gail, a retailer, were made at a price inclusive of VAT at the standard rate of 17.5% and all purchases and expenses bore VAT at the standard rate. For the three months ended 31 March 2005 gross sales were £23,500, purchases were £12,000 (net) and expenses £800 (net).

How much is due to the tax authority for the quarter?

A £1,260

B £1,400

C £1,594

D £1,873

(2 marks)

Q 18 **The sales account is:**

A credited with the total of sales made, including VAT

B credited with the total of sales made, excluding VAT

C debited with the total of sales made, including VAT

D debited with the total of sales made, excluding VAT

(1 mark)

Q 19 **If sales (including VAT) amounted to £27,612.50 and purchases (excluding VAT) amounted to £18,000, the balance on the VAT account, assuming all items are subject to VAT at 17.5%, would be:**

A £962.50 debit

B £962.50 credit

C £1,682.10 debit

D £1,682.10 credit

(2 marks)

Q 20 **A business commenced with capital in cash of £1,000. Stock costing £800 net of VAT at 17.5% is purchased on credit. Half of this stock is then sold for £1,000 plus VAT, the customer paying promptly in cash.**

The accounting equation after these transactions would show:

A assets £1,775 less liabilities £175 equals capital £1,600

B assets £2,775 less liabilities £975 equals capital £1,200

C assets £2,575 less liabilities £800 equals capital £1,775

D assets £2,575 less liabilities £975 equals capital £1,600

(2 marks)

Chapter 6: Accruals and prepayments

Q 21 **The electricity account for the year ended 30 April 2005 was as follows:**

	£
Electricity accrued at 1 May 2004	250
Payments made during the year in relation to:	
Quarter ending 30 June 2004	400
Quarter ending 30 September 2004	350
Quarter ending 31 December 2004	425
Quarter ending 31 March 2005	450

Which of the following is the appropriate entry for electricity?

	Accrued at 30 April 2005	Charge to profit and loss account for year ended 30 April 2005
A	£Nil	£1,375
B	£150	£1,525
C	£300	£1,675
D	£450	£1,825

(2 marks)

Q 22 The year end of Lansdown is 31 December. The company pays for its electricity by a standing order of £100 per month. On
1 January 2005 the statement from the electricity supplier showed that the company had overpaid by £25. Lansdown received electricity bills for the four quarters starting on 1 January 2005 and ending on 31 December 2005 for £350, £375, £275 and
£300 respectively.

Which of the following is the correct entry for electricity in Lansdown's profit and loss account and balance sheet for the year ending 31 December 2005?

Profit and loss account	Balance sheet
A £1,300	£75 accrual
B £1,300	£75 prepayment
C £1,200	£125 accrual
D £1,200	£125 prepayment

(2 marks)

Q 23 At 1 January 2005, Michael had a prepayment of £200 in respect of rent. He paid £1,200 on 1 March 2005 in respect of the year ended 28 February 2006.

What is the charge to the profit and loss account in respect of rent for the year ended 31 December 2005?

A £1,400

B £1,200

C £1,100

D £1,300

(1 mark)

Q 24 At 31 December 2003, Tony had accrued £240 in respect of light and heat for the quarter ending 31 December 2003. In January 2004 he discovered that he had under-accrued by £10.

The bills for the next four quarters were as follows (q.e. = quarter ended):

Amount	Relating to	Date paid
£260	q.e. 31 March 2004	15 April 2004
£220	q.e. 30 June 2004	17 July 2004
£210	q.e. 30 September 2004	14 October 2004
£230	q.e. 31 December 2004	19 January 2005

Tony always accrues for expenses based on the last bill.

What is the charge to the profit and loss account in respect of light and heat for the 15-month period ended 31 March 2005?

A £1,160

B £1,150

C £930

D £920

(2 marks)

Q 25 Stationery paid for during the year amounted to £1,350. At the beginning of the year there was a stock of stationery on hand of £165 and an outstanding stationery invoice for £80. At the end of the year there was a stock of stationery on hand of £140 and an outstanding stationery invoice for £70. The stationery figure to be shown in the profit and loss account for the year is:

A £1,195

B £1,335

C £1,365

D £1,505

(1 mark)

Chapter 7: Bad and doubtful debts

Q 26 At 30 April 2005, Gareth has a debtors balance of £50,000 and a provision for doubtful debts of £800. Following a review of debtors, Gareth wishes to write off a bad debt of £1,000 and adjust his provision to 5% of debtors.

What will be the adjusted balance of the provision for doubtful debts account?

A £1,650

B £2,450

C £2,500

D £3,450

(1 mark)

Q 27 As at 31 March, Phil had debtors of £82,500. Following a review of debtors, Phil has decided to write off the following bad debts:

John	£1,000
Beatrice	£500
Peter	£3,250

Phil would like to provide against a specific debt of £250 and based on past experience, make a general provision at 2% of debtors. The current balance on the provision for doubtful debts account is £2,000. Phil also received £300 from a debt that had been previously been written off.

What is the charge to the profit and loss account in respect of bad debt expense and the entry on the balance sheet for debtors at 31 March?

	Profit and loss account charge	Balance sheet
A	£4,250	£75,950
B	£4,450	£77,750
C	£4,450	£75,950
D	£4,250	£77,750

(2 marks)

KAPLAN PUBLISHING

Q 28 At the start of the year Joe had a provision of £700 against debtors. During the year £450 of this amount went bad and £150 was received; the balance remained unpaid at the year end. Another amount of £170 went bad. At the year end it was decided to provide for a new debt of £240.

What was the total bad debt expense for the year?

A £170

B £260

C £410

D £710

(2 marks)

Q 29 Doris currently has a debtors balance of £47,800 and a provision for doubtful debts of £1,250. She has received £150 in respect of half of a debt that she had provided against. She now believes the other half of the debt to be bad and wishes to write it off. She also wishes to maintain her provision at 2% of debtors.

What is the total charge to the profit and loss account in respect of these items?

A £150 debit

B £150 credit

C £300 debit

D £300 credit

(2 marks)

Q 30 At the year end, Harold has a debtors balance of £100,000 and a provision for doubtful debts of £5,000. He has not yet accounted for a receipt of £500 in respect of a debt which he had previously provided against or a receipt of £1,000 in respect of a debt which had been written off in the previous year. Harold wishes to maintain his provision for doubtful debts at 7% of debtors.

What balances will be shown in his balance sheet at the year end for debtors and the provision for doubtful debts?

	Debtors	Provision for doubtful debts
A	£98,500	£6,465
B	£99,500	£6,465
C	£98,500	£6,965
D	£99,500	£6,965

(2 marks)

Q 31 James has been advised that one of his customers has ceased trading and that it is almost certain that he will not recover the balance of £720 owed by this customer.

What entry should James make in his general ledger?

A	Dr Debtors	£720
	Cr Bad debt expense	£720
	Being write off of bad debt	
B	Dr Bad debt expense	£720
	Cr Debtors	£720
	Being write off of bad debt	
C	Dr Debtors	£720
	Cr Bank	£720
	Being write off of bad debt	
D	Dr Bank	£720
	Cr Debtors	£720
	Being write off of bad debt.	

(1 mark)

Q 32 Gordon's debtors owe a total of £80,000 at the year end. These include £900 of long-overdue debts that might still be recoverable, but for which Gordon has created a provision for doubtful debts. Gordon has also provided £1,582, which is the equivalent of 2% of the other debtors' balances.

What best describes Gordon's provision for doubtful debts as at his year end?

A a specific provision of £900 and a general provision of £1,582 based on past history

B a specific provision of £1,582 and a general provision of £900 based on past history

C a specific provision of £2,482

D a general provision of £2,482

(1 mark)

Chapter 8: Fixed assets

Q 33 At 1 January 2005, Mary has motor vehicles which cost £15,000. On 31 August 2005 she sells a motor vehicle for £5,000 which had originally cost £8,000 and which had a NBV of £4,000 at the date of disposal. She purchased a new motor vehicle which cost £10,000 on 30 November 2005.

Her policy is to depreciate motor vehicles at a rate of 25% pa on the straight-line basis, based on the number of months' ownership.

What is the depreciation charge for the year ended 31 December 2005?

A £3,750

B £3,291

C £4,250

D £3,500

(2 marks)

Q 34 Which of the following best explains what is meant by 'capital expenditure'?

A expenditure on fixed assets, including repairs and maintenance

B expenditure on expensive assets

C expenditure relating to the issue of share capital

D expenditure relating to the acquisition or improvement of fixed assets

(1 mark)

Q 35 A fixed asset was purchased at the beginning of Year 1 for £2,400 and depreciated by 20% pa by the reducing-balance method. At the beginning of Year 4 it was sold for £1,200. The result of this was:

A a loss on disposal of £240.00

B a loss on disposal of £28.80

C a profit on disposal of £28.80

D a profit on disposal of £240.00

(2 marks)

Q 36 Giles bought a new machine from abroad. The machine cost £100,000 and delivery and installation costs were £7,000. Testing it amounted to £5,000. Training employees on how to use the machine cost of £1,000.

What should be the cost of the machine in the company's balance sheet?

A £100,000

B £107,000

C £112,000

D £113,000

(1 mark)

Q 37 Joseph's machinery cost account showed a balance of £5,000 at
1 January 2005. During the year he had the following transactions:

28 February	Disposed of machine costing £300
31 March	Acquired machine costing £1,000
1 November	Disposed of machine costing £600

Joseph depreciates machines at a rate of 10% pa on the straight-line basis based on the number of months' ownership.

What is the depreciation charge in respect of machinery for the year ended 31 December 2005?

A £545

B £540

C £510

D £630

(2 marks)

Q 38 B acquired a lorry on 1 May 20X0 at a cost of £30,000. The lorry has an estimated useful life of four years, and an estimated resale value at the end of that time of £6,000. B charges depreciation on the straight-line basis, with a proportionate charge in the period of acquisition.

What will the depreciation charge for the lorry be in B's ten-month accounting period to 30 September 20X0?

A £3,000

B £2,500

C £2,000

D £5,000

(1 mark)

Q

Chapter 9: From trial balance to financial statements

The following is the extract of Jessie's trial balance as at 31 December 2005:

	Dr £	Cr £
Buildings	580,000	
Buildings accumulated depreciation		116,000
Plant and machinery	50,000	
Plant and machinery accumulated depreciation		12,500
Debtors	25,800	
Provision for doubtful debts		1,900
Rent	34,000	
Insurance	30,000	
Bad debt expense	1,800	

The following notes are provided:

(i)   Buildings are depreciated at 2% pa on a straight-line basis.

(ii) Plant and machinery is depreciated at 25% pa on a reducing-balance basis.

(iii) Additional bad debts of £3,200 were discovered at the year end. It has been decided to make a provision for doubtful debts of 5% on the adjusted debtors at the year end.

(iv) The monthly rental charge is £3,000.

(v)   The insurance charge for the year is £24,000.

Using the above information attempt the following questions 39 to 42.

....

Q

39 The depreciation charge for buildings for the year and the net book value (NBV) at the year end will be:

	Depreciation charge £	NBV £
A	11,600	568,400
B	9,280	464,000
C	11,600	452,400
D	11,600	464,000

(2 marks)

Q **40** The depreciation charge for plant and machinery for the year and the NBV at the year end will be:

	Depreciation charge £	NBV £
A	9,375	37,500
B	12,500	25,000
C	9,375	40,625
D	9,375	28,125

(2 marks)

Q **41** The total bad debt expense for the year and the closing debtors balance will be:

	Bad debt expense £	Debtors £
A	4,230	21,470
B	5,000	21,470
C	5,770	21,830
D	2,430	19,670

(2 marks)

Q **42** What is the charge for rent and insurance for the year and the closing accrual and prepayment?

	Charge for the year	£	Closing accrual/prepayment	£
A	Rent	30,000	Rent accrual	3,000
	Insurance	24,000	Insurance prepayment	6,000
B	Rent	36,000	Rent accrual	2,000
	Insurance	24,000	Insurance prepayment	6,000
C	Rent	36,000	Rent accrual	3,000
	Insurance	24,000	Insurance prepayment	6,000
D	Rent	30,000	Rent accrual	3,000
	Insurance	30,000	Insurance prepayment	6,000

(2 marks)

Chapter 10: Books of prime entry and control accounts

Q 43 Which of the following is not the purpose of a sales ledger control account?

A A sales ledger control account provides a check on the arithmetic accuracy of the debtors ledger.

B A sales ledger control account helps to locate errors in the trial balance.

C A sales ledger control account ensures that there are no errors in the debtors ledger.

D Control accounts deter fraud.

(1 mark)

Q 44 Which one of the following is a book of prime entry and part of the double-entry system?

A the journal

B the petty cash book

C the sales day book

D the purchase ledger

(1 mark)

Q 45 On 1 January 2005 the balance of debtors was £22,000. Calculate the closing debtors after taking the following into consideration:

	£
Sales	120,000
Bank receipts	115,000
Discount allowed	1,000
Discount received	3,000
Dishonoured cheque	9,000
Contra – Set off	5,000

A £30,000

B £23,000

C £12,000

D £28,000

(1 mark)

Chapter 11: Control account reconciliations

Q **46** A sales ledger control account had a closing balance of £8,500. It contained a contra to the purchase ledger of £400, but this had been entered on the wrong side of the control account.

The correct balance on the control account should be:

A £7,700 debit

B £8,100 debit

C £8,400 debit

D £8,900 debit

(1 mark)

Q **47** The sales ledger control account at 1 May had balances of £32,750 debit and £1,275 credit. During May sales of £125,000 were made on credit. Receipts from debtors amounted to £122,500 and cash discounts of £550 were allowed. Refunds of £1,300 were made to customers. The closing credit balance is £2,000.

The closing debit balances at 31 May should be:

A £35,175

B £35,675

C £36,725

D £34,725

(1 mark)

Q **48** A supplier sends you a statement showing a balance outstanding of £14,350. Your own records show a balance outstanding of £14,500.

The reason for this difference could be that:

A The supplier sent an invoice for £150 which you have not yet received.

B The supplier has allowed you £150 cash discount which you had omitted to enter in your ledgers.

C You have paid the supplier £150 which he has not yet accounted for.

D You have returned goods worth £150 which the supplier has not yet accounted for.

(1 mark)

Q 49 A credit balance of £917 brought forward on Y's account in the books of X means that:

A X owes Y £917

B Y owes X £917

C X has paid Y £917

D X is owed £917 by Y

(1 mark)

Q 50 In a sales ledger control account, which of the following lists is composed only of items which would appear on the credit side of the account?

A Cash received from customers, sales returns, bad debts written off, contras against amounts due to suppliers in the creditors ledger

B Sales, cash refunds to customers, bad debts written off, discounts allowed

C Cash received from customers, discounts allowed, interest charged on overdue accounts, bad debts written off

D Sales, cash refunds to customers, interest charged on overdue accounts, contras against amounts due to suppliers in the creditors ledger.

(1 mark)

Chapter 12: Bank reconciliations

Q 51 The following information relates to a bank reconciliation.

(i) The bank balance in the cash book before taking the items below into account was £5,670 overdrawn.

(ii) Bank charges of £250 on the bank statement have not been entered in the cash book.

(iii) The bank has credited the account in error with £40 which belongs to another customer.

(iv) Cheque payments totalling £325 have been correctly entered in the cash book but have not been presented for payment.

(v) Cheques totalling £545 have been correctly entered on the debit side of the cash book but have not been paid in at the bank.

What was the balance as shown by the bank statement before taking the items above into account?

A £5,670 overdrawn

B £5,600 overdrawn

C £5,740 overdrawn

D £6,100 overdrawn

(2 marks)

Q 52 At 31 August 2005 the balance on the company's cash book was £3,600 credit. Examination of the bank statements revealed the following:

- Standing orders amounting to £180 had not been recorded in the cash book.
- Cheques paid to suppliers of £1,420 did not appear on the bank statements.

What was the balance on the bank statement at 31 August 2005?

A £5,200 overdrawn

B £5,020 overdrawn

C £2,360 overdrawn

D £3,780 overdrawn

(1 mark)

Q 53 An organisation's cash book has an operating balance of £485 credit. The following transactions then took place:

- cash sales £1,450 including VAT of £150
- receipts from customers of debts of £2,400
- payments to creditors of £1,800 less 5% cash discount
- dishonoured cheques from customers amounting to £250.

The resulting balance in the bank column of the cash book should be:

A £1,255 debit

B £1,405 debit

C £1,905 credit

D £2,375 credit

(2 marks)

Q 54 The cash book shows a bank balance of £5,675 overdrawn at 31 March 2005. It is subsequently discovered that a standing order for £125 has been entered twice and that a dishonoured cheque for £450 has been debited in the cash book instead of credited.

The correct bank balance should be:

A £5,100 overdrawn

B £6,000 overdrawn

C £6,250 overdrawn

D £6,450 overdrawn

(1 mark)

55 The attempt below at a bank reconciliation statement has been prepared by Q Limited. Assuming the bank statement balance of £38,600 to be correct, what should the cash book balance be?

A £76,500 overdrawn, as stated

B £5,900 overdrawn

C £700 overdrawn

D £5,900 cash at bank

	£
Overdraft per bank statement	38,600
Add: deposits not credited	41,200
	79,800
Less: outstanding cheques	3,300
Overdraft per cash book	76,500

(1 mark)

56 After checking a business cash book against the bank statement, which of the following items could require an entry in the cash book?

1 Bank charges

2 A cheque from a customer which was dishonoured

3 Cheque not presented

4 Deposits not credited

5 Credit transfer entered in bank statement

6 Standing order entered in bank statement.

A 1, 2, 5 and 6

B 3 and 4

C 1, 3, 4 and 6

D 3, 4, 5 and 6

(1 mark)

Chapter 13: Correction of errors and suspense accounts

57 Faulty goods costing £210 were returned to a supplier but this was recorded as £120 in the ledger accounts.

What is the journal entry necessary to correct the error?

	Dr	£	Cr	£
A	Suspense	90	Purchases returns	90
B	Purchases	90	Creditors	90
C	Creditors	90	Suspense	90
D	Creditors	90	Purchases returns	90

(1 mark)

Q 58 A suspense account was opened when a trial balance failed to agree. The following errors were later discovered:

- a gas bill of £420 had been recorded in the gas account as £240

- discount of £50 given to a customer had been credited to discounts received

- interest received of £70 had been entered in the bank account only.

The original balance on the suspense account was:

A debit £210

B credit £210

C debit £160

D credit £160

(2 marks)

Q 59 Molly starts up in business as a florist on 1 April 2004. For the first six months, she has a draft profit of £12,355.
On investigation you discover the following:

- Rent paid for the 12 months ending 31 March 2005 of £800 has not been recorded in the accounts.

- Closing stock in the accounts at a cost of £1,000 has a net realisable value of £800.

What is the adjusted profit for the period?

A £11,355

B £11,755

C £12,155

D £12,555

(1 mark)

Q 60 In an accounting system where individual debtors and creditors ledger accounts are maintained as an integral part of the double entry, which of the following errors will not be identified by a trial balance?

A overcasting of the sales day book

B undercasting of the analysed cash book

C failure to transfer a fixed asset to the disposal account when sold

D transposition error in an individual debtors account

(1 mark)

Q 61 A trial balance has been extracted and a suspense account opened. One error relates to the misposting of an amount of £400, being discount received from suppliers, which was posted to the wrong side of the discount received account

What is the correcting journal entry?

		Dr	Cr
A	Discount received	£400	
	Suspense		£400
B	Suspense	£400	
	Discount received		£400
C	Discount received	£800	
	Suspense		£800
D	Suspense	£800	
	Discount received		£800

(1 mark)

Q 62 A company, Y, purchased some plant on 1 January 20X0 for £38,000. The payment for the plant was correctly entered in the cash book but was entered on the debit side of plant repairs account.

Y charges depreciation on the straight-line basis at 20% pa, with a proportionate charge in the year of acquisition and assuming no scrap value at the end of the life of the asset.

How will Y's profit for the year ended 31 March 20X0 be affected by the error?

A Understated by £30,400

B Understated by £36,100

C Understated by £38,000

D Overstated by £1,900

(2 marks)

Q **63 The trial balance of Z failed to agree, the totals being:**

Debit   £836,200

Credit   £819,700

A suspense account was opened for the amount of the difference and the following errors were found and corrected:

1 The totals of the cash discount columns in the cash book had not been posted to the discount accounts. The figures were discount allowed £3,900 and discount received £5,100.

2 A cheque for £19,000 received from a customer was correctly entered in the cash book but was posted to the customer's account as £9,100.

What will the remaining balance on the suspense account be after the correction of these errors?

A £25,300 credit

B £7,700 credit

C £27,700 credit

D £5,400 credit

(2 marks)

Q **64 The trial balance of C did not agree, and a suspense account was opened for the difference. Checking in the bookkeeping system revealed a number of errors.**

1 £4,600 paid for motor van repairs was correctly treated in the cash book but was credited to motor vehicles asset account.

2 £360 received from B, a customer, was credited in error to the account of BB.

3 £9,500 paid for rent was debited to the rent account as £5,900.

4 The total of the discount allowed column in the cash book had been debited in error to the discounts received account.

5 No entries had been made to record a cash sale of £100.

Which of the errors above would require an entry to the suspense account as part of the process of correcting them?

A 3 and 4

B 1 and 3

C 2 and 5

D 2 and 3

(2 marks)

questions

Chapter 14: Applications of IT

Q 65 **Which of the following is not a quality of information?**

   A Accuracy

   B Colourfulness

   C Cost effectiveness

   D Timeliness

(1 mark)

Q 66 **Match the different types of input device listed in column 1 with the relevant applications listed in column 2.**

Column 1

Optical mark reader

Bar code reader

Scanner

Optical character recognition

Column 2

Cheque processing

Examination answer sheets

Capturing images

Point of sale systems

(1 mark)

Q 67 **'User friendly' is an expression which is used to describe functionality which has been designed specifically to make the system easier to use for those who are not IT-trained. Both hardware and software features can be considered.**

Which of the following is an example of hardware user friendliness (the others are examples of software)?

   A Icon

   B Touch screen

   C Pull down list

   D Default value

(1 mark)

Chapter 15: Incomplete records

Q 68 **Ashley started a business on 1 January 2005. He acquired the following assets:**

Van	£2,000
Stock	£1,000
Debtors	£500
Prepaid insurance for stock	£100

He also opened a business bank account and paid in £4,000. At the end of the first year of trading, he had the following:

Van	£1,800
Fixtures	£500
Stock	£840
Debtors	£600
Creditors	£400
Cash	£3,400

He had drawn £1,000 in cash during the period.

What was Ashley's profit or loss for the year?

A £140 loss

B £140 profit

C £1,860 loss

D £1,860 profit

(2 marks)

Q 69 **George started a business by investing £10,000 into a business bank account. At the end of his first year's trading he had earned a profit of £5,000 and had the following assets and liabilities:**

Fixed assets	£20,000
Current assets	£15,000
Current liabilities	£8,000

During the year he had withdrawn £2,000 from the business.

How much further capital had he introduced in the year?

A £20,000

B £24,000

C £10,000

D £14,000

(1 mark)

Q 70 If Harry's mark-up on cost of sales is 15%, what is his gross profit margin?

A 12.5%

B 13.04%

C 15%

D 17.65%

(1 mark)

Q 71 A sole trader had opening capital of £10,000 and closing capital of £4,500. During the period the owner introduced capital of £4,000 and withdrew £8,000 for her own use.

Her profit or loss during the period was:

A £9,500 loss

B £1,500 loss

C £7,500 profit

D £17,500 profit

(1 mark)

Q 72 From the following information, calculate the value of purchases:

	£
Opening creditors	142,600
Cash paid	542,300
Discounts received	13,200
Goods returned	27,500
Closing creditors	137,800

A £302,600

B £506,400

C £523,200

D £578,200

(2 marks)

Q

73 Carol owns a shop. The only information available for the year ended 31 December 2005 is as follows:

Stock at 1 January 2005	£3,500
Stock at 31 December 2005	£1,350
Sales	£17,000
Gross profit margin	25%

What were the purchases of the shop for the year?

A £11,450

B £12,750

C £14,900

D £10,600

(1 mark)

Q

74 The following information is relevant to the calculation of the sales figure for Alpha, a sole trader who does not keep proper accounting records:

	£
Opening debtors	29,100
Cash received from credit customers and paid into the bank	381,600
Expenses paid out of cash received from credit customers before banking	6,800
Bad debts written off	7,200
Refunds to credit customers	2,100
Discounts allowed to credit customers	9,400
Cash sales	112,900
Closing debtors	38,600

The figure which should appear in Alpha's profit and loss account for sales is:

A £525,300

B £511,700

C £529,500

D £510,900

(2 marks)

Q 75 A sole trader who does not keep full accounting records wishes to calculate her sales revenue for the year.

The information available is:

1 Opening stock   £17,000

2 Closing stock   £24,000

3 Purchases   £91,000

4 Standard gross profit percentage   40% on sales revenue

Which of the following is the sales revenue figure for the year calculated from these figures?

A £117,600

B £108,000

C £210,000

D £140,000

(1 mark)

Q 76 A business compiling its accounts for the year to 31 January each year pays rent quarterly in advance on 1 January, 1 April, 1 July and 1 October each year. After remaining unchanged for some years, the rent was increased from £24,000 per year to £30,000 per year as from 1 July 20X0.

Which of the following figures is the rent expense which should appear in the profit and loss account for the year ended 31 January 20X1?

A £27,500

B £29,500

C £28,000

D £29,000

(1 mark)

Q 77 On 31 December 20X0 the stock of V was completely destroyed by fire. The following information is available:

1 Stock at 1 December 20X0 at cost £28,400.

2 Purchases for December 20X0 £49,600.

3 Sales for December 20X0 £64,800.

4 Standard gross profit percentage on sales revenue 30%.

Based on this information, which of the following is the amount of stock destroyed?

A £45,360

B £32,640

C £40,971

D £19,440

(2 marks)

Chapter 16 : Partnerships

Q 78 Alf, Ben, Connie and Dora are in partnership. The capital they have invested in the partnership is £45,000, £30,000, £20,000 and £15,000 respectively. Their partnership agreement states the following terms:

- Interest is to be allowed on capital at a rate of 10% pa.
- Connie and Dora are to receive salaries of £5,000 each.
- Any remaining profits are to be shared in the ratio 4:3:2:1 respectively.

In the year ended 31 December 2005, the partnership earned profits of £56,000.

What is the total share of the profits each partner is entitled to in the year ended 31 December 2005?

	Alf	Ben	Connie	Dora
A	£14,000	£14,000	£14,000	£14,000
B	£22,400	£16,800	£11,200	£5,600
C	£22,500	£16,500	£11,000	£6,000
D	£18,500	£13,500	£14,000	£10,000

(2 marks)

Q 79 Warren, Hall and Oates are in partnership. In the year ended 31 December 2005 the partners received the following shares of the profits:

	Warren	Hall	Oates
Interest on capital	£5,200	£4,940	£4,550
Remaining share of profits	£12,656	£9,492	£3,164
Total	£17,856	£14,432	£7,714

The capital accounts of Warren, Hall and Oates were £40,000, £38,000 and £35,000 respectively.

Which of the following best describes the terms for appropriating profits in the partnership?

A Interest on capital at 13%, PSR of 4:3:1

B Interest on capital at 10%, PSR of 4:3:1

C Interest on capital at 13%, PSR of 3:2:1

D Interest on capital at 10%, PSR of 3:2:1

(2 marks)

Q **80** Alpha, Beta and Gamma are in partnership. The profits of the partnership for the year ended 30 June 2005 have currently been appropriated as follows:

Alpha   £30,000
Beta   £10,000
Gamma   £8,000

The partnership agreement states that Beta is entitled to a guaranteed minimum profit share (GMPS) of £14,000. The profit sharing ratio is 3:2:1.

What share of the profits is each partner entitled to in the year ended 30 June 2005?

	Alpha	Beta	Gamma
A	£30,000	£14,000	£8,000
B	£27,000	£14,000	£7,000
C	£26,000	£14,000	£8,000
D	£28,000	£14,000	£6,000

(2 marks)

Q **81** D, E and F are in partnership, sharing profits in the ratio 5:3:2 respectively, after charging salaries for E and F of £24,000 each per year.

On 1 July 20X0 they agreed to change the profit-sharing ratio to 3:1:1 and increase E's salary to £36,000 per year, F's salary continuing unchanged.

For the year ended 31 December 20X0 the partnership profit amounted to £480,000.

Which of the following correctly states the partners' total profit shares for the year?

	D	E	F
A	£234,000	£136,800	£109,200
B	£213,000	£157,800	£109,200
C	£186,000	£171,600	£122,400
D	£237,600	£132,000	£110,400

(2 marks)

Q 82 J and K are in partnership sharing profits and losses in the ratio of 4:1. They decide to admit L to the partnership. The new partnership ratio is to be 4:3:3. At the time of admission of L goodwill is valued at £80,000. It has been decided not to maintain a goodwill account.

What is the overall net double entry in the capital accounts of the partners for the adjustment of goodwill after admission of L is taken into account?

A	Dr Capital a/c – J	£32,000
	Cr Capital a/c – K	£8,000
	Cr Capital a/c – L	£24,000
B	Dr Capital a/c – K	£8,000
	Dr Capital a/c – L	£24,000
	Cr Capital a/c – J	£32,000
C	Dr Capital a/c – K	£24,000
	Dr Capital a/c – L	£32,000
	Cr Capital a/c – J	£8,000
D	Dr Capital a/c – K	£0
	Dr Capital a/c – L	£42,000
	Cr Capital a/c – J	£32,000

(2 marks)

Chapter 17: Company accounts

Q 83 Geese's trial balance shows an overprovision in respect of corporation tax for the year ended 31 December 2004 of £5,000. Geese estimates that tax liability in respect of the year ended 31 December 2005 will be £23,000.

What is the tax charge in Geese's profit and loss account and the balance sheet entry for the year ended 31 December 2005?

	Profit and loss account charge	Balance sheet liability
A	£5,000	£18,000
B	£23,000	£18,000
C	£18,000	£23,000
D	£28,000	£23,000

(1 mark)

Q 84 The correct journal entry to record the issue of 100,000 50p shares (fully paid) at an issue price of £2.50 a share is:

			£	£
A	Dr	Bank	250,000	
	Cr	Share capital		100,000
	Cr	Share premium		150,000
B	Dr	Bank	250,000	
	Cr	Share capital		50,000
	Cr	Share premium		200,000
C	Dr	Bank	50,000	
	Cr	Share premium		50,000
D	Dr	Share capital	100,000	
	Dr	Share premium	150,000	
	Cr	Bank		250,000

(1 mark)

Q 85 A company has the following share capital:

	Authorised	Issued
	£000	£000
25p ordinary shares	8,000	4,000
6% 50p preference shares	2,000	1,000

In addition to providing for the year's preference dividend, an ordinary dividend of 2p per share is to be paid.

What are total dividends for the year?

A £140,000

B £380,000

C £440,000

D £760,000

(1 mark)

Q 86 Revenue reserves are:

A accumulated and undistributed profits of a company

B amounts which cannot be distributed as dividends

C amounts set aside out of profits to replace revenue items

D amounts set aside out of profits for a specific purpose

(1 mark)

Q 87 On 1 April 2004 the balance on B's accumulated profit account was £50,000 credit. The balance on 31 March 2005 was £100,000 credit. On 10 March 2005 dividends of £50,000 were declared in respect of the year ended 31 March 2005, payable on 31 May 2005.

Based on this information, profit after tax (but before dividends) for the year ended 31 March 2005 was:

A Nil

B £50,000

C £100,000

D £150,000

(1 mark)

Chapter 18: Accounting standards

Q 88 Jackson's year end is 31 December 2005. In February 2006 a major credit customer went into liquidation and the directors have suspicions that they will not be able to recover the £450,000 owed to them.

How should this item be treated in the financial statements of Jackson for the year ended 31 December 2005?

A The bad debt should be disclosed by note.

B The financial statements are not affected.

C The debt should be provided against.

D The financial statements should be adjusted to reflect the bad debt.

(1 mark)

Q 89 A former employee is claiming compensation of £50,000 from Harriot, a limited liability company. The company's solicitors have stated that they believe that the claim is unlikely to succeed. The legal costs relating to the claim are likely to be in the region of £5,000 and will be incurred regardless of whether or not the claim is successful.

How should these items be treated in the financial statements of Harriot Ltd?

A Provision should be made for £55,000.

B Provision should be made for £50,000 and the legal costs should be disclosed by note.

C Provision should be made for £5,000 and the compensation of £50,000 should be disclosed by note.

D No provisions should be made but both items should be disclosed by note.

(1 mark)

Q 90 Cowper has spent £20,000 researching new cleaning chemicals in the year ended 31 December 2005. It has also spent £40,000 developing a new cleaning product which will not go into commercial production until next year. The development project meets the criteria laid down in SSAP 13.

How should these costs be treated in the financial statements of Cowper for the year ended 31 December 2005?

A £60,000 should be capitalised as an intangible asset on the balance sheet.

B £40,000 should be capitalised as an intangible asset and should be amortised; £20,000 should be written off to the profit and loss account.

C £40,000 should be capitalised as an intangible asset and should not be amortised; £20,000 should be written off to the profit and loss account.

D £60,000 should be written off to the profit and loss account.

(1 mark)

Q 91 The directors of ABC estimated that stock which had cost £50,000 had a net realisable value of £40,000 at 30 June 2005 and recorded it in the financial statements for the year ended 30 June 2005 at this lower value in accordance with SSAP9. They have since found out that the net realisable value of the stock is only likely to be £30,000.

What adjustments, if any, should be made in the financial statements in respect of this stock?

A No adjustments required.

B Increase the value of stock by £10,000.

C Decrease the value of stock by £10,000.

D Decrease the value of stock by £20,000.

(1 mark)

Q **92** **Which of the following items are non-adjusting items per FRS 21?**

(a) the issue of new share or loan capital

(b) financial consequences of losses of fixed assets or stock as a result of fires or floods

(c) information regarding the value of stock sold at less than cost thus resulting in a reduction in the value of stock

(d) mergers and acquisitions

(e) bankruptcy of a credit customer

A (a), (b) and (d)

B (c) and (e)

C (a), (d) and (e)

D (b), (c) and (e)

(1 mark)

Q **93** **Which of the following correctly describes how research and development expenditure should be treated in accordance with SSAP 13?**

A Research and development expenditure must be written off to the profit and loss account as incurred.

B Research and development expenditure should be capitalised as an intangible asset on the balance sheet.

C Research expenditure should be written off to the profit and loss account; development expenditure must be capitalised as an intangible asset provided that certain criteria are met.

D Research expenditure should be capitalised as an intangible asset provided that certain criteria are met; development expenditure should be written off to the profit and loss account.

(1 mark)

Q **94** **Who issues Financial Reporting Standards?**

A The Auditing Practices Board

B The Stock Exchange

C The Accounting Standards Board

D The government

(1 mark)

Q **95** Which of the following statements concerning the accounting treatment of research and development expenditure are true, according to SSAP 13 Intangible Assets?

1 If certain criteria are met, research expenditure may be recognised as an asset.

2 Research expenditure, other than capital expenditure on research facilities, should be recognised as an expense as incurred.

3 In deciding whether development expenditure qualifies to be recognised as an asset, it is necessary to consider whether there will be adequate finance available to complete the project.

4 Development expenditure recognised as an asset must be amortised over a period not exceeding five years.

5 The financial statements should disclose the total amount of research and development expenditure recognised as an expense during the period.

A 1, 4 and 5

B 2, 4 and 5

C 2, 3 and 4

D 2, 3 and 5

(2 marks)

Q **96** FRS 21 Events after the Balance Sheet Date regulates the extent to which events after the balance sheet date should be reflected in financial statements.

Which of the following lists of such events consists only of items that, according to FRS 21 should normally be classified as non-adjusting?

A Insolvency of a debtor whose account balance was outstanding at the balance sheet date, issue of shares or loan notes, a major merger with another company.

B Issue of shares or loan notes, changes in foreign exchange rates, major purchases of fixed assets.

C A major merger with another company, destruction of a major fixed asset by fire, discovery of fraud or error which shows that the financial statements were incorrect.

D Sale of stock giving evidence about its value at the balance sheet date, issue of shares or loan notes, destruction of a major fixed asset by fire.

(2 marks)

Chapter 19: Cash flow statements

Q 97 In the year ended 31 December 2005, Lamb bought new vehicles from Warwick Motors with a list price of £100,000 for £70,000 cash and an allowance against old motor vehicles of £30,000. The value of the vehicles taken in part exchange was £27,000.

Lamb sold other vehicles with a net book value of £12,000 for £15,000 cash.

In Lamb's cash flow statement for the year ended 31 December 2005, how would the above transactions be presented under the heading 'Investing activities'?

	Cash inflow	Cash outflow
A	–	£76,000
B	£45,000	£100,000
C	£15,000	£70,000
D	£15,000	£100,000

(2 marks)

Q 98 **Baldrick has the following balances in its balance sheet as at 30 June 2004 and 30 June 2005:**

	30 June 2005 £	30 June 2004 £
Current liabilities		
Taxation payable	600	400
Dividends (declared before the year end)	3,300	2,500
Fixed liabilities		
8% Loan notes	50,000	40,000
Capital and reserves		
Accumulated profits	65,500	45,500

In the year ended 30 June 2005 taxation of £550 was paid. The additional loan notes were issued on 30 June 2005.

What is the operating profit of Baldrick for the year ended 30 June 2005?

A £27,250

B £26,450

C £28,050

D £27,100

(2 marks)

Q 99 At 31 December 2004, Topaz had provided £50,000 in respect of corporation tax. At 31 December 2005, the company estimated that its corporation tax bill in respect of the year would be £57,000. The amount charged in the profit and loss account for the year ended 31 December 2005 in respect of corporation tax was £60,000.

How much will appear in the cash flow statement for the year ended 31 December 2005 in respect of corporation tax?

A £50,000

B £53,000

C £57,000

D £60,000

(1 mark)

Q 100 Evans had the following balances in its balance sheets as at 30 June 2004 and 2005:

	2004	2005
10% Loan notes	£150,000	£130,000
Share capital	£100,000	£120,000
Share premium	£35,000	£45,000

How much will appear in the cash flow statement for the year ended 30 June 2005 under the heading of 'Financing activities'?

A £nil

B £10,000 inflow

C £30,000 inflow

D £40,000 inflow

(1 mark)

The following information relates to Questions 101 and 102.

Scents had the following balances in its balance sheets as at 30 September 2004 and 2005:

	2004	2005
Loan interest accrual	£5,000	£3,000
Proposed ordinary dividends	£20,000	£25,000
10% Loan notes	£100,000	£100,000
Ordinary share capital	£150,000	£150,000
8% Preference share capital	£50,000	£50,000

Q **101 How much will appear in the cash flow statement for the year ended 30 September 2005 for the loan interest and preference dividend paid?**

A £10,000

B £12,000

C £16,000

D £32,000

(2 marks)

Q **102 How much will appear in the cash flow statement for the year ended 30 September 2005 for the ordinary dividend paid?**

A £20,000

B £24,000

C £25,000

D £29,000

(1 mark)

Q **103 FRS 1 Cash Flow Statements requires the cash flow statement prepared using the indirect method to include the calculation of net cash from operating activities.**

Which of the following lists consists only of items which could appear in such a calculation?

A Depreciation, increase in debtors, decrease in creditors, proceeds of sale of plant.

B Increase in creditors, decrease in stock, profit on sale of plant, depreciation.

C Increase in creditors, depreciation, decrease in debtors, proceeds of sale of plant.

D Depreciation, interest paid, equity dividends paid, purchase of plant.

(1 mark)

Chapter 20: The regulatory and conceptual framework

Q **104** When preparing financial statements under historic cost accounting in periods of inflation, directors:

A must reduce asset values

B must increase asset values

C must reduce dividends

D need make no adjustments

(1 mark)

Q **105** If the owner of a business takes goods from stock for his own personal use, the accounting concept to be considered is the:

A relevance concept

B capitalisation concept

C money measurement concept

D separate entity concept

(1 mark)

Q **106** A 'true and fair view' is one which:

A presents the accounts in such a way as to exclude errors which would affect the actions of those reading them

B occurs when the accounts have been audited

C shows the accounts of an organisation in an understandable format

D shows the assets on the balance sheet at their current market price

(1 mark)

Q **107** Which concept is followed when a business records the cost of a fixed asset even though it does not legally own it?

A substance over form

B prudence

C accruals

D going concern

(1 mark)

Q 108 **The ASB Framework for the Preparation and Presentation of Financial Statements gives five characteristics that make financial information reliable.**

These five characteristics are:

A prudence, consistency, understandability, faithful representation, substance over form

B accruals basis, going concern concept, consistency, prudence, true and fair view

C faithful representation, neutrality, substance over form, completeness, consistency, faithful and free

D free from material error, prudence, faithful representation, neutrality, completeness

(1 mark)

Q 109 **The accounting concept or convention which, in times of rising prices, tends to understate asset values and overstate profits, is the:**

A going concern concept

B prudence concept

C realisation concept

D historical cost concept

(1 mark)

Answers

Chapter 1: Practice questions

A 1 D

A 2 A

Chapter 2: Balance sheet and profit and loss account

A 1 C

A 2 C

A 3 A

A 4 C

A 5 C

Chapter 3: Double entry bookkeeping

A 6 D

A 7 D

A 8 C

A 9 B

A 10 D

A 11 C

Chapter 4: Stock

A **12 D**

	A	B	C	Total
	£	£	£	£
Cost	7	10	19	
NRV	13	8	14	
Lower of cost or NRV	7	8	14	
x Number of units	20	25	15	
Valuation	140	200	210	550

A **13 A**

$(35 \times £15) + (30 \times £20) = £1,125$

A **14 C**

A **15 The correct answer is D**

A **16 The correct answer is C**

400 items		£
Cost	400 x £4	1,600
NRV	(400 x £3) – £200	1,000
Therefore use NRV.		

200 items		£
Cost	200 x £30	6,000
NRV	(200 x £35) – £1,200 – £300	5,500
Therefore use NRV.		

Total stock figure = £116,400 + £1,000 + £5,500 = £122,900.

Chapter 5: Value Added Tax (VAT)

A **17 A**

VAT

	£		£
Purchases	2,100	Sales	3,500
(17.5 % x 12,000)		23,500 x 17.5/117.5	
Expenses	140		
(17.5% x 800)			
Bal c/f	1,260		
	3,500		3,500
		Bal b/f	1,260

A **18** B

A **19** B

VAT

	£		£
Purchases (17.5 % x 18,000)	3,150.00	Sales 27,612.50 x 17.5/117.5	4,112.50
Bal c/f	962.50		
	4,112.50		4,112.50
		Bal b/f	962.50

A **20** D

			£	£
Assets	Cash (1,000 + 1,175)			2,175
	Stock			400
				2,575
Liabilities	Creditors (800 x 1.175)		940	
	VAT (175 − 140)		35	
				(975)
				1,600
Capital	Capital			1,000
	Profit (1,000 − 400)			600
				1,600

Chapter 6: Accruals and prepayments

A **21** B

Electricity

	£		£
Bank	400	Bal b/f	250
Bank	350		
Bank	425	Profit and loss account (ß)	1,525
Bank	450		
Bal c/f	150		
	1,775		1,775
		Bal b/f (450/3)	150

A **22 A**

Electricity

	£		£
Bal b/f	25		
Bank (12 x 100)	1,200		
		Profit and loss account	1,300
		(350 + 375 + 275 + 300)	
Bal c/f (ß)	75		
	1,300		1,300
		Bal b/f	75

A **23 B**

Rent

	£		£
Bal b/f	200		
Bank	1,200	Profit and loss account (ß)	1,200
		Bal c/f	200
	1,400		1,400
Bal b/f (2/12 x 1,200)	200		

A **24 A**

Light and heat

	£		£
Bank (240 + 10)	250	Bal b/f	240
Bank	260		
Bank	220		
Bank	210	Profit and loss account (ß)	1,160
Bank	230		
Bal c/f	230		
	1,400		1,400
		Bal b/f	230
		(last quarter's bill)	

A **25 C**

Stationery payable

	£		£
		Bal b/f	80
Bank	1,350	Purchases of stationery (ß)	1,340
Bal c/f	70		
	1,420		1,420
		Bal b/f	70

Opening stock + Purchases − Closing stock = £165 + £1,340 − £140 = £1,365

Chapter 7: Bad and doubtful debts

A **26 B**

5% x (50,000 − 1,000) = £2,450

A **27 A**

Debtors

	£		£
Bal b/f	82,500	Bad debt expense	4,750
		Bal c/f	77,750
	82,800		82,800
Bal b/f	77,750		

Bad debt expense

	£		£
Debtors (1,000 + 500 + 3,250)	4,750	Decrease in provision	200
		Profit and loss account	4,250
	4,750		4,750

Provision at 31 March	£
Specific provision	250
General provision (2% x (77,750 − 250))	1,550
	1,800
Current provision balance	2,000
Movement in provision balance	200 decrease

Net debtors = £77,750 − £1,800 = £75,950

A **28 B**

Provision for doubtful debts

	£		£
		Bal b/f	700
Profit and loss account (ß)	360		
Bal c/f	340		
	700		700
		Bal b/f	340

Bad debt expense

	£		£
Debtors	450		
Debtors	170		
		Profit and loss account	260
	620		620

Provision required at end of year = £700 − £450 − £150 + £240 = £340

Irrecoverable Debts

	£		£
Receivables	450	Reduction in allowance	360
Receivables	170	Income statement	260
	620		620

A **29 B**

Debtors

	£		£
Bal b/f	47,800	Bank	150
		Bad debt expense	150
		Bal c/f	47,500
	47,800		47,800
Bal b/f	47,500		

Bad debt expense

	£		£
		Decrease in provision	300
Debtors	150		
Profit and loss account	150		
	300		300

A **30 D**

Debtors

	£		£
Bal b/f	100,000	Bank	500
		Bal c/f	99,500
	101,000		101,000
Bal b/f	99,500		

Provision for doubtful debts

	£		£
Bal c/f	6,965	Bal b/f	5,000
		Profit and loss account (ß)	1,965
	6,965		6,965
		Bal b/f (7% x 99,500)	6,965

A **31 B**

This is an example of a bad debt being written off. Credit the debtors account in order to clear the debt and debit the bad debt expense account with the amount of the debt written off.

A **32 A**

There is a specific provision for the debt of £900 which has still not been written off as bad, and a general provision equivalent to 2% of the remaining balance based on past history.

Chapter 8: Fixed assets

A **33 B**

	£
Assets held all year (£15,000 – 8,000) x 25%	1,750
Asset disposed of £8,000 x 25% x 8/12	1,333
Asset acquired £10,000 x 25% x 1/12	208
Total depreciation	3,291

A **34 D**

KAPLAN PUBLISHING

A **35 B**

	£
Proceeds of sale	1,200.00
NBV at disposal (2,400 − 480 − 384 − 307.20)	(1,228.80)
Loss on disposal	(28.80)

Depreciation to disposal

Yr 1: £2,400 x 20% = £480

Yr 2: £(2,400 − 480) x 20% = £384

Yr 3: £(2,400 − 480 − 384) x 20% = £307.20

A **36 C**

£100,000 + £7,000 + £5,000 = £112,000

A **37 B**

	£
Assets held all year (5,000 − 300 − 600) x 10%	410
Disposals	
£300 x 10% x 2/12	5
£600 x 10% x 10/12	50
Acquisition £1,000 x 10% x 9/12	75
Total depreciation	540

A **38 B**

$$\frac{£30,000 - £6,000}{4} \times 5/_{12} = £2,500$$

Chapter 9: From trial balance to financial statements

A **39 C**

Depreciation charge = £11,600 (2% x £580,000)

NBV = £452,400 [£580,000 − (£116,000 + £11,600)]

A **40 D**

Depreciation charge = £9,375 [25% x £37,500
(£50,000 − £12,500)]

Net book value = £28,125 [£50,000 − (£12,500 + £9,375)]

A | **41 A**

	£
Bad debt expenses £1,800 + 3,200 =	5,000
Decrease in provision for doubtful debts	(770)
Total bad debt expense	**4,230**
Debtors (£25,800 − 3,200)	22,600
Less: Closing provision for doubtful debts	(1,130)
Net closing debtors	**21,470**

Closing provision for doubtful debts	
[5% x (£25,800 − 3,200)]	1,130
Opening provision for doubtful debts	1,900
Decrease in provision for doubtful debts	770

A | **42 B**

	Charge for the year £				Closing Balance £
Rent	36,000	Rent accrual			2,000
	(12 x £3,000)	Due		36,000	
		Paid		34,000	
		Accrual		2,000	
Insurance	24,000	**Insurance prepayment**			6,000
		Paid		30,000	
		Due		24,000	
		Prepayment		6,000	

Chapter 10: Books of prime entry and control accounts

A | **43 C**

A | **44 A**

A | **45 A**

Debtors

	£		£
Bal b/f	22,000	Bank	115,000
Sales	120,000	Discounts allowed	1,000
Dishonoured cheque	9,000	Contra	5,000
		Bal c/f	30,000
	151,000		151,000
Bal b/f	30,000		

Chapter 11: Control account reconciliations

A **46 A**

$£8,500 - (£400 \times 2) = £7,700$

A **47 C**

Sales ledger control account

	£		£
Bal b/f	32,750	Bal b/f	1,275
Sales	125,000	Bank	122,500
Refunds	1,300	Discounts allowed	550
Bal c/f	2,000	Bal c/f	36,725
	161,050		161,050
Bal b/f	36,725	Bal b/f	2,000

A **48 B**

A **49 A**

A **50 A**

The other three lists all contain one item which should appear on the debit side of the account.

Chapter 12: Bank reconciliations

A **51 D**

Bank – cash book

	£		£
		Bal b/f (i)	5,670
		Bank charges (ii)	250
Bal c/f	5,920		
	5,920		5,920
		Bal b/f	5,920

	£
Balance per bank statement (ß)	(6,100)
Add: Error (iii)	(40)
Add: Outstanding cheques (iv)	(325)
Less: Outstanding lodgements(v)	545
Balance per cash book	(5,920)

A   52 C

Balance per bank statement (ß)	(£2,360) o/d
Add: Outstanding cheques	(£1,420)
Balance per cash book (3,600 + 180)	(£3,780) o/d

A   53 B

Bank – cash book

	£		£
Sales	1,450	Bal b/f	485
Debtors	2,400	Creditors (0.95 x 1,800)	1,710
		Dishonoured cheques	250
		Bal c/f	1,405
	3,850		3,850
Bal b/f	1,405		

A   54 D

Bank – cash book

	£		£
Standing order	125	Bal b/f	5,675
		Dishonoured cheque	900
		(£450 x 2)	
Bal c/f	6,450		
	6,575		6,575
		Bal b/f	6,450

A   55 C

The bank reconciliation should have been calculated as follows:

	£
Overdraft per bank statement	(38,600)
Add deposits not yet credited	41,200
	2,600
Less outstanding cheques	(3,300)
Overdraft per cash book	(700)

A   56 A

Items 3 and 4 relate to timing differences only and would appear in the bank reconciliation.

Chapter 13: Correction of errors and suspense accounts

A **57 D**

A **58 A**

Suspense

	£		£
Bal b/f (ß)	210	Gas (420 – 240)	180
Interest receivable	70	Discounts (50 x 2)	100
	280		280

A **59 B**

Draft profit for the period	£12,355
Six months' rent 6/12 x 800	(£400)
Closing Stock adjustment (1,000 – 800)	(£200)
	£11,755

A **60 C**

A **61 D**

A **62 B**

The profit will be understated by the following amount:

	£
Amount charged in error to the repairs account	38,000
Less depreciation chargeable on the plant (3/12 x 20% x £38,000)	(1,900)
	£36,100

A **63 D**

	£	
Opening balance on suspense account (£836,200 – £819,700)	16,500	Cr
Difference remaining after postings to the discount accounts (£5,100 – £3,900)	(1,200)	
Difference from cheque incorrectly posted (£19,000 – £9,100)	(9,900)	
	£5,400	Cr

A **64 B**

Items 1 and 3 would result in an imbalance in the trial balance and therefore require an entry to the suspense account. Items 2, 4 and 5 do not affect the balancing of the accounts.

Chapter 14: Applications of IT

A **65 B**

All of the other options are vital for the information to be understood by the user. Although colour might make the information to easier to understand, it often only improves the presentation.

A **66**

Input device	Application
Optical mark reader	Examination answer sheets
Bar code reader	Point of sale systems
Scanner	Capturing images
Optical character recognition	Cheque processing

A **67 B**

Touch screen is an example of hardware which can be installed and used for a number of applications such as purchasing a ticket, ATM (Automatic Teller Machines) and flight check in. All of the other examples (icon, pull down list and default values) are functions of the software.

Chapter 15: Incomplete records

A **68 B**

Closing net assets – Opening net assets = Capital Introduced + Profit for year – Drawings

£6,740 – £7,600 = 0 + Profit for year – 1,000

Profit for year = £140

A **69 D**

Closing net assets – Opening net assets = Capital Introduced + Profit for year – Drawings in year

£27,000 – £10,000 =Capital Introduced + £5,000 – £2,000

Capital Introduced = £14,000

A **70 B**

	%
Sales	115
Cost of Sales	100
Gross profit	15

15/115 = 13.04%

A **71 B**

Closing net assets – Opening net assets = Capital Introduced + Profit for year – Drawings

£4,500 – £10,000 = £4,000 + Profit/(loss) – £8,000

Loss for year = £1,500

A **72 D**

Creditors

	£		£
Bank	542,300	Bal b/f	142,600
Discounts received	13,200		
Returns outwards	27,500	Purchases (ß)	578,200
Bal c/f	137,800		
	720,800		720,800
		Bal b/f	137,800

A **73 D**

Cost of Sales = 75% x £17,000 = £12,750

Purchases = £12,750 + £1,350 – £3,500 = £10,600

A **74 A**

Credit sales can be calculated as a balancing figure on the sales (debtors) ledger control account.

Sales (debtors) ledger control account

	£		£
Balance b/f	29,100	Bank takings	381,600
Bank – refunds	2,100	Expenses	6,800
Credit sales	412,400	Bad debts	7,200
(balance)		Discounts allowed	9,400
		Balance c/f	38,600
	443,600		443,600

Credit sales = £412,400, cash sales = £112,900, total sales = £525,300

A 75 D

	£
Opening stock	17,000
Purchases	91,000
Closing stock	(24,000)
Cost of sales	84,000

Sales = £84,000 x 100/60 = £140,000

A 76 A

The rent expense for the year should be:

(5/12 x £24,000) + (7/12 x £30,000) = £27,500

A 77 B

Cost of sales = 70% x £64,800 =	£45,360
	£
Opening stock	28,400
Purchases	49,600
Cost of sales	(45,360)
Loss of stock	32,640

Chapter 16 : Partnerships

A 78 D

	Alf	Ben	Connie	Dora	Total
	£	£	£	£	£
Profit					56,000
Salaries			5,000	5,000	(10,000)
Interest on capital	4,500	3,000	2,000	1,500	(11,000)
					35,000
PSR 4:3:2:1	14,000	10,500	7,000	3,500	(35,000)
Total	18,500	13,500	14,000	10,000	

A 79 A

£5,200/£40,000 = 13%

£12,656/£3,164 = 4

£9,492/£3,164 = 3

A **80 B**

	Alpha £	Beta £	Gamma £
Appropriated	30,000	10,000	8,000
GMPS	(3,000)	4,000	(1,000)
Total	27,000	14,000	7,000

A **81 A**

	D £000	E £000	F £000	Total £000
First 6 months' profit				240
Salaries		12	12	(24)
Balance in PSR (5:3:2)	108	64.8	43.2	216
Second 6 months' profit				240
Salaries		18	12	(30)
Balance in PSR (3:1:1)	126	42	42	210
Total profit shares	234	136.8	109.2	

A **82 B**

(i) Before admission of L record goodwill as follows:

    Dr   Goodwill   £80,000

    Cr   Capital a/c – J   £64,000

    Cr   Capital a/c – K   £16,000

    Credit old partners in their old profit share ratio (4:1)

(ii) After admission of L write off goodwill as follows:

    Dr   Capital a/c – J   £32,000

    Dr   Capital a/c – K   £24,000

    Dr   Capital a/c – L   £24,000

    Cr   Goodwill   £80,000

    Debit new partners in their new profit share ratio (4:3:3)

(iii) Net double entry is (i) less (ii)

    Dr   Capital a/c – K   £8,000

    Dr   Capital a/c – L   £24,000

    Cr   Capital a/c – J   £32,000

Chapter 17: Company accounts

A **83 C**

	£
Profit and loss account charge	
2005 estimate	23,000
Overprovision 2004	(5,000)
	18,000
Tax liability	23,000

A **84 B**

A **85 B**

		£
Preference dividends (6% x 1,000,000)	=	60,000
Ordinary dividends (16,000,000 x 0.02)	=	320,000
Total dividend	=	380,000

A **86 A**

A **87 C**

	£
Profit after tax (balancing figure)	100,000
Dividends	(50,000)
Profit for year	50,000
Accumulated profit b/f	50,000
Accumulated profit c/f	100,000

Chapter 18: Accounting standards

A **88 D**

A **89 C**

A **90 C**

A **91 C**

A **92 A**

A **93 C**

A **94 C**

A **95 D**

Statements 2, 3 and 5 are correct

A **96 B**

The other lists contain adjusting items

Chapter 19: Cash flow statements

A **97 C**

A **98 A**

	£
Retained profit for the year £(65,500 – 45,500)	20,000
Dividends	3,300
Taxation £(600 + 550 – 400)	750
Interest payable (8% x £40,000)	3,200
Operating profit	27,250

A **99 B**

Corporation tax

	£		£
		Bal b/f	50,000
Bank (ß)	53,000	Profit and loss account	60,000
Bal c/f	57,000		
	110,000		110,000
		Bal b/f	57,000

A **100 B**

	£
Issue of share capital £(20,000+10,000)	30,000 inflow
Repayment of loan notes	20,000 outflow
	10,000 inflow

A 101 C

Loan interest payable

	£		£
		Bal b/f	5,000
Bank (ß)	12,000	Profit and loss account (100,000 x 10%)	10,000
Bal c/f	3,000		
	15,000		15,000
		Bal b/f	3,000

Preference dividends 8% x £50,000 = £4,000
Total payments = £12,000 + £4,000 = £16,000

A 102 A

A 103 B

All other lists contain one or more items that would not appear in the calculation of net cash from operating activities

Chapter 20: The regulatory and conceptual framework

A 104 D

A 105 D

A 106 A

A 107 A

A 108 D

The other three contain items which are not considered to contribute towards reliability.

A 109 D

Index

Index

Index

Index

Index

Index